The International Behavioural and Social Sciences Library

THE POLITICS OF
ORGANIZATIONAL
DECISION-MAKING

TAVISTOCK

The International Behavioural and Social Sciences Library

ORGANIZATIONAL BEHAVIOUR
In 10 Volumes

THE POLITICS OF ORGANIZATIONAL DECISION-MAKING

ANDREW M PETTIGREW

First published in 1973 by
Tavistock Publications Limited

Reprinted in 2001 by
Routledge
2 Park Square, Milton Park, Abingdon, Oxon, OX14 4RN

Transferred to Digital Printing 2009

Routledge is an imprint of the Taylor & Francis Group

British Library Cataloguing in Publication Data
A CIP catalogue record for this book
is available from the British Library

The Politics of Organizational Decision-Making
ISBN10: 0–415–26468–5 (hbk)
ISBN10: 0–415–48835–4 (pbk)

ISBN13: 978–0–415–26468–6 (hbk)
ISBN13: 978–0–415–48835–8 (pbk)

Organizational Behaviour: 10 Volumes
ISBN 0-415-26513-4
The International Behavioural and Social Sciences Library
112 Volumes
ISBN 0-415-25670-4

The Politics of Organizational Decision-making

ANDREW M. PETTIGREW

LONDON: TAVISTOCK
ASSEN: VAN GORCUM

First published in 1973
by Tavistock Publications Limited
2 Park Square, Milton Park, Abingdon, Oxon, OX14 4RN
in association with Van Gorcum & Comp. N.V
10/12pt Times New Roman
by Willmer Brothers Limited, Birkenhead

© *Andrew M. Pettigrew 1973*

ISBN 0 422 74120 5

Distributed in the USA by
HARPER & ROW PUBLISHERS, INC.
BARNES & NOBLE IMPORT DIVISION

For

Martha Ann

Contents

viii   *Contents*

Figures and Tables

Acknowledgements

This book is the result of research carried out between September 1966 and December 1969. Data were collected from a single firm using a variety of methods. I wish to acknowledge my gratitude to those members of Brian Michaels[1] who, at a time of great stress, gave generously of their time and patience. In particular, I should like to express my deep appreciation to Jim Kenny, the head of Management Services in the above firm. Without Jim Kenny's reasoned belief in research this piece of work would never have been completed.

Between September 1966 and August 1968 I was a member of the Computer Research Unit at the Manchester Business School. The opportunity to do this research arose from the aims of that unit and, in particular, through the achievements and guidance of its director, Enid Mumford. The intellectual debt I owe her should be obvious to anyone remotely familiar with the field of industrial sociology.

The research was completed while I was a visiting faculty member at the Department of Administrative Sciences, Yale University. I am deeply indebted to Professors Chris Argyris, Douglas T. Hall, Edward E. Lawler III, and Benjamin Schneider for reading and commenting on the first draft of the book. Particular thanks are due to Ben Schneider for making available his extensive knowledge of data analysis in the behavioural sciences.

Jean Miller and Anna Raeburn expertly, interestedly, and cheerfully typed the manuscript through all its revisions.

My wife Ethna and my daughter Martha were merely indispensable. Ethna helped to collect and analyse some of the data and was a stringent editor.

[1] All company and personal names mentioned in this volume are pseudonyms.

Preface

This volume explores the issues of power and conflict in organizational life. It is almost a truism to say that the concept of power is one of the neglected areas of empirical study in the social sciences. Certainly there are still few detailed studies of the mobilization and dissolution of power in organizations.

Faced with this characterization of the organizational literature, the layman might argue, is this not a strange state of affairs? In one sphere of our life or another are we not all both users and recipients of power? A visit to any factory tea-break, office lunch gathering, or faculty meeting would seem to indicate that we are all familiar with shop-floor or office politics and bureaucratic gamesmanship.

The problem for the student of social behaviour is that power and politics are difficult nettles to grasp. Therein lies the challenge. The present work attempts to explore the political dimension in the context of a series of innovative decisions in a single firm. The approach is eclectic, not only in its conceptual sources but also in its use of a variety of research methods. Above all, it has been guided by a belief in the value of longitudinal research designs for highlighting social processes in organizations.

The study has interdisciplinary aims. I have attempted to weave the various theoretical contributions of sociology, social anthropology, social psychology, and political science into my general argument. That argument suggests that an organization or any other social system may profitably be explored as an ongoing system with a past, a present, and a future. The generalized implication is that man's behaviour at time t_2 may be explained with reference to his past actions at time t_1 and his future designs at time t_3, as well as to the particular set of forces impinging on him at time

t_2. Sound theory must therefore take into account the history and the future of a system and relate them to the present.

The concern is with social process: the behaviour of men over time. Data are presented on two social processes, decision-making and specialization. The data were gathered to span the lifetime of computer activities in one firm, Brian Michaels. In the period 1957-68 Brian Michaels made four computer-purchase decisions. From 1966-8 I studied in great detail the last of these decisions. The overall argument of the book is that the behaviour observed in relation to that decision could not be satisfactorily explained without reference to the past. In particular, changes in the distribution of power and status between the various groups and role incumbents up to and including the decision affected the level of conflict before and throughout the decision process and ultimately the decisional outcome. In addition, the allegiances certain individuals had made in respect of previous decisions were seen to have an impact, and did have an impact, on their and others' behaviour in the 1966-8 decision.

The material is presented in ten chapters. Chapter 1, 'Conceptual Orientations', begins by introducing the idea of time and social structure. The main body of the chapter critically reviews the relevant literature on organizational decision-making. The focus of the discussion is the most developed theoretical work in the filed, March and Simon (1958) and Cyert and March (1963). The remainder of the chapter looks at the theoretical problems raised by non-programmed innovative decisions and at the organizational literature on the problems of specialist groups. Consideration is also given to the way in which the particular groups here studied – programmers and systems analysts – fit into this literature.

Chapter 2, 'Decision-making as a Political Process', sets out to add to the Cyert and March approach by discussing, first of all, the meaning and determinants of the political behaviour the Carnegie authors describe. Added precision is given to the term 'political', in the context of innovative decision-making, through a discussion of the analytical potential of the concepts of power and authority. The chapter concludes by suggesting that this work can complement existing writing on innovative decision-making in two main ways: first, by exploring the demand-generating process in decision-making and, second, by looking at the mobilization of power in a decision-making process.

Chapter 3, 'The Setting', is descriptive. Its aim is to give the reader an overview of the main events in Michaels in the period 1955-68 before the analysis begins in Chapter 5.

Chapter 4, 'The Research Process', falls neatly into two sections. The first section discusses the methods used in studying the 1966-8 Michaels computer decision. The second section explains the scope and methods of the historical part of the research. The underlying themes are that theory and method are necessarily interdependent and that the use of multiple methods can improve the validity of the findings in a project of this kind and, it is hoped, the reliability of the conclusions.

Chapters 5, 6, and 7 explore how the specialities of programming and systems analysis developed in Michaels. Specific attention is given to changes in the power, status, and level of perceived hostility between the two groups. The Michaels data are compared and contrasted with national data on status changes between programmers, O & M officers, and systems analysts. One of the aims of Chapter 7 is to show that the differences between the Michaels case and the national data can largely be accounted for in terms of the successful power-maintenance strategies of the Michaels programmers.

Chapters 8 and 9 offer an analysis of the determinants of the conflict and of the influence of the various parties' strategic behaviour on the 1966-8 decisional outcome. The theoretical core of Chapter 8 rests on factors producing disparity in the demand-generating process of an innovative decision. Chapter 9 deals with the issue of power mobilization in the Michaels 1966-8 computer decision. Both chapters seek to relate present behaviour to previous behaviour and to future designs in terms of the general theoretical approach of the book.

Chapter 10 considers the conclusions that can be drawn from this piece of work.

B

CHAPTER 1

Conceptual Orientations

Harold Wilensky (1967) comments in the preface to his book: 'Despite centuries of concern with policy, we have little solid understanding of the relation of experts and intellectuals to men of power.' The same might also be said of relations between experts in different disciplines. This study attempts to deal at an exploratory level with both. In the language of organization theory, we are concerned here with the vertical and with what Landsberger (1961) calls the horizontal dimension in a bureaucracy.

The analytical approach is based upon a longitudinal research design. The interest is in social process, the behaviour of men over time. Conceptually the study cuts across several domains. In this context, the analysis of social process, the field of social anthropology has offered considerable help. Anthropologists, however, have not always been interested in time and social structure. In 1952 Radcliffe-Brown was arguing for a synchronic description of social life. The aim was 'to give an account of a form of social life as it exists at a certain time, abstracting as far as possible from changes that may be taking place in its features' (1952: 4). M. G. Smith (1962: 77) has pointed out that 'under these circumstances many social anthropologists have undertaken to study social systems as if they were closed and changeless. They begin by excluding historical interests from their field of enquiry. They next exclude all changes that may be currently under way in the units they investigate.' Smith describes such a theoretical scheme as 'the fallacy of the ethnographic present' (1962: 77). He recommends that the appropriate field of anthropological study should be a 'unit over time, not merely a unit at a particular point in time' (p. 81). In this way, structural regularities may be abstracted from the succession of relatively unique events 'to reveal the outlines of an order within processes of simultaneous continuity and change'

1

(p. 84). Turner (1957) uses the mechanism of the social drama to delve into social process. The drama performs a dual function. First, it sheds light: 'The social drama is a limited area of transparency on the otherwise opaque surface of regular, uneventful social life' (1957: 93). A sequence of such dramas may also be used to observe the crucial principles of the social structure in their operation, and their relative dominance at successive points in time.

Van Velsen (1967) advocates the use of the extended case method and situational analysis. Unlike Smith and Turner, he tries in addition to break down the firm hold that normative functionalism has had on structural–functional analysis. He argues that there will always be a certain amount of choice, in the sense of selection by the individual of alternative norms of behaviour within a persisting social structure: 'Situational analysis will be useful for the study of social process including the study of regularities in the variety of actual individual behaviour within the social structure' (1967: 142). Like Smith, Van Velsen is careful to point out that such an approach is aimed at illuminating certain regularities of social process, not at highlighting personal idiosyncrasies.

The use of historical material in the study of organizations is rare. Lipset, Trow, and Coleman (1956) in their study of *Union Democracy* show what can be done with historical data. To answer their original question why there is democracy in the International Typographical Union, they say this 'can be found only by combining the structural and historical analyses' (1956 : 441): 'The historical analysis explains how the system, in this case two-party democracy, came into existence, while the sociological analysis accounts for the ways in which structural factors . . . operate to maintain it' (p. 451). It is at this point that the theoretical approach set out here differs from that of Lipset, Trow, and Coleman. The concern here is not with system maintenance but with the analysis of processes located in changing structures of social relationships, norms, values, and ideas over time.

Jobling (1969) also makes a plea for the use of historical material in the study of organizations. Talking of university development in the UK, he maintains that 'historical data provide first insight into problems and intimations of fruitful hypotheses as well as being sociologically valuable in their own right' (1969 : 11). Mouzelis (1967) notes that 'present organization theory is not only predominantly ethnocentric but ahistorical as well. The organizations studied seem to exist in a timeless dimension' (1967: 165).

It would seem futile, however, to argue for a methodological strategy that included the collection of historical data and the observation of social processes if the theoretical assumptions that were being made about *homo sociologicus* restricted the analysis of change. Merton (1957a) is clear on this point when he discusses the bearing of empirical research on sociological theory. Van Velsen (1967 : 145) notes that 'it is one of the assumptions of situational analysis that the norms of society do not constitute a consistent and coherent whole. They are vague and discrepant. It is this fact which allows for their manipulation by members of a society in furthering their own aims.' Blumer (1953 : 199) holds that 'the human being is not swept along as a neutral and indifferent unit by the operation of a system. As an organism capable of self-interaction he forges his actions out of a process of definition involving choice, appraisal and decision. . . . Cultural, status positions and role relationships are only frameworks inside of which that process of formative transaction goes on.' Gross, Mason, and McEachern (1958) dismiss the postulate of consensus on role definition and provide evidence from the school superintendent role of the great deal of choice behaviour possible within a role. Goode (1960a) sees institutional process as a resolution of role strain. Faced with the felt difficulty of fulfilling role demands, individuals attempt to make bargains with the other members of their role set about their respective rights, privileges, and obligations. Strauss *et al.* (1963) argue in favour of a negotiated order. A hospital can be seen like any other organization as a hierarchy of status, power, rules, roles, and organizational goals. It may also be considered as an ordered environment 'which has to be worked at and continually reconstituted' (Buckley, 1967 : 149). Such a negotiation process was found to have patterned and temporal features. Agreements were ordered in terms of 'who contracts with whom, about what, as well as when' (Strauss *et al.*, 1963: 162).

The recognition of choice and variability in social interaction leaves the way open for a strategic conception of behaviour in organizations. Exchange theory offers some conceptual assistance here. The major theoretical antecedents of Blau's (1964) version of exchange theory are the rational choice models of economics and game theory. The major assumption is that individuals make choices which accord best with their self-interest. Blau is quick to point out, however, that not all individuals act in their own interests (1964 : 5). Not all human behaviour is dominated by individuals' pursuit of social rewards in their associations. He also acknowledges Luce and Raiffa's (1957) and Schelling's (1960) criticisms of game theory and modifies his rational choice model in two ways. Individuals' choices are limited, first, by their perception of the situation in which they act and, second, by the amount of information they have at hand (Blau, 1964 : 18-19). I would also add a third, very important, restriction on rationality: the constraints of access imposed by man's location in a social structure. Nevertheless, Blau's heuristic approach 'that men seek to adjust social conditions to achieve their ends' (1964 : 19) is one of the major theoretical assumptions of this work.

As Kapferer (1969b) notes, individuals' actions may be directed in their self-interest but often their actions so directed have an effect contrary to their interests. Consideration of the way in which they perceive the situation of their action and of the extent to which they have sufficient and accurate information as to how their interests can best be achieved is essential to any analysis of social behaviour. In their attempts to operate various strategies, individuals continually commit errors because of misperception through lack of information or miscalculation. They can also be manoeuvred into committing errors. Finally, individual action may lead to unintended consequences. Somebody obviously striving for power will encourage others to consider their own interests more carefully and perhaps enable them to generate sufficient resources to maintain those interests in the face of the new threat.

In the analysis so far, then, man is presented not merely as being governed by the structure of the situation in which he participates but also as attempting, at least to some extent, to shape and mould that structure over time to suit his own interests. As a later discussion will attempt to show, an individual's ability to achieve this moulding is very much a function of his ability to generate sufficient power and influence to impose his will on others in the face of opposition.

The neglect of the analysis of social processes in organizations has already been stressed. It is difficult, however, to analyse social process unless the situation of one's sociological analysis is treated as part of a process in the first place. The two major substantive processes dealt with here are decision-making and specialization. Decision-making is considered first.

The literature in the field of decision-making is immense. In 1959 Gore and Silander talked about a generous list running to five thousand entries. By 1964 Wasserman and Silander had produced a 178-page bibliography. Gore and Silander were not impressed by any unity of purpose: 'In short, the literature dealing with decision-making, impressive in relation to one man's ability to deal with it, appears to be uneven and chaotic, and in no respect comprehensive' (1959 : 121). They note that such 'critical factors as a typology of decision, models of various decisional processes, the function of ideology and the basis of power and its generation receive only infrequent and inadequate attention' (p. 121).

The oft-made statement that decision-making is *the* organizational activity (Barnard, 1938; Simon, 1957) has encouraged scholars from many disciplines to its study. Work from psychology is usefully summarized by Collins and Guetzkow (1964) and Edwards and Tversky (1967); from public administration, by Mailick and Van Ness (1962), with notable other contributions by Gore (1956), Lindblom (1959), Braybrooke and Lindblom (1963), and Chapman (1968). Snyder and Paige (1958), Dahl (1961), Polsby (1963), and Hawley and Wirt (1968) have worked in the areas of community decision-making and foreign policy decision-making using a political science approach; while, notably, March and Simon (1958), Cyert and March (1963), and Gore and Dyson (1964) have attempted to use an interdisciplinary framework. Further well-established and expanding fields are the mathematical-economic approaches of Cooper *et al.* (1958) and Wagner (1969), and the game theoretical work of Von Neumann and Morganstern (1944), Shubik (1959), Siegel and Fouraker (1960), and Cross (1969).

One of the most general statements that can be made about the theories of organizational decision-making is that they fall into two broad classes. There are the normative mathematical–economic theories and the so-called behavioural theories. It is the second of these two approaches that informs the present study. The interest here is in tracing decisions empirically to find out what actually happens rather than what is ideally expected to happen. In this connection, the work of March and Simon (1958) and Cyert and March (1963) offers the most material assistance.

March and Simon

As Burns (1965) points out, the Carnegie group attempt to put forward a general theory that will make sense of a wide range of empirical experience of business concerns obtained through research and consultancy. Their model, 'derived from the conventions of the computer simulation of business decision-making', is an attempt 'to elaborate a rational model of the business concern' (1965 : 168).

In spite of its interdisciplinary aims, the main point of March and Simon's book *Organizations* is that the interrelation of motivation and cognition must be of central concern for organization theory (1958 : 135). The book has a consistently strong psychological bias. As Udy (1959 : 222) observes: 'Half the book is devoted to motivation and much of the remainder to personal decision-making. Furthermore, the impression is given that all problems of administration are reducible either to the rational allocation of values or individual psychology. Relatively little attention is given to the social organization of administration.'

March and Simon's thorough critique of the instrumental man put forward in the writings of Taylor, Gulick, and Urwick sets the tone of their book. These authors are criticized for their incomplete and inaccurate motivational assumptions, for ignoring human limitations on information-processing, and for giving little attention to the role of cognition in task identification (1958 : 33). In turn, the theories of Merton, Selznick, and Gouldner are deemed incomplete because they do not systematically explore the different modes of influence over individual motivation in organizational behaviour. These must be examined in terms of two critical individual decisions, the decision to participate and the decision to produce.

March and Simon summarize their position thus (p. 11): 'This, then, is the general picture of the human organism that we will use to analyse organizational behavior. It is a picture of a choosing, decision-making, problem-solving, organism that can do only one or a few things at a time, and that can attend to only a small part of the information recorded in its memory and presented by the environment.' There is here too much emphasis on reconstructing the organization from the perspective of the individual, and not enough on demonstrating how the organizational structure impinges on the individual's perspective. March and Simon show too much concern with the individual as an information-processing system and not enough with the organization in these terms. It is this basic weakness in their approach that leads me to suggest that their conception of organizational decision-making is but a partial theory.

The central theme of their chapter on decision-making is 'that the basic features of organization structure and function derive from the characteristics of human problem-solving processes and rational human choice' (p. 169). Their two main points are that people seek to satisfice and not maximize in making decisions and that there are various cognitive limits on rational behaviour. They suggest that the highly specified and clearly defined environment in which the rational man of economics and statistical decision theory makes 'optimal' choices is highly unrealistic. Decision-makers do not have all the alternatives laid out before them from which to choose, nor all the consequences of these alternatives. It is not just a matter of setting a utility function and selecting the alternative leading to the preferred set of consequences (p. 137).

Instead, 'Choice is always exercised with respect ot a limited, approximate, simplified model of the real situation' (p. 139). The alternatives generated and the way they are evaluated are a function of the decision-maker's definition of the situation. This, in turn, is influenced by selective perception and sub-goal identification.

A critical and novel part of March and Simon's theory is the existence of search behaviour. They argue that information is not given to the firm but must be obtained, that alternatives are searched for and discovered sequentially, and that the order in which the environment is searched determines to a substantial extent the decisions that will be made. This is tied up, as are other areas of their theory of choice, with their ideas on organizational conflict. To March and Simon, conflict is necessarily dysfunctional for rational problem-solving. Conflict is defined as 'a breakdown in the standard mechanisms of decision-making so that an individual or group experiences difficulty in selecting an action alternative' (p. 112). From the perspective of the individual, as well as from that of the organization, 'where conflict is perceived, motivation to reduce conflict is generated' (p. 115). 'As in the case of the individual, we assume that internal conflict is not a stable condition for an organization and that effort is consciously directed toward resolving both individual and intergroup conflict' (p. 129). Such statements lead Krupp (1961 : 165) to accuse March and Simon of being interested fundamentally in 'harmony and continuity'. The authors' three sources of conflict, unacceptability, incomparability, and uncertainty (p. 113), all pinpoint the inability to reach agreement on a preferred alternative and set in motion the search for a 'satisfactory' alternative. Unfortunately, it is never made clear in an operational sense what satisfaction means. For a similar critical view of March and Simon's 'satisficing man', see Shubik (1961) and Loasby (1968).

Given an organizationally relevant state of interdependence, March and Simon hold that 'a felt need for joint decision-making' will arise. For conflict to occur, however, one or both of two additional conditions must also be present: first, a difference in goals, and, second, a difference in knowledge and perceptions, between groups in an interdependent relationship. What they fail to recognize is that conflict may arise because of a felt need, not for joint decision-making, but for transference of authority over a particular area from one sub-unit to another. Dimock (1952), Scheff (1961), and Strauss (1962, 1964) provide empirical examples of such a process. Unfortunately, to March and Simon, interdependence is always given, never problematic. It is this inability to accommodate structural sources of conflict in their decision theory that leads both Krupp (1961) and Ephron (1961) to suggest that March and Simon's theory of conflict is incomplete. Certainly the key place they attach to cognitive and value predispositions in the creation of conflict tends to ignore the theoretical possibility that such factors may only be reinforcing differences of opinion and interest that have been generated by organizational relationships.

Their tendency to neglect structural sources of instability in organizational decision-making is tied to their neglect of another major variable. As Rex (1961 : 112) has noted: 'If there is a conflict of ends the behaviour of actors towards one another may not be determined by shared norms but by the success each has in compelling the other to act in accordance with his interests. Power then becomes a crucial variable in the study of social systems.' The consideration of power leads the argument away from woolly notions of satisficing towards the possibility of explaining choice among alternatives as a product of the strategic mobilization of power resources. The issue of power in a theory of organizational decision-making will be dealt with later. For the moment there is the major work of Cyert and March (1963) to consider.

Cyert and March

In certain respects, *A Behavioral Theory of the Firm* is a considerable advance on the already well-codified, if somewhat partial, approach of *Organizations*. Above all, as both Lupton (1966: 85) and Loasby (1968: 355) point out, it has 'political realism'. As with all great path-finding books, however, time and further thinking usually reveal areas that are found wanting.

The theoretical antecedents of the proposed behavioural theory of the firm are mixed, but the one that shines through most strongly is learning theory from individual psychology. The model of the firm the authors develop behaves as an entity, like the model of the goal-directed, economizing, and learning individual. The authors modify the individual learning model in two ways: they make it a decision-making coalition model, and they focus it on price and output decisions of the firm. Like March and Simon (1958) they stress both a theory of search and a theory of choice (1963: 120). Their theory posits multiple, changing, acceptable-level goals, the sequential examination of alternatives with the acceptance of the first satisfactory alternative, and the avoidance of uncertainty through the use of standard operating procedures.

Cyert and March differ from March and Simon in one major respect: the stress that the former give to their conception of an organization as a coalition (p. 27). To Cyert and March, decision-making is very much a political process. Unlike March and Simon, they regard conflicts of interest based on sub-goal differentiation as 'normal' parts of organizational life. They discuss mechanisms of conflict resolution but accept that such resolution can be only partially successful: 'Most organizations most of the time exist and thrive with considerable latent conflict of goals' (p. 117).

While pointing out the importance of coalition formation and the desire of any sub-group to generate support for its particular interests, the authors give scant attention to the processes involved. They are aware of this. They admit (p. 27) that they pay 'only limited attention to the process by which the coalition is changed' and justify this by stating that their model is concerned only with organizational decision-making for the short run. Later (p. 32) they argue that coalition formation is a product of bargaining over side-payments and policy agreements. Finally, however, the reader is left with the ambiguous statement that 'Patently, therefore, the composition of the viable set of coalitions will depend on environmental conditions' (p. 39).

The reader is not made aware of the significance of power until later (p. 79) when the authors note that 'any alternative that satisfies the constraints and secures suitably powerful support within the organization is likely to be adopted'. Critical questions related to the generation of support and how the structure of the organization might limit such a process are ignored. This makes it difficult to explain why a particular alternative is raised at a specific time, by whom, and with what consequences. Again the reader is left with a vague statement: 'Support came about through a rather complex mixture of personal, organizational, and general organizational goals' (p. 79).

Soelberg (1963) notes that Cyert and March's theory of goals is suspect because they assume that organizational goals are made up of a small number of departmental aspiration levels 'which appear to exist entirely separate from the organization members' individual goals' (1963: 21). He also states in a footnote (p. 31) that Cyert and March leave the description of the process of sub-unit goal formation entirely 'to the reader's imagination'. His own conclusion is that 'desire for power and concern for personal advancement represent goals which are of central concern to an organizational theory of decision-making' (p. 22).

In short, then, it may be said that Cyert and March paint a broad picture which savours of reality but leaves many interesting questions unanswered. They ignore role and communication structures and how they are devised and changed. There is little mention of the influence of external affiliations on organizational behaviour. There is no mention of the organizational structure of the firm, nor therefore of the membership of the bargaining subgroups in the coalition. Finally, their reliance on Simon's (1955a) hypothesized model of a sequential search for aspiration-level goals, without setting down the determinants of such aspiration levels, allows them to dodge the issue of the potential role that powerful interests are likely to have in the search and choice processes. All the above factors are likely to have implications for the alternatives raised, the timing of their appearance, how they are justified and attacked, and by whom, and, ultimately, for which alternative is chosen.

NON-PROGRAMMED INNOVATIVE DECISIONS

The concern here is not with decision-making as a universalistic phenomenon but with one particular type of decision, namely, innovative decision-making. Following Knight (1967: 478), innovation is defined as 'the adoption of a change which is new to an organization and to the relevant environment'. The process of innovation is considered by Knight as a special case of the process of change in an organization. Such innovative decision processes are likely to have many of the features of Simon's (1960) definition of non-programmed decisions.[1] After making a distinction between programmed and non-programmed decisions, Simon (1960: 5) asserts that they 'are not really distinct types, but form a continuum'. He acknowledges shades of grey. Programmed decisions are seen as 'repetitive and routine, to the extent that a definite procedure has been worked out for handling them' (p. 5). 'Decisions are non-programmed to the extent that they are novel, unstructured, and consequential' (p. 6). Simon follows these definitions with comments on the different techniques used for handling each type of decision. If such distinctions are to have any real analytical worth, however, they require further elaboration.

It is hypothesized that uncertainties are inherent in making non-programmed decisions. In the present work, interest does not lie in the conception of uncertainty found in the economics literature, where concepts of utility and probability are used to explain choice among uncertain alternatives; neither is March and Simon's (1958: 113) refinement of this employed: 'In the case of uncertainty, the individual does not know the probability distribution connecting behavior choices and environmental outcomes.' Rather, the concern here is to analyse the nature and determinants of uncertainty in an innovative decision. Frischmuth and Allen (1968: 1) describe the problem well:

'For a technical problem there is no correct, or even best, solution

---

[1] Simon first raises the programmed–non-programmed distinction in a paper (1955a). It is developed further in March and Simon (1958: 136-210) and again in Simon (1960).

in the long run. In fact, there is frequently no terminal state; the solutions themselves are often dynamic. The interaction of the researchers with their environment is also continual and changing. The goals for the problem's solution may be established when the process is initiated, but they are subject to change as the process proceeds. They do not explicitly contain the criteria by which the solution is to be evaluated, since the criteria are a matter of judgement and differ among individual evaluators.'

In short, a complex and changing task environment is likely to lead to uncertainty in decision-making. It will be argued later that the area of computer technology and its use provided such a complex and changing task environment for the systems analysts and programmers trying to make the computer purchase decision studied. It will also be hypothesized that the amount of uncertainty in this particular task environment helped to sustain the power conflicts lying in the very structure of the relationships formed over time between the various interested parties – in this case between what Ramsoy (1963) calls an inclusive system, the organization, and its innovative subsystem, and also between subsystems within the innovative system itself.

Uncertainty within his own task environment is just one of many problems faced by the specialist involved in an innovative decision-making process. As Dill (1962: 106) points out: 'Individuals and subgroups within organizations do not have the same task environments. . . . Instead of representing a common exposure to a common environment, the actions that they take in interaction with one another represent the direct confrontation of different exposures.' In short, structural differentiation and the consequent task differentiation in a condition of interdependence are likely to lead to the development of particularistic subgroup attitudes and values and intergroup conflict. This process has been well documented in the role set by Merton (1957b), Evan (1962), Kahn *et al.* (1964), Snoek (1966), and Pettigrew (1968). As a group phenomenon it has received attention in work by Dalton (1950), Miller (1959), Burns and Stalker (1961), White (1961), Barnes (1963), Hower and Orth (1963), Strauss (1964), Dutton and Walton (1966), Lawrence and Lorsch (1967), Miller and Rice (1967), Pondy (1967), and more recently Lynton (1969).

For Miller (1959: 245), 'an essential preliminary to differentiation of a managing system is the formation of subsystems with discrete sub-tasks within the simple system'. The components of such differentiation are seen to be technology, territory, and time. Lawrence and Lorsch (1967) split the firm analytically into three subsystems: production, sales, and research and development. Using environmental uncertainty as an independent variable, they then suggest that each of these three subsystems is likely to vary on some structural dimensions, time orientations, goal and inter-personal orientations. Many authors discuss the normative systems that support such structural differentiation. Much of this literature uses the R & D scientist–manager relationship as an example of the linking problem between an innovative subsystem and its inclusive system. To Kornhauser (1962) the central problem posed by the interdependence of scientists and organizations is that of autonomy versus integration. Associated with functional autonomy is the emphasis on free inquiry, scientific standards, research creativity, and responsibility to the scientific community. Associated with functional integration is the emphasis on research organization, administrative standards, research utility, and responsibility to the organization. Differences in age and formal education (Dalton, 1950), and in working hours, dress, and leisure pursuits (Burns and Stalker, 1961: 186) tend to compound value differences noted by Kaplan (1959), Kornhauser (1962), and Hower and Orth (1963). A feature of much of this literature, as Bumstead (1969: 12) has indicated, is that it assumes 'that these men [scientists] have the same values and goal orientations as the ideal-type pure scientist, instead of using this ideal type as a yardstick to measure against'. This point has also been made, and evidence gathered to show differentiation *within* professional value systems, by Glaser (1964), Kaplan (1965), Miller (1967), and Box and Cotgrove (1966).

If the problem of the professional in the organization was analysed somewhat simplistically in the early literature, in terms of what Box and Cotgrove (1966: 21) have called 'various hyphenated neologisms', this is not to argue that in fact the issue is not a real one. Given structural differentiation there is the problem of coordination. Specialists operating across system boundaries are faced with role conflict, role ambiguity, and intergroup conflict (Kahn *et al.*, 1964; Pettigrew, 1968). Using data gathered from operational researchers, Pettigrew (1968: 216) shows that, in addition to being exposed to role conflicts and ambiguity in organizational place and function, the OR man is faced with interpersonal conflicts arising from his attempts to introduce change on an often unwilling management.

Computer technologists are another group of innovating specialists likely to encounter resistance to and suspicion of their ideas. Mumford and Ward (1968b: 101) note that 'managers, like everyone else, see change and innovation as highly ambiguous and react to it in terms of their interpretation of how it will affect their own jobs, status and ambitions'. In their empirical study published in 1967, Mumford and Banks reveal the fears and hostilities of those who become the victims of an electronic data-processing (EDP) change. They find three major reasons for such anxieties and antagonisms (1967: 14-15): first, lack of awareness of the social implications of the change being introduced; second, poor communication and consultation policies; and, finally, the pressures of the change period itself.

From the computer technologist's perspective, hostilities from managers may be complicated by his assumed dependence on their formal authority. Like other specialists, computer technologists are regarded as staff officers. Only advice from them is legitimate. Pettigrew (1968) and Mumford and Ward (1966) have argued that the staff–line description is neither descriptively nor analytically useful. The exact nature of the computer technologist–manager relationship is likely to be characterized as much by persuasion, consultation, and influence as by the unitary term of advisory. The extent of the dependence of the specialist on the manager is here assumed to be subject to empirical verification. It is especially important to stress this point in the case of the computer technologist. As Mumford and Ward (1966) observe, the computer technologist performs a role very different from the role of the traditional staff adviser: 'These specialists are not there merely to assist line management to perform its existing duties in a more efficient way. . . . Their task is something more basic and fundamental to the commercial success of the enterprise. . . . Their slogan could be said to be "if it works, it's obsolescent".' The changes computer technologists recommend may alter 'the functions of management and perhaps eliminate some management positions altogether. Therefore, unlike normal staff advisers, the new specialists represent a threat to the jobs and power positions of many line managers' (Mumford and Ward, 1966: 245-6).

Given the uncertain nature of the task facing the computer technologists and managers here studied, the making of a large-scale computer-investment decision, and allowing for the hypothesized differences in interests, attitudes, and values between the two groups, we can expect their decision-making deliberations to be characterized by tension, conflict, and misunderstanding. Pondy (1967: 319) has remarked that joint decision-making processes between specialist groups and managers are more likely to be characterized by bargaining than by problem-solving. Lynton (1969: 402) notes that such bargaining is likely to include 'careful rationing of information and its deliberate distortion; rigid, formal, circumscribed relations; and suspicion, hostility and dissociation'. Walton (1965: 414) talks of minimum disclosures, manipulation, defensiveness, and distrust. In a field-study, Weber (1965: 870) noted less bargaining than he had expected: 'There were conflicts and "politics", but these appeared to be due to differences in judgments about goal expectations of others, especially supervisors.'

Hypotheses about the likely extent, form, and determinants of power conflicts in an innovative decision-making process are presented in the following chapter.

C

CHAPTER 2

Decision-making as a Political Process

THE ORGANIZATION AS A POLITICAL SYSTEM

The idea of analysing organizations as political systems is not yet a popular one. In 1962 Norton Long noted: 'People will readily admit that governments are organizations. The converse – that organizations are governments – is equally true but rarely considered' (1962: 110). Long gives two main reasons for this neglect· first, a lack of concern with the 'political' structure of the organization and a consequent over-attention to the formal structure of power and legitimacy; second, a heavy reliance on a psychological orientation with a lack of emphasis on sociological analysis. Burns (1961) has also made a plea for the study of the 'political' in organizations. He raises the issue of the difficulty of studying such behaviour: 'The problem is no one regards himself as a politician, or as acting politically, except of course on occasions when he is led into accounts of successful intrigue and manoeuvering when he bolsters his self-esteem and reputation by projecting the whole affair into the safe social context of a game or joke' (p. 260). There is, in addition, the problem that those who are politically involved usually claim that they are acting in the interests of the company as a whole. This is how they legitimate their behaviour.

Nevertheless, a few empirical studies of political behaviour in organizations have appeared. Dimock (1952) provides a rather extreme example. He sees the executive as a tactician and philosopher who 'must live by his wits, his competitive instincts, his understanding of social forces, and his ability as a leader' (1952: 290). The bureaux that Dimock talks of are engaged in conflict as a result of overlapping jurisdictions, competing loyalties, and incompatible objectives. Strauss (1962) in a study of lateral organizational relationships deals with what he calls 'office politics' and 'bureaucratic gamesmanship'. He describes the various tactics used by purchasing agents to control the inputs to their role and thereby increase their status. Dalton (1959) provides further dramatic examples of the informal nature of power relations between production and maintenance and between line and staff. Crozier (1964), dealing with the triadic relationship, demonstrates how a person with formally the lowest power and prestige is able, in part at least, to control the initiation of action by others. His main explanatory variables are uncertainty, immobility, and commitment. The technical engineer, because of his control over the major source of uncertainty in the routine of factory life, his relative immobility, and his high commitment to his job, is able to exert some power over his superiors. Finally, Dutton and Walton (1966), using what they call a tactical-instrumental approach to behaviour, describe and analyse the conflicts between sales and production departments in two firms.

In the present study the organization is considered an open political system. The division of work in an organization creates sub-units. These sub-units develop interests based on specialized functions and responsibilities. Although such sub-units have specialized tasks, they may also be interdependent. This interdependence may be played out within a joint decision-making process. Within such decision-making processes, interest-based demands are made. Given heterogeneity in the demand-generating process and the absence of a clearly set system of priorities between those demands, conflict is likely to ensue. Sub-units with differential interests make claims on scarce organizational resources. The extent of the claims is likely to be a reflection of the unit's perception of how critical the resources up for negotiation are to its survival and development. The success any claimant has in furthering his interests will be a consequence of his ability to generate support for his demand.

It is the involvement of sub-units in such demand- and support-generating processes within the decision-making processes of the organization that constitutes the political dimension. Political behaviour is defined as behaviour by individuals, or, in collective terms, by sub-units, within an organization that makes a claim against the resource-sharing system of the organization. As Burns (1961) has succinctly put it:

'Corporations are co-operative systems assembled out of the

usable attributes of people. They are also social systems within which people compete for advancement; in so doing they make use of others. . . . The hierarchic order of rank and power that prevails in them is at the same time a single control system and a career ladder. . . . Politics are the exploitation of resources, both physical and human, for the achievement of more control over others, and thus of safer, or more comfortable, or more satisfying terms of individual existence.'

In later papers (1962, 1965) Burns develops a theory to explain this political behaviour. He goes well beyond the simple sub-goal identification and bargaining model set out by March (1962) and Cyert and March (1963):

'The notion either of a hierarchy of sub-goals which, although generated within, and by the existence of, the organization, wander out of line so far as organizational goals are concerned, or of an organizational goal generated by the consensus reached by individuals, each with personal goals, bargaining and learning their way towards a satisfactory equilibrium between their goals and those of the working community can *itself* [author's emphasis] only be realized and made operational if we accept the fact that the organization represents only one of several means–end systems for realizing the goals of the individual . . .' (Burns, 1965: 176).

To Burns, the individual has commitments other than those that enlist him as a resource of the working organization. He calls these political and career commitments. The aim of political commitments is to increase the individual's personal power by attaching him to parties of people who represent the same kind of resource and wish to enhance its exchange value, or to cabals[1] that seek to control or influence the exercise of patronage in the firm. Career commitments, while not necessarily different in their ultimate goals, refer to the advancement or defence of the individual's status. These two systems are regarded as interdependent. They act upon and react to the others; in particular, the political system and the career structure will influence the constitution and operation of the working organization. The issues in which they are involved arise from the conflicting demands on the rewards of the enterprise, its uncommitted

[1] For an analysis of the functions of cliques and cabals, see Burns (1955).

resources (or the allocation of capital), the direction of the activities of others, and patronage (promotion, new appointments, and the distribution of rights and privileges).

In *White Collar*, C. Wright Mills offers a biting description of career advancement in an organizational context. Success no longer specifically implies becoming an independent entrepreneur. With this change in emphasis has come a change in ideology to justify it:

> 'Now the stress is on agility rather than ability, on "getting along" in a context of associates, superiors, and rules, rather than "getting ahead" across an open market; on who you know rather than what you know; on techniques of self display and the generalized knack of handling people. But the most important single factor is "personality," which commands attention . . . by charm . . . force of character, or . . . demeanor. . . . Accomplishment without personality is unfortunate. . . . Personality without industry is undesirable. Getting ahead becomes a continual selling job. . . . You have a product and that product is yourself' (Mills, 1951: 260-5).

Glaser (1968) also is concerned with the sources and strategies of career development. He notes that procedures for promotion may be fairly well ordered and even printed out in detail for those in a particular career. The formality of those procedures, however, does not prevent the individual from attempting to exert pressure on those who process the procedures: 'The resort to strategic sponsors and their power is an important strategy here' (Glaser, 1968: 193). Martin and Strauss (1956) give an illuminating account of the reciprocity involved in the sponsor and protégé relationship. The protégé may complement his superior by being strong in an area of activity where his sponsor is weak; he may serve in a role as detail man, adviser, and confidant. A given sponsor may have a cluster of protégés surrounding him. Ties of loyalty as well as need compel him to push for advancing 'his men' as he moves up: 'As a result, top management echelons of many companies are made up of inter-locking cliques – certain powerful sponsors and their adherents' (1965: 109). In this way, the power structure of the organization is superimposed upon the formal structure of relations.

Clearly, power plays and strategies of career development are subject to various forms of social control. Crozier (1964) criticizes Dalton (1959) for his neglect of these controls: '[Dalton] is so haunted by the fear of being misled by the formal structure and the formal definitions of the roles that, in his analysis of the ways managers really behave, he reports only irregularities, back-door deals, and subtle blackmail. . . . No organization could survive if it were run solely by individual and clique back-door deals' (1964: 166). Crozier goes on to note (p. 167) four main stabilizing factors: 'The necessity for the members of the different groups to live together; the fact that the existence of each group's privileges depends to quite a large extent on the existence of other groups' privileges; the general consensus among all groups about keeping certain minimum standards of efficiency; and, finally, the very stability of group relationships.' Time is a further limit on aggrandizement, as is location in the organization's structure; not all possible sponsors are approachable; not all sources of information can be reached to be tapped. At some point, even in the most hard-fought power conflicts, those who perceive the struggle to be going against them will consider the aftermath of the conflict. It is not always convenient for the losers to leave. Both parties will sooner or later acknowledge that they will have to live together when the conflict is over. Coser (1964) has suggested that the power struggle itself may be a very necessary part of achieving a new stability of relations between the parties over time. Accommodation, he believes, can be reached only when the contenders have assessed their respective strength in conflict. Eventually 'the parties must agree upon rules and norms allowing them to assess their respective power position in the struggle. Their common interest leads them to accept rules which enhance their mutual dependence in the very pursuit of their antagonistic goals. Such arguments make their conflict, so to speak, self-liquidating' (Coser, 1964: 405).

Nevertheless, as long as organizations continue as resource-sharing systems where there is an inevitable scarcity of those resources, political behaviour will occur: 'The specialization of function not only proceduralizes and so restrains power, it also creates functionaires with a function to defend and a constituency to represent and draw strength from' (Long, 1962: 114). If the dominant occupational ideology defines success as career mobility and if people continue to be rewarded for that mobility, they will attempt to influence the procedures for mobility established in any occupation.

One of the major hypotheses of this study is that such political behaviour is likely to be a special feature of large-scale innovative decisions. These decisions are likely to threaten existing patterns of resource-sharing. New resources may be created and appear to fall within the jurisdiction of a department or individual who has not previously been a claimant in a particular area. This department, or its principal representative, may see this as an opportunity to increase its, or his, status and rewards in the organization. Those who see their interests threatened by the change may invoke resistance in the joint decision process. In all these ways new political action is released and ultimately the existing distribution of power is endangered.

The impact of a large-scale computer installation, it is suggested, will have substantially similar consequences for the organization concerned. In the joint decision process involving the Old Guard and the New Guard (Kahn *et al.*, 1964: 128), the issues that are likely to arise will have to do with the relative contribution that either side can claim for its knowledge or skill contributed as resources, and the right thereby to the greater or lesser share of command over total resources. In the present case, the control problem involving the inclusive leadership system and its innovating subsystem is complicated by the control problem within the innovating subsystem itself. In the fifteen or so years in which computers have been used commercially, there have been dramatic changes in computer technology. These changes have not only kept user task environments in a considerable state of flux and uncertainty, but also brought changes in the occupational structure of the industry. The relative statuses of the various occupational groups have changed: programmers no longer occupy the high status they once did. Status systems, however, are slow to adjust, and recognition frequently lags behind capabilities. Newer specialties are often more expansionist than older ones, since they have not been accepted and are still trying to prove themselves. To use Thompson's (1961) phrase, power conflicts thus arise over perceptions of 'the reality of interdependence'. In a changing technological environment the right to review or to be consulted may be distributed in a manner inconsistent with the distribution of ability. This may lead to jurisdictional struggles until a further balance in the state of interdependence is achieved.

It was pointed out in the previous chapter that the theoretically most developed analyses of organizational decision-making, those of

March and Simon (1958) and Cyert and March (1963), are lacking in certain respects. While the earlier more detailed discussion made it clear that the above theories are by no means identical, and that certain criticisms are more applicable to one theory than another, for the sake of brevity here the criticisms will be lumped together.

First, the above theories are virtually untestable on an aggregate basis because they are presented in a universal and non-structural form. Theories, even in a universal form, should be specified in a societal context and related to societal structures and organizations. Second, decisions are not made by individuals or by role occupants, but via processes which are affected by properties of the unit or units in which the decision is to be made. Information failures that characterize 'bounded rationality' are rooted in structural problems of hierarchy, specialization, and centralization, and do not just reflect the malfunctioning of thought processes. Conflict in a joint decision-making process may arise not only as a result of differences in goals and perceptions but with regard to the transference of authority over a particular area from one sub-unit to another. While 'satisficing man' may be a considerable advance in realism over the economist's maximizing man, the former is never operationally defined. In consequence, the role that powerful interests might play in the search and choice processes tends to be played down. Finally, although Cyert and March (1963) discuss conflict they are never specific about its determinants. They offer only vague discussions of sub-goal identification. Their model of coalition formation, while smacking of realism, lacks depth of presentation. There is no mention of the organizational structure of the firm, nor therefore of the membership of the bargaining subgroups in the coalition. Little attention is given to how and why coalitions are formed and changed, or to the generation of support and how the structure of the organization might limit such a process.

While our analysis has gone much further than Cyert and March in discussing the determinants of the political behaviour they describe, if it is going to add to existing work, an attempt must be made to explain processually the relationship between the strategies pursued by the various interested parties and the final decisional outcome. Such an analysis involves tracing out the generation of demands and the mobilization of support for those demands. Finally, for the sake of analytical precision the concept of politics requires differentiation into the elements of power and authority.

POWER AND ORGANIZATIONAL DECISION-MAKING

In 1964, Kahn wrote: 'The descent from theory to data is often painful. With respect to power, there are a few extra twinges involved in that downward journey because the research results so far available are few and modest' (1964: 52).[1] He then went on to describe three studies of superior–subordinate relationships and a study of control in a trade union, all carried out at Michigan. By 1968, Silverman was arguing for a social action approach to the study of organizations and, in particular, for 'an analysis of the balance of power within an organization and of the factors that govern it' (1968: 234). Mouzelis (1967) talked of feats already achieved as far as intraorganizational power relations were concerned: 'What is most needed ... is to combine in a more systematic way this new awareness of the internal power structure of an organization with the wider problems of power in modern societies' (1967: 162). However, he could cite only Dalton (1959) and Crozier (1964) to back up his argument about a 'new awareness'. In 1968-9 seven papers on power appeared in the four major sociology journals in Britain and the USA. Six of these – Wrong (1968), Giddens (1968), Marshall (1969), Lehman (1969), Zald (1969), and Bannester (1969) – are theoretical articles. Only Warren (1968) supports his theoretical ideas with data. Only political scientists appear to have collected extensive data with the concept of power in mind, and even in these instances the operational measures used have generated much controversy.[2]

As far as organizational studies of power are concerned, one of the main problems is gaining access to do research. In many cases, sociologists rely upon the cooperation and financial support of those who control the organizations they seek to study. As Mouzelis (1967: 163) has stated, the practical issue then becomes whether 'groups would systematically oppose and hinder the sociologists' attempts to bring into the open the power structure and political struggles taking place in the organization'. The present research did in fact suffer a multitude of hindrances for exactly those reasons.

Aside from the practical problem of limited research access, the concept of power has received scant empirical attention because of controversy over its conceptual elaboration and operational defini-

[1] Crozier (1964: 145-50) presents a similar argument.
[2] Much of the argument has been over ways of operationalizing community power. For a summary of this literature, see Hawley and Wirt (1968).

tion. The latter aspect is discussed in Chapter 4, which describes the research methods used. We turn now to consider concepts of power and authority in relation to innovative decision-making.

There are as many different definitions of the concepts of authority and power as there are of the concept of role. This is not the place to effect yet another survey of them.[1] However, a number of important theoretical distinctions must be made if our analysis is to move off on a sound footing. For Talcott Parsons, authority refers to the legitimate position of an individual or group: 'Authority is essentially the institutional code within which the use of power as medium is organized and legitimized' (1967: 319). Authority is then, for Parsons, a basis of power, in fact the only basis of power, rather than a kind of power. The use of power is restricted entirely to the achievement of collective goals: 'Power rests on the consensual solidarity of a system . . . in this sense it is the capacity of a unit in the social system, collective or individual, to establish or activate commitments to performance that contributes to, or is in the interest of, attainment of the goals of a collectivity' (1967: 504). Giddens (1968) holds that Parson's collectivistic orientation to power shares some of the basic difficulties and deficiencies of his general theory: 'By treating power as necessarily (by definition) legitimate, and thus starting from the assumption of consensus of some kind between power-holders and those subordinate to them, Parsons virtually ignores . . . the necessarily hierarchical character of power, and the divisions of interest which are frequently consequent upon it' (1968: 264). Clearly, positions of power offer to their incumbents definite material and psychological rewards, and thereby stimulate conflicts between those who want power and those who have it. This brings into play a multiplicity of possible strategies of coercion, deceit, and manipulation which can be used either to acquire or to hold on to power: 'Any sociological theory which treats such phenomena as "incidental", or as "secondary and derived", and not as structurally intrinsic to power differentials, is blatantly inadequate' (Giddens, 1968: 264).

The extent of the consensus between those with legitimated power (authority) and those subordinate to them is a major variable in the present study. The formal structure of power and legitimacy

[1] The interested reader might consult Peabody (1964) for authority, and Wrong (1968) or Lehman (1969) for power.

is regarded as problematic. This issue has been expressed in the literature in a number of ways. Barnard (1938) talks of the authority of position and the authority of leadership, while Bass (1960) distinguishes between power of position and personal power. More recently, Peabody (1964) has discussed the differences between formal and functional authority. All these authors imply that authority requires to be fortified in interaction. A position may give a leader authority, but the exercise of authority requires interaction. It is at this point that the leader's problems begin. Blau (1955) has posited that a superior's ability to exercise authority depends on the willingness of his subordinates to obey him. The superior not only controls but is controlled. Crozier (1964: 150) similarly considers subordinates as 'free agents who can discuss their own problems and bargain about them, who not only submit to a power structure but also participate in that structure'.

It has already been argued that if certain groups within a social system compare their share of power, wealth, and status with that of other groups and question the legitimacy of this distribution, discontent and overt conflict are likely to ensue. The critical consideration is, then, what factors lead groups and individuals to question at a certain point the legitimacy of the system of distribution of authority and rewards? A further source of discontent in certain poorly institutionalized social systems is the possibility that individuals may not know what either their superiors or their subordinates regard as legitimate behaviour.

The present question is, however, how superiors attain and sustain legitimacy. The key issue is the norms and values adhered to by both superior and subordinate. According to Blau (1964: 199): 'Compliance is a cost that is judged on the basis of social norms of fairness. Excessive demands lead to disapproval.' As a group representative the superior will be expected to some extent to symbolize the values and standards of the group. And yet the contact the superior has with the norms of the external environment, coupled with his need for some acceptance by that environment if he is to be an effective group representative, may place on him pressures to conform to norms contrary to his group's. Michels (1949: 311), quoting the example of the 'deproletarianization' of socialist leaders, suggests that this is a special problem for minority group leaders. Other empirical examples of this same phenomenon have been provided by Gluckman (1949) in discussing the village headman's role, and more recently by Kaplan (1959) and Evan (1965) in examining the research administrator's role. Data will be presented shortly to demonstrate that the head of a Management Services department is faced with a similar problem.

Evidence from experimental psychology has established that 'competence in helping the group achieve its goals, and early conformity to its normative expectations for members, provide the potential for acting as a leader and being perceived as such' (Hollander and Julian, 1969). Dubno (1965) has provided further evidence that a superior's legitimation is aided by his competence in a major group activity. Julian and Hollander (1966) found that, aside from the significance of task competence, a leader's 'interest in group members' and 'interest in group activity' were significantly related to group members' willingness to have him continue in that position. While it is doubtful that in a non-laboratory situation subordinates could exert sufficient pressure to remove their superior, the above findings certainly support the conclusion that the leader's source of authority is perceived and reacted to as a relevant element in the leadership process.

In contrast to prestige and authority structures, power strucures rest primarily not on a social consensus concerning expectations about privileges or rights between superiors and subordinates, but on the distribution of the resources by means of which compliance with demands can be enforced. Following Dahl (1957: 203), power involves 'A having power over B to the extent that he can get B to do something that B would not otherwise do'. Power is, then, a property of social relationships, not an attribute of the actor. An essential aspect of this theory of power is the notion of dependency. Emerson (1962) supplies the initial exploration of dependency. Blau (1964: 118) interprets him as follows: 'By supplying services in demand to others, a person establishes power over them. If he regularly renders needed services they cannot readily obtain elsewhere, others become dependent on and obligated to him for these services' – unless they in turn can supply him with services that he needs. The power of one individual over another thus depends on the social alternatives, or lack of them, available to the subjected individual. This involves a conception of power somewhat wider than the one expressed in dyadic form by Dahl (1957). There is here a basis of a systems view of power. To understand the relative power of A and B one needs to know details of this dyad's relations with X, Y, Z to *n*. In this way the power network or power structure is revealed.

An examination of the determinants of dependency should uncover the power base of an actor in respect of his role set: 'The base of an actor's power consists of all the resources, opportunities, acts, objects that he can exploit in order to affect the behavior of another' (Dahl, 1957: 203). Dependency is, then, a product of an imbalance of exchange between individuals and the ability of one actor to control others through his possession of resources. Such resources must not only be possessed by the power aspirant, but also be controlled by him. Bannester (1969: 386) makes this point succinctly: 'It is immaterial who owns the gun and is licensed to carry it; the question is who has his finger on the trigger.'

Mechanic (1962: 352) has shown that within organizations dependency can be generated by controlling access to the resources of 'information, persons and instrumentalities'. To the extent that these resources can be controlled, 'lower participants make higher-ranking participants dependent upon them. Thus, dependence together with the manipulation of the dependency relationship is the key to the power of lower participants' (1962: 256). Unfortunately there are few empirical examples describing such a process. Scheff (1961) analyses the failure of a state mental hospital to bring about intended reform because of the opposition of the hospital attendants. The power of the ward attendants largely derived from the dependence on them of the physicians. This dependence resulted from the physicians' short tenure, their lack of interest in administration, and the large amount of administrative responsibility they had to assume. An agreement developed between the physicians and the attendants whereby the attendants would take on some of the responsibilities and obligations of the physicians in exchange for increased power in decision-making processes concerning patients. If a physician failed to honour his part of the agreement, the attendants would disrupt his contact with patients by withholding information and being disobedient and generally uncooperative. Sykes (1961) quotes a similar example, this time describing the dependence of prison guards on inmates. Although guards could report prisoners for disobedience, too many reports from a particular guard would give his superiors the impression that he was ineffective. The result was a trading agreement whereby the guards allowed violation of certain rules in return for co-operative behaviour.

Control over information is a critical resource for mobilizing power in a decision-taking situation. McCleery (1960) has provided interesting data on power relations in a prison. His main point is that the formal system of authority relations could be considerably modified by the location and control of communication channels. Because all reports had to pass through the custodial hierarchy, this group was able to subvert the industrial and reform goals represented by the Prison Professional Services and Industry Programs. The head of the custodial hierarchy, the prison captain, was for the same reason able to exert considerable control over decisions made by his immediate superior, the warden. McCleery concludes that while 'the institutional autocrat is not responsible to his subordinates, he is no less responsible than any other executive to those who define the premises of his discretion' (1960: 51).

The pertinent research question for present purposes is: Under what conditions is a superior likely to be most dependent on his subordinates? Walter (1966), in a study of decision-making in two cities, confirmed his hypothesis that 'the influence of subordinates over superiors on non-programmed choices is greater than the influence of superiors over subordinates' (p. 206). His reasons for this were somewhat inconclusive: 'This outcome is apparently a function of the subordinate's greater knowledge, or, perhaps, the shared presumption by superiors that subordinates know more than they do.'

Given our interest in innovative decision-making jointly involving executives and computer experts, what power the experts have over their immediate superior and the executives is likely to be consequent upon the amount of dependency in the relationship. The expert can maintain a power position over high-ranking persons in the organization as long as they are dependent upon him for special skills and access to certain kinds of information. It is expected that innovative decisions will be characterized by uncertainty. Such uncertainty can be used as a major power resource by the expert. Crozier (1964: 131) cites the example of the technical engineer who is able to control the actions of his director by setting technical limits on what it is and what it is not possible to do. Others also have referred to the role of uncertainty in power relations. Talking of power relations among prisoners, McCleery (1960: 58) noted: 'Leadership in the inmate society involved the ability to explain, predict or control to some degree a situation in which others were uncertain and helpless.' Zald (1962) found that the degree of uncertainty in the relation of administrative means to organizational ends was a contributory factor to both the power balance and the level of conflict in five correctional institutions. Gordon and Becker (1964) draw attention to the instability of expert power. They attribute shifts in power within hospitals from physicians to administrators to the impact of modern medical techniques. These enable administrators to specify the procedures and resources to be used in treatment. Specified procedures improve administrative coordination, but mounting conflict may be anticipated as physicians defend their discretionary prerogatives against the encroaching rules.

In a joint decision process the expert is unlikely to be omnipotent even with the most technically uncertain problem. There is the factor of political access. The position the expert occupies in the structure of relationships in the organization will affect his ability to control and direct the actions of others, as will his position in the communication structure of the organization. Furthermore, executives generally have ultimate power to hire and fire experts. This is likely to exert a major control over the power strategies of the experts. Also, a superior may attempt to reduce his dependence on any group of experts by arranging to pick up the specialist information they possess from other sources. In doing so, however, he will create an exchange imbalance in his relationship with them. He may, of course, attempt to coerce his experts into giving him advice or, alternatively, resign himself to doing without it. Dahl (1967: 238) has noted that a further strategy used by leaders 'is to co-opt[1] rivals into the central leadership group. Another is to buy them off, or to undercut their support by making concessions to their followers.' Georg Simmel (1950), in his discussion of coalition formation in triads, describes the strategy of divide and rule used by a leader faced with a coalition of subordinates. All these strategies may be used by an executive seeking to reduce his dependence on an expert group.

The expert, however, need not simply rely upon the presumed dependency of others that his mystical powers can give him. He can

[1] This strategy is discussed most fully by Selznick (1966).

seek support for the demands he is making. Again, the amount of support a person achieves in a situation will be conditional on the structure and nature of his organizational relationships. Respect might be an important factor here, as will be general personal acceptability and particular feelings of indebtedness felt by relevant others. Even the timing of a demand and the way in which it is presented (Devons, 1950) may be decisive in terms of the support it receives. In short, 'where support is lacking, it may be mobilized; where attention is unfocused, it may be directed by advertising; where merits are not obvious, they may be presented in striking form' (Wildavsky, 1964: 177).

Crozier (1964) has analysed the evolution of power relationships in systems. He underlines the self-defeating nature of expert power: 'The invasion of all domains by rationality, of course, gives power to the expert who is an agent of this progress. But the expert's success is constantly self-defeating. The rationalization process gives him power, but the end results of rationalization curtail this power. As soon as a field is well covered, as soon as the first intuitions and innovations can be translated into rules and programs, the expert's power disappears' (p. 165). Crozier also hypothesizes that, 'in the long run, power will tend to be closely related to the kind of uncertainty upon which depends the life of the organization' (p. 164). It has already been hypothesized that innovative decisions will be characterized by uncertainty. Expert power might be expected to be maximal when the expert is involved in an innovative decision in that area of the business upon which the life of the organization depends.

THEORETICAL BEARINGS

The analyses of organizational decision-taking proposed by March and Simon (1958) and Cyert and March (1963), while noteworthy for their political realism, have been found wanting. The present analysis seeks to complement existing work by exploring the nature of the 'political' in the context of an innovative decision process. For reasons already given, such political behaviour is likely to be especially pronounced in the uncertain task environment surrounding an innovative decision. The political dimension will be analysed with reference to authority and power relations in the decision process.

Particular emphasis will be given to the part played by individuals in the structuring of social action over time. By their ability to exert power over others, individuals can change or maintain structures as well as the norms and expectations upon which these structures rest. An individual's behaviour is therefore governed not only by the structure of the situation in which he participates but also by his ability to shape and mould that structure to suit his own interests. He can do this only if he has sufficient power to impose his will on others despite their opposition. The weapons of such contests are the resources that individuals possess, control, and can manipulate, and the ties of dependency that they can form with relevant others

Within decision-taking processes, power *strategies* are employed by the various interested parties through their *demands*. Strategies 'are the links between the intentions and perceptions of officials and the political system that imposes restraints and created opportunities for them' (Wildavsky, 1964: 63). A demand 'is an expression of opinion that an authoritative allocation with regard to a particular subject matter should or should not be made by those responsible for doing so' (Easton, 1965: 38). The more complex, heterogeneous, and differentiated a political structure is, the more likely are disparate demands to be made. Such disparities are a product of organizational position, professional training, and adherence to subgroup values and reference groups. A joint decision process involving an inclusive leadership system and an innovative subsystem will be characterized by disparate demands. Not all demands can be met. A competitive struggle will develop in which the innovating subsystem (which may be differentiated itself) will attempt to utilize its various resources to generate support for its demands. Where a demand is voiced, who articulates it, who hears it, and how widely it is diffused are all matters of signal importance for the future stages of its career. The processing of demands and the generation of support are the principal components of the general political structure through which power may be wielded. The final decisional outcome will evolve out of the processes of power mobilization attempted by each party in support of its demand.

CHAPTER 3

The Setting:
Overview of Events 1955-68

Brian Michaels was founded by the present chairman's father just before World War I. The first store was located in Wolverhampton. Slowly throughout the 1920s and 1930s the business expanded and more and more clothing stores were opened in the Midlands. In these early days the company's head office was in Wolverhampton. By the late 1940s a new head office had been built in the centre of Birmingham.

Throughout this period the company had been expanding but always in the clothing trade. Early in the 1950s, on the death of his father, the present chairman, also called Brian Michael, made the decision to diversify his interests into furniture. The focal point for this activity became the London area and an administrative office was set up there to cope with this work. Michaels now had a show-piece head office in Birmingham and two large administrative offices, one in Wolverhampton and the other in south London. The 1950s brought unparallelled expansion for both the clothing and furniture divisions of the company. In the early and mid 1960s two further administrative offices were opened to cope with the rapid expansion of business.

HISTORY OF COMPUTER DEVELOPMENTS IN MICHAELS STORES 1955-64

The massive increase in company business between 1952 and 1968, in both clothing and furniture, put a great deal of strain on all sections of the company's labour force. Many of the computer specialists and line managers today acknowledge that the phenomenal growth in that time period would not have been possible without the assistance of computers.

The first interest in computers was shown in 1955 when Brian Michael was contacted by a business friend, Sam Miller, who was about to install one of the first commercial computer systems in Britain. It was suggested that furniture stock control might be a profitable area to investigate for a computer application. Brian Michael expressed provisional interest. In September 1955 Harry Bell was taken from his O & M (organization and methods) job in the office of the furniture division in London and asked to make a study of the possible use of computers in the company. He began by paying a number of visits to Miller's computer installation. The area that Miller was dealing with, while not strictly comparable with the kind of work carried out at Michaels, did indicate that the computer could no longer be considered a 'toy' or tool for mathematicians.

Harry Bell, who was, he says, 'operating as a one-man-band at this time', worked on the subject until April 1956 when he produced a report for the Michaels management. In this he suggested that a computer should be used for stock control. He saw the main advantage of running a stock-control system on a computer not as a saving of staff but as a means of running on a reduced inventory balance, i.e. a more efficient stock. Further, he believed that if the computer could successfully tackle the nub of the retail problem – getting the right stock in the right place at the right time – then it could tackle any other job that the firm was likely to consider suitable for electronic data-processing.

This report persuaded the Michaels directors that they must investigate the feasibility and economic possibilities of a computer system as opposed to the existing manual system. Bell, realizing that the firm's knowledge of electronics was non-existent, asked Miller to work on a consultancy basis with Michaels, and to help to establish whether the job was practical, economic, and possible of attainment within a reasonable period of time.

It must be understood here that, while the firm's existing stock-control system was working most efficiently with manual procedures, Michaels was faced with three imminent problems. These were:

– the rapid expansion of the business
– an increasing shortage of suitably trained staff
– a need for more information than the manual system could supply.

The more Michaels increased in size, the more it overloaded its existing methods. It was therefore imperative that a way be found to increase efficiency for less time and less cost. Operating a computer would give the firm vital breathing-space. This would be made possible by developing, on a computer, a system of control by exception, which would make the efforts of existing staff more effective and also enable them to cope with extra work.

Harry Bell was joined by Ted Morgan, a stock controller, also from the London office. They set out to investigate what machines were available and which of these would be most appropriate for the firm's purposes. At this time there were only ten to fifteen machines on order in the country. Morgan described how he and Bell felt as if they were operating in 'inventor's land'. After following up some of the more obvious alternatives they eventually 'stumbled' on a small electronics firm called Scientific Electronics. Morgan described their first contact with a representative from Scientific Electronics called Scott:

'He was the scruffiest character I'd ever seen. His suit was worn and creased and his Balliol tie was splattered with egg. He was completely unlike the smooth sales types we'd run into from the other companies. We tried out the cross-talk routine we'd used before in similar meetings and the darned bloke appeared to be going to drop off to sleep. This went on for about an hour, with Harry and I getting more and more exasperated, until finally Scott picked up an old envelope, wrote down a few symbols on it, and said, "Here's the answer to your problem".

We didn't understand his solution but when he'd explained what the symbols meant it looked as if he'd done it. We couldn't believe it! We'd been working on this for months by now and then this scruffy nut comes along in a few minutes and wraps it all up! We went more or less immediately to see Scientific Electronic's hardware and found they were way ahead of the others technically. They had magnetic film and magnetic disc. Their whole storage concept was superior to the others in this country.'

By now the Michaels directors were finding it increasingly difficult to understand computer jargon and to decide which, if any, of the available machines warranted further consideration. The directors, somewhat suspicious of the claims made by the computer manufacturers, demanded a test run. Morgan takes up the story from here:

'Finally, on 4, 5, and 6 of July 1956 we arranged for the three remaining manufacturers to demonstrate that they could do the job with their existing equipment. We gave them some specimen data for a simple run through, and then the demonstration was to be followed by discussion between them and the directors.

We knew before the demonstration that Scientific Electronics were technically the best but we were worried about their lack of organization – their basic lack of a commercial approach would become apparent to our directors. We tried to chivvy them up a bit by having some practice runs before the big day but you just couldn't get through to them the urgency of it all. They were just a bunch of boffins.'

Eventually it was decided to order a machine from Scientific Electronics, hereafter called the SE 100. This decision was not popular with many of the board members. Nor was it popular with Brian Michael himself because of his friendship with Miller and therefore his preference for Miller's machine.

Thus, although the directors did agree to the purchase of a computer, their decision was brought about, in effect, by the personality and enthusiasm of Bell. The Michaels directors knew nothing of computers; their expertise lay in the fields of buying and selling. Bell described himself during this period as 'an island surrounded by a hostile sea':

'Management didn't understand what was going on. They didn't even know what to call me. At one time it was suggested that I should be called "consultant to Michaels".'

In September 1956 Bell and Morgan recruited three programmers. All had degrees in mathematics, one with first-class honours. The following year, two O & M officers (Bill Reilly and Tim Philby) were recruited from within the company (from the Work Study department at Wolverhampton), and a computer operator was recruited from outside. By 1958 the team had increased to ten programmers, two O & M officers, two liaison officers with the user departments, and several computor operators. Meanwhile the directors had decided that the first computer job should be applied to the clothing side of the business rather than the furniture side. This change probably reflects the tremendous pressure on the clothing side at that time. Initially, Bell, Morgan, and Reilly, and the three original programmers spent a great deal of time in London where the SE 100 was being manufactured. Morgan and Reilly then began to find the technical demands made on them in London more than they could cope with, and gradually the three programmers spent more and more time on their own.

The SE 100 was finally delivered on 1 April 1958. A Computer department was formed, and all concerned were brought together in the main administrative office of the Michaels clothing division in Wolverhampton.

Even in those early days, the clothing stock-control job was seen as only the first stage of a progressive electronic data-processing programme. It was hoped to go on to integrate management, accounting, and costing. Bell now thinks that this Michaels stock-control application was probably the first successful computer operation in the country – in the sense that it paid off financially. He says:

'The early computers were mechanizing existing processes. We tried to use a computer as a computer and not as an accounting machine. Also, we were better able than most to design a system for a computer. I'd studied problems of distribution and linear programming in my previous firm. Most firms, at this time, were looking to computers for prestige. Also many put them under the accountant, who acted as a "dead hand" on computer developments.'

But although the system was a good one and proved a financial success, the stock controllers, whose work was being changed, were very unhappy at the idea of a computerized system. Reilly commented:

'We started off with a pretty high error rate on output but eventually got this down to 1·5 per cent. The stock controllers took every opportunity to throw this 1·5 per cent at us while refusing to recognize that they had for years had a 4 per cent error rate on the manual system. This was a delaying tactic; they were faced with a big unknown device and a crowd of peculiar characters saying that they could put stock control on a computer in a couple of years. In their minds it was a matter of, "Jesus, what's going to happen to us now?" '

In 1959 Harry Bell left the company for a better job elsewhere. The Computer department was now given joint heads. Ted Morgan was put in charge of the data preparation and computer output while

Gerald Lane, the senior of the three original programmers, was given control of programming and operations.

About the same time as Bell left, Jim Kenny arrived to set up an O & M department. Kenny had been asked to take the appointment by the chief personnel officer at Michaels, who had been worried for some time about relations between the Computer department and the rest of the company. It was felt that an O & M department could better represent the interests, experiences, and feelings of user departments than was being permitted by way of the present direct relations with the programmers. Only the very unusual event of the direct personal intervention of Brian Michael persuaded Kenny to take the post. The O & M department was set up in the new head office of the company in Birmingham. The Computer department was twenty miles away in the Wolverhampton administrative office. The new department thus had direct contact with all the major centralized company functions. Its first four recruits came from within the company, and in the following year (1960), Bill Reilly and Tom Reagan were recruited from the Computer department.

Kenny was much more aware than Bell had been of the difficult human relations factors associated with the introduction of change. Bell, of course, had had to face a great deal of resentment. He recalled how the then chief personnel manager had reassured him that the company would not make him 'a machine minder'. Bell had a reputation of mythical proportions among the early staff for being the original 'political animal'. One O & M officer commented with both awe and nostalgia:

'The thing you have to remember about Harry is that he was a superb politician. He played the art of brinkmanship superbly.'

Kenny was less than satisfied with what he saw on his arrival:

'When I came, the computer was operating but in a meaningless way. It was obvious that we must study what the stock controllers were actually doing. The stock controllers still had their manual records; the computer output was irrelevant.'

There were tremendous arguments with the stock controllers during this period, for the latter were still very chary of entrusting their work to this new and completely untried system. Kenny, however, avoided using a sharp, surgical approach with the new system. For a while, he produced computer runs which gave the stock controllers all the information they thought they required, even though much of it was superfluous. Then slowly he cut this down, demonstrating to the stock controllers all the time that they did not really need it. Kenny described with some relish the end-point of this process:

> 'The actual changeover to computer documentation took place over one weekend. I just sent in my four O & M bods and told them to remove the lot [the manual records].'

Today the attitude of the chief stock controller is:

> 'I do not know how we would begin to operate without a computer. It would be impossible. In the early days Mr Kenny and I had very serious disagreements. He was able to overrule me by saying, "You will do it". Our hidden fear was that the computer would take over and that the Stock Control department would become virtually redundant. This is the fear that was in everybody's mind. It wasn't clear what was going to happen. Now, however, it is we who are pushing the computer whereas before it was the computer people who were pushing us.'

Although the principal financial saving of the computer was in the reduced level of stock held, the computer also secured a reduction in the number of clerks required to deal with the stock-control operation. The Stock Control department was able to dispense with eighty-five records clerks. None of the clerks had to be dismissed, however. Many became responsible for checking the output of the computer, for making out contracts, and for checking progress with manufacturers – all rather more interesting jobs than they had had before. The remainder were absorbed elsewhere in the company.

The successful implementation of the SE 100 reflected well on Kenny and his O & M department. By early 1961 some of the original programmers were beginning to feel short of up-to-date experience and moved on. About this time the company set up an Operational Research (OR) department. The first manager hit disaster with the firm. He apparently fell out of favour with his fellow specialists and the board. Kenny described this OR manager as 'an impossible guy':

> 'I said to Brian Michael, "This guy has got to go". He went there and then that Friday. I was now in charge of O & M and OR.'

The year 1961 turned out to be an eventful one. Kenny resigned in order to take up another appointment; but he was subsequently persuaded to stay on by Brian Michael himself. In the meantime, however, Fred Ramsbottom had been recruited to manage the O & M department. Kenny was given a vague assignment in management development.

Ramsbottom was quickly given the go-ahead to do a systems investigation of the furniture stock-control and accounting functions. By April 1962 an NTL 200 had been bought and installed, largely on the insistence of a board member who had close contacts with NTL. The NTL 200 was placed in an auxiliary office in Birmingham, near but not in the head office. It was given its own contingent of programmers, punch girls, and operators to match the team on the SE 100 at Wolverhampton.

During 1963 and early 1964 Ramsbottom campaigned for further computerization of the business. The administrative offices of the clothing division seemed the most obvious area for the next development. These offices, which employed between 400 and 500 people, the majority of them females under twenty-one years, did all the day-to-day clerical and financial work. Ramsbottom later recalled his lack of success:

'The directors weren't too keen on having computers in the administrative offices. This was the main side of the business where feelings were strongest and where the most entrenched systems were to be found. To me it was a prolific area for computerization, but in the minds of the entrenched this was the heart and soul of the business. The directors were afraid of the effects of computerization.'

By this time the SE 100 was quickly becoming obsolete. Ramsbottom was informed on one of his infrequent visits to the Computer department that it was costing £50,000 per year just for maintenance. Spares were becoming more and more difficult to find and its workload was building up beyond its capacity. Kenny later quipped: 'In the end, we couldn't even give the damned thing away, even to a university! '

Ramsbottom was told to look for a machine to replace the SE 100. At the same time, Kenny and the Computer department did their own investigations of the market. Ramsbottom, after consulting the programmers, opted for BCD. He later changed in favour of the Victor 300. Meanwhile, Kenny worked his way into the decision process. After a meeting with Henry de Ville, a sales director of Newton EDP, and various other members of the Newton board, he managed to persuade the Michaels directors to buy a Newton 350 computer.

Two weeks later Ramsbottom was dismissed. Brian Michaels purchased, in 1964, a Newton 350 – the first in Britain. Subsequently, in 1968, this model was upgraded to a Newton 1500. This was the first Newton 1500 purchased in Europe. Thus Kenny's meeting with de Ville in 1964 turned out to be fateful. As we shall see, it had significant long-term consequences for both computer developments and managerial relationships in Brian Michaels.

THE STRUCTURE OF THE MANAGEMENT SERVICES DEPARTMENT

Prior to the arrival of the Newton 350 in 1964, computer activities in Michaels were spread around three departments in three different locations (see diagram below). There was one computer manager responsible for the SE 100 and the NTL 200. As the diagram shows, these computers were twenty miles apart.

There were those who considered the computer manager's job to be an on-the-spot one. Now that Ramsbottom had left, Kenny took

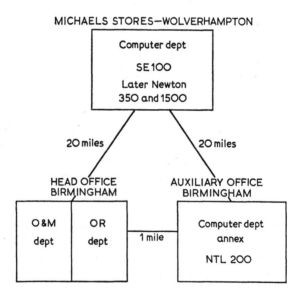

over again and immediately carried through a major structural change. The existing computer manager was transferred to another part of the business. Kenny appointed a computer manager for each of the two computers and made them responsible for operational problems only. Once the SE 100 had been replaced, the cream of the programmers were transferred to development work in a new department called Management Services. This was located in the company's head office. Kenny's justification for these changes at the time was twofold. First, he wanted to reduce the level of conflict that existed between the O & M department and the programmers. He thought that 'knocking their heads together under the same roof' would achieve this. Second, he thought 'the programmers' day-to-day concern with computer operations was impeding programming development'. He did not disclose his principal motive until much later. In 1966 the structure of the Management Services department was as shown below.

Management Services dept Head: J. Kenny		
O & M or Systems dept Manager: B. Reilly 15 systems analysts	Programming dept Manager: N. Turner 11 programmers	O R dept Manager: T. Carr 5 OR staff

It should be noted that the Michaels O & M officers had their title changed first, in 1965, to O & M analysts and then, in 1966, largely for market reasons, to systems analysts. Although the department retained the title of O & M in all official company reports throughout the period of the study, from 1966 onwards it was almost always referred to by Michaels employees as the Systems department. In the text, both department titles are used, and the department staff are referred to in a general way as 'analysts' except where the historical context is specific. These terminological uncertainties reflect the general uncertainty at the time about the specialties and skills involved, as will be shown later.

THE 1966-8 COMPUTER DECISION

In July 1968 an announcement appeared in the national press concerning the computer plans of Brian Michaels. It stated that initial capital outlay would be in the region of £1·5 million, and that planned expenditure would eventually run to over £5 million. Michaels had apparently been making some hefty decisions about computer developments. The terse announcement concealed all the interesting and relevant action. In fact, it had taken the company seven years to reach this decision, the last two and a half of which had cost it around £20,000 in staff time alone. Three of the six computer manufacturers who had been involved in the tendering process must have spent at least that amount in putting together a series of proposals for Michaels. Presumably the successful company would recoup its costs.

Developments prior to August 1966: After the decision had been announced, I asked the systems manager, Bill Reilly, if there had been any previous attempts to computerize the administrative offices of the clothing division. Characteristically, I received an excitable reply:

> 'By God there had! We didn't start off with a clean sheet by any means. Thompson [an early senior programmer] had a go. So did Ramsbottom later on.'

The first recorded attempt to computerize the administrative offices was found to have been made in September 1961 by the then Computer department. It was in respect of the Wolverhampton office, but by the early months of 1962 the application had been judged not technically feasible. There is no trace of a formal report made to the directors on the subject. However, a letter dated October 1963, from Ramsbottom to Hall, a clothing director, indicates that about this time an investigation was started in another of the clothing administrative offices. In early 1964, reports relating to two of the offices were produced by Ramsbottom and sent to the directors. It is not clear whether this second investigation was requested by the directors or not. This episode was closed with the directors indicating firmly that the question of replacing the SE 100 was entirely separate from the question of applying a computer to the work of the administrative offices. Ramsbottom, who was doing the pushing at this time, explained, as noted above, that to 'the entrenched' the administrative offices represented 'the heart and soul of the business'. Later in 1964 the Newton 350 was ordered to replace the SE 100.

On 18 May 1965 the O & M department produced terms of reference, but these were rejected by the managing director. Eventually, a report was prepared by the O & M department for the computerization of one of the clothing offices. Although the report was well received by the directors, they decided that further investigations were required. While these investigations were going on, the Management Services department was to undertake another investigation into the Wolverhampton office. No sooner had this project got under way, however, than the Michaels board received the news that one of its competitors had recently tried to computerize its administrative office procedures and had got in such a tangle that it had been unable to meet demands over Christmas. The Management Services department was obliged to keep quiet about future computer developments on the administrative side until the impact of this event had disappeared. The matter was not raised again until 1966.

Nevertheless, because the initial stock-control system had proved so successful, Management Services was anxious to take computer developments further and to put the accounting procedures of one of the administrative offices onto a computer. The Wolverhampton office (clothing division) was chosen for this purpose since it was physically closest to Michaels head office, where Management Services was located. During 1966 the systems analysts did a great deal of work analysing the procedures of the Wolverhampton office so that a brief could be given to those computer manufacturers who were in a position to supply suitable hardware.

August 1966: It was decided to obtain proposals from seven computer manufacturers. Brochures were prepared setting out the system of accounting in the Wolverhampton office and these were sent to computer manufacturers with a letter inviting them to submit quotations in December. The following companies, who had been recommended by a firm of computer consultants, were approached:

1. NTL
2. BCD
3. Newton
4. Wilson Electric

5. American Electronics
6. Victor
7. Alpha.

Of the seven manufacturers, all but Victor decided to tender for the job. The remaining six submitted proposals for the computer system in mid-November.

November 1966: The staff of the Management Services department – mainly the systems analysts – were now faced with the task of reading and evaluating these proposals, a mammoth task because of the sheer size of the reports. Most of the analysts had to work evenings and at weekends on the job and they believed, perhaps unjustly, that computer manufacturers operated from the premise that the thickest report would make the greatest impression. Many of the reports were found to contain arithmetic errors and the systems analysts had to spend three weeks laboriously checking each arithmetic calculation concerned with the flow of data into or out of the computer.

The process of revising the computer manufacturers' proposals caused a certain amount of strain to develop among the staff of the Management Services department. Discussions and informal meetings held among the systems analysts became increasingly emotional as the level of work increased, particularly as the time approached when a decision would have to be taken as to which of the manufacturers should be placed on the hardware shortlist. Five staff left during this period and work stress could have been a factor in their decision to terminate their employment with Michaels at this time. Systems analysts who were asked to look at the proposals of particular manufacturers tended to identify with those manufacturers, and in this way conflict was exacerbated.

December 1966: In an effort to secure as unbiased and accurate an assessment of the six proposals as possible, the Management Services department decided to send all the proposals to an outside company who had devised a computer simulation program known as SWIFT. This program would check the hardware and software claims of the systems proposed by the computer manufacturers. The systems analysts, for a short period, now had little to do. This alternation of a period of tremendous rush followed by a period of comparative inactivity, while decisions were taken or tests made, proved characteristic of their experience throughout the development of the project.

On 16 December the systems analysts met together informally to select their shortlist before the SWIFT results arrived on the following Monday. At this stage they believed that input was likely to be the most difficult feature of the new system, and therefore that they could most usefully compare the manufacturers' proposals from this point of view. After much discussion, they decided that the two most suitable manufacturers appeared to be BCD and Wilson Electric, both of which used some form of reading device. Teletype input was queried because it was felt that it would require well-trained operators who would be under considerable strain in operating the machines at the speed at which the input would be coming at them. The BCD reading device was seen as particularly advanced but it had the drawback of being six times as expensive as the Wilson Electric reader.

So far in the decision process the amount of contact between the programming team and the systems analysts had been negligible. This was to be a continuing feature of the process in spite of the fact that the two groups had adjoining offices. Turner and Reilly, the two managers, respectively, met more regularly, but Reilly made it clear that he trusted neither Turner nor Kenny.

Over the Christmas period further meetings were held, and the systems analysts and programmers each produced a list of the computer manufacturers in order of preference.

The systems analysts' list:
    1st   Wilson Electric and BCD
    2nd   Alpha
    3rd   Newton
    4th   NTL and American Electronics.

The programmers' list:
    1st   Wilson Electric and BCD
    2nd   Newton
    3rd   Alpha
    4th   NTL and American Electronics.

The SWIFT analysis influenced their thinking very little. Although it had cost Michaels several thousand pounds, its conclusion, in essence, was that any of the suggested configurations could do the job. It can be seen that, if a shortlist of two machines were accepted, there would be no disagreement between the two groups. Kenny, however, felt strongly that it would be most unwise to eliminate Newton at this stage, particularly since Michaels was already successfully using a Newton machine. He therefore exercised his prerogative as head of Management Services and insisted that Newton should go on the list. To say the least, this action was not popular with Reilly or Turner.

January-February 1967: During the early months of 1967, Reilly and Turner, the systems and programming managers, were convinced that the contract should not be awarded to Newton and they gave their respective allegiances to Wilson Electric and BCD. It seemed that Kenny, Reilly, and Turner were at this time using quite different criteria by which to assess the suitability of the' various computers. Kenny placed great importance upon the need for a cooperative relationship with the manufacturer concerned, and stressed that such a relationship had already been established with Newton. Reilly and Turner, in contrast, thought much more in terms of the relative technical capacities of the different systems as they perceived them. These divergent views led to a great deal of argument and, on occasion, to strained relationships.

On 9 January, Kenny, Reilly, and Turner met two of the directors (one from the clothing division and one from the furniture division). At this meeting it was decided that all the manufacturers except Wilson Electric and Newton should be told that Michaels was no longer interested in their services. Newton was to be asked to consider upgrading the existing 350 machine while Wilson Electric was to be asked to quote for the Wolverhampton job plus one-half of the work of another of the administrative offices. Both manufacturers reacted to these proposals in the same way: each suggested that the other had been given the easier job to do. Wilson Electric was the most worried of the two, believing that Newton had been chosen not so much because of the excellence of the Newton proposals as because the Michaels directors had decided that it was time the company fixed on one computer manufacturer for the provision of all its future hardware.

During this period Kenny was giving a great deal of attention to the input problem. He was very interested in, and attracted by, CRT (cathode ray tube) equipment, but after investigation he concluded that it was too expensive. He believed that the only solution to the input problem was to find some kind of document reader that was compatible with a Newton computer. In this respect the Wilson Electric Smith reader was suitable, but it was unlikely that Wilson Electric would sell one of its readers to Newton, knowing that Newton was to be given the Michaels contract. Eventually Turner came across a reader manufactured by a very small company called Larco. He became enthusiastic about the idea of getting this firm to make a special reader for the Michaels job, and Kenny thought the idea worth considering. Reilly, however, was becoming more and more favourably disposed towards Wilson Electric, and he was not at all keen on this suggestion.

By the end of January, Kenny, Reilly, and Turner had given a great deal of thought to the relative merits of the two selected computer manufacturers and Kenny and Turner had begun to have serious doubts about Wilson Electric. The reason for this was that one of the rejected computer manufacturers had visited Michaels and had expressed great astonishment at the choice of Wilson Electric, pointing out that the Wilson Electric machine had no software. Kenny was very worried about this, and wondered if Michaels now had, as its second choice, a machine that could not do the job. The Wilson Electric machine was a new one and there were few examples of it in use in this country.

March 1967: One of the senior programmers left the firm and this caused anxiety among the Management Services staff. The latter were still not convinced that the Michaels directors were wholly in favour of the new computer system and they wondered if the directors would take the resignation as a sign that there were going to be staffing difficulties in Management Services and, in consequence, become more cautious about the project. One or two members of Management Services thought that the directors might see computers as taking away some of their traditional areas of control. For example, very complex mathematical procedures were now being used for sales-forecasting and it was not easy for a layman to understand them. Their use could be interpreted as taking power away from the buying department and transferring it to the statistical section of the company. Staff turnover, together with feelings of uncertainty concerning the acceptability of their work to top management, caused a drop in the morale of the systems analysts during this month.

Coincidentally with this drop in morale, those systems analysts

E

who were working on the Newton and Wilson Electric hardware proposals appeared to identify even more with the virtues of the machines they were evaluating. Those who were working on the Wilson Electric proposal started talking of resigning if Newton got the order.

By the middle of March, Kenny was in favour of buying a Newton machine, provided the input problem could be solved; Reilly was in favour of Wilson Electric; and Turner was becoming increasingly convinced that they had been wrong to eliminate BCD at such an early stage and that this company should be reconsidered.

April 1967: Between them, Kenny and Turner now decided that mark-sensing would be a wrong approach. It would be backward-looking and would not take account of future needs. Turner argued that in five years' time the most advanced computer systems would be on-line, real-time applications and that this would be impossible with a mark-sensing form of input. Teletype on-line would be a step in this direction and would allow for real-time development with CRT equipment.

May-June 1967: This shift from reading devices back to teletype input caused further morale problems among the systems analysts. Many of them had been working extremely hard testing the various reading devices and they now felt that this work had been to no purpose.

Towards the end of June, BCD, one of the rejected manufacturers, tried to make a comeback. In fact this was a propitious time for the company to reapproach Michaels because the Larco reading tests were being continually postponed by Larco, and the Management Services department was becoming disillusioned about the interest and efficiency of this small company. It now seemed less likely that Newton would be able to solve the input problems by means of a Larco document reader. BCD believed that it might be able to interest Michaels in a new BCD reader that was shortly to appear on the market. This reader would be compatible with Newton hardware.

July-August 1967: Eventually, the systems analysts began to test and to get good results from the Larco reader. They also began testing the Wilson Electric reader in order to see if it would be suitable as an interim reading device. Kenny could not finish his report and send it to the directors until these tests were completed.

Now that a viable solution appeared to have been found, Reilly, who until now had still preferred a Wilson Electric to a Newton computer, came out in support of Newton.

September 1967: On 2 September a report prepared by Reilly's department, recommending Newton hardware and the Larco reading device, went to the directors. The systems team believed that this report was well received. The directors asked for further information on certain points, which the analysts had no difficulty in supplying. There was a feeling of satisfaction in the department at a job well done.

From 2 to 24 September there was silence from the directors. Then, on 24 September, Kenny saw the managing director and found that a demonstration of CRT equipment on television had aroused his interest in the possibilities of this equipment. Kenny pointed out that no one had been able to justify the use of CRT equipment on economic grounds. He told the managing director that he had investigated this type of input at an early stage in the project but had rejected it because of its high cost. The managing director replied that he thought that CRT equipment should be looked at again.

October 1967: At the beginning of October, Kenny met the deputy chairman, the managing director, and the two divisional directors in order to discuss the report he had sent them on 2 September. They told him that it was a good report, but that it was directed at doing only a limited job, namely accounts. The directors had come to the conclusion that, in view of the amount of upheaval that was going to be involved in introducing a new system, the company should try to initiate something more ambitious. Their proposal was that Newton should be asked to quote for CRT input equipment related to a 'total' as opposed to a limited job. By 'total' they meant an integrated data-processing operation that would eventually cater for all the procedures in all the administrative offices. Newton was to be asked four questions:

1. Is it practical?
2. Can you do it?
3. What will it cost?
4. Do you advise it

Newton was asked to provide answers to these questions within two weeks. The company met this deadline and quoted £3·25 million as the cost of its proposed configuration for a 'total' job.

November 1967: Now that the Michaels directors had widened the parameters of the job, Turner suggested that BCD should be reconsidered. He maintained that BCD's enormous research expenditure must mean that it would push ahead of other computer manufacturers. Turner believed that this would be especially the case with software, which to him was the most difficult part of implementing a new data-processing system.

December 1967: On 1 December BCD held a seminar for the Michaels directors. Although the manufacturer had arranged to bring some of its senior marketing men from Europe and the United States, only one Michaels director attended the meeting. The BCD people were left talking to the staff of the Management Services department.

On 7 December the Michaels directors met to take a final decision. In fact they did not do this but asked the Management Services department to provide more information on the suggested alternatives. The managing director favoured CRT input, but the chairman himself was questioning the economics of this method. However, it now seemed reasonably certain that the directors wished to go ahead with the larger system.

January 1968: On 30 January the managing director and the two divisional directors met with Kenny and told him to go ahead with the total system. This would cover all administrative office procedures. No decision was taken on the input problem.

February 1968: On 2 February the directors met again to consider input. The managing director and Kenny favoured the use of CRT equipment, but the chairman was still worried about the cost. The directors therefore decided to ask the Newton sales director to visit the company and answer some questions about CRT. This was an important stage in the decision-making process since until this event no top computer man had been formally received by the Michaels directors.

On the wider problem of what to computerize first, now that the project had become so much larger, the directors opted for introducing the new system by computerizing the Wolverhampton administrative office of the clothing division. After this had been completed, the system would be extended to the other administrative offices of the clothing and furniture divisions. The directors asked the Management Services department to look into the costs of this approach.

During this period BCD was trying hard to convince Michaels that it was the company, and not Newton, who should have the contract. Turner supported the use of BCD equipment and Reilly agreed with him, but Kenny remained convinced that the firm must stick to Newton.

March 1968: On 1 March the directors took a final decision to go ahead with the proposed new system. They accepted the Management Services department's recommendation that the project should incorporate data links and CRT equipment. They did not specify which computer manufacturer should be given the contract.

Kenny still could not get his own managers to accept the Newton solution. He decided that he must make this decision himself. He therefore wrote a memo to the managing director pointing out that the proposed new system was highly complex and that Michaels had no experience in handling this kind of change. He also explained that there were many external pressures on his department which had led to an absence of agreement on the choice of computer. He then set out his case for purchasing a Newton machine. The essence of this was that the claims that BCD made could not be validated. If Michaels bought from BCD, therefore, it would be placed in the paradoxical position of having based its choice of expensive technical equipment on hunch and belief instead of on knowledge. The firm had knowledge and experience of Newton equipment and he strongly recommended that the relationship with this company should be continued. Reilly and Turner were offered the opportunity to sign this memo. Both refused.

CHAPTER 4

The Research Process

People who write about methodology often forget that it is a
matter of strategy, not of morals. There are neither good nor
bad methods but only methods that are more or less effective
under particular circumstances in reaching objectives on the
way to a distant goal.

George C. Homans (1949:330)

Every data-gathering class – interviews, questionnaires, observation, performance records, physical evidence – is potentially
biased and has specific to it certain validity threats. Ideally, we
should like to converge data from several different data classes,
as well as converge with multiple variants from within a single
class.

Eugene J. Webb (1966: 35)

The research design for this study has been guided by the spirit of
the above quotations. An attempt has been made both to relate the
methods used to the problems under study and to relate the methods
to one another in order to improve the validity of the findings. Such
an approach has had its advocates among those who write on how
research ought to be done. In a now celebrated paper, Campbell and
Fiske (1959) discuss the validation process in terms of the multitrait-
multimethod matrix. Webb *et al.* (1966: 1) observe: 'The issue is
not choosing among individual methods. Rather it is the necessity
for a multiple operationalism, a collection of methods combined to
avoid sharing the same weaknesses.' The most recent and most
extensive discussion of what he calls 'strategies of multiple triangulation' is offered by Denzin (1970). What matters, however, is not the
elegance or the neologisms with which the problem is stated and
restated, but whether there are accomplishments at the end of it all.

Some have doubted the accomplishments: 'Today, the dominant mass of social science research is based upon interviews and questionnaires. We lament this overdependence upon a single, fallible method' (Webb *et al.*, 1966: 1).

The problem of validity need not just be approached, as Campbell and Fiske (1959) and Webb *et al.* (1966) imply, through the use of multiple methods in the analysis of the same empirical events. In addition to multiple methods, a research design might include multiple data sources. For example, a study using the content analysis of documents as a method might seek out documents from a variety of sources in order to test a particular hypothesis. The use of multiple observers and multiple levels of analysis may achieve the same result. Where practicable the present study has employed multiple methods, multiple data sources, multiple observers, and multiple levels of analysis.

THE INTERDEPENDENCE OF THEORY AND METHOD

Another major influence on the planning of this research has been the assumption that methods are not atheoretical. Research methods have a differential ability to shed light on theory. It is no accident that those concerned either with the symbolic interactionist perspective or with the analysis of social process have preferred to use observational methods.[1] Olesen and Whittaker (1968: 19) state: 'Since the choice of method should be suggested at all times by the subject matter, and the subject matter in our case was process, the choice of participant observation as the principle way of investigating seemed a good choice. Our rationale was that the best way to understand a process was to become part of it.'[2] Just as certain methods may aid the development of theory, so the neglect of these or other methods may impede that development. Role theory has suffered from those whose imagination could take them no further than the questionnaire. Conceptualization in role theory at the moment is essentially static. This is largely because questionnaires

[1] See, for example, Becker (1963), Glaser and Strauss (1965), and Olesen and Whittaker (1968).
[2] Denzin (1970: 12) suggests that surveys better measure static and stable forms of behaviour while life-histories and participant observation more adequately lend themselves to processual analyses.

have traditionally been used to stop the social structure and take a snapshot of it at a particular point in time.[1]

Customarily, anthropologists have been one of the few groups of social scientists willing to spend extended periods of time in the field to test their hypotheses. Even they, however, are only just beginning to tear themselves away from the static conceptualization of structural functionalism. For many years anthropologists like Lowie (1917) and Radcliffe-Brown (1952) allowed themselves to wallow in the convenient fictions of this concept. They ensured their intellectual comfort by rejecting methodological and analytical approaches that would have upset some of the more questionable parts of their theories. One way of dealing with the charge that one's theory is static is to maintain that primitive tribes have no sense of history, and no sense of historical perspective (Lowie, 1917: 165); or to say, as Radcliffe-Brown did, that 'in the primitive societies that are studied by social anthropology there are no historical records' (1952: 3). Both M. G. Smith (1962: 75) and Vansina (1965: 12-15) contend that such statements rest on a misunderstanding of the nature of history and historical records. Vansina puts forward an imaginative argument in favour of the use of oral tradition, an aspect of social reality that Radcliffe-Brown would have been content to call myth while asking what function it performed (1952: 49-50).

Latterly, anthropologists like Vogt (1960), Turner (1957, 1969), and Van Velsen (1967) have become interested in social process. 'If we start off with the assumption that the basic tendencies in social and cultural systems are toward change rather than equilibrium', says Vogt (1960: 19), 'we would realize that to use only structural concepts is like arbitrarily stopping a movie to study the patterns of a single frame instead of studying patterned sequences of events that comprise the whole movie. . . . The more we look at the frames on either side, the more meaning the structure of the single frame has.' Van Velsen (1967) emphasizes that such an approach does not imply the end of structural analysis: rather, the latter 'should be supplemented and enlivened by an account of the actions – both "normal"

---

[1] A notable exception to this trend is a study of policemen by Preiss and Ehrlich (1966), which uses the language of role theory but combines questionnaire and observational methods. The result is some attempt to deal with the theoretical issues of role adaptation.

and "exceptional" – of the individuals who operate the structure, i.e., the processes going on within the structure' (1967: 140).

The present research has been guided by a concern for the elaboration of social structure; for social process. An underlying theme is that theories of organizational decision-making, power, and conflict require a processual form. Operationalizing such concepts necessitates a longitudinal research design. It was felt that participant observation, interviewing, and the content analysis of documents would meet the basic theoretical requirements of the study as well as the methodological aim of validation through convergence.

A further reason for the choice of these methods is the flexibility they offer. I was not driven into the field with a neatly labelled and rigidly constructed set of hypotheses and operational definitions. Such an approach would have been unsuitable, given the little that is known about innovative decision-making processes and about the two occupational groups that form the basis of the study.[1] A limited number of questions were formulated before the field-work began; these were suggested by the area to be studied and the theoretical problems this area presented. Further questions, in many ways those most fundamental to the study, emerged during the field-work itself. Some of these questions considerably modified earlier conceptualizations.[2] In a few cases additional methods had to be used to gather data to test these refinements. In this sense the research design was as processual as the theories it was testing.

The field-work was carried out in two stages. Between 1966 and 1968 the Michaels innovative decision was studied by observation and other methods. The historical part of the research was begun in 1968, overlapping the study of the ongoing decision process, and was completed in 1969. The methods used to study the process of decision-making are discussed first.

[1] I was faced with a similar problem in an earlier study of a previously unresearched group (see Pettigrew, 1967, 1968), and in that case there was almost complete reliance on questionnaires. It was largely as a result of that experience that multiple methods were used here.
[2] Glaser and Strauss (1967) argue strongly against developing theory from *a priori* assumptions. They note that there has been an over-concern with the verification of *a priori* theory to the neglect of generating theory grounded in social research.

STUDY OF THE ONGOING DECISION PROCESS

The Participant–Observer Role

The choice of participant observation as the principal method[1] in this stage of the research was related to the early conceptualization of decision-making as a political process. The aim was to penetrate the veil of formal position in order to determine, as far as possible, who *really* had the power, in which part of the decision process, and for what reasons. In fact, it was possible to identify the power-holders by gathering data in this way. It was not so easy, however, to answer the question why they appeared to have more power than did others. This was one of the reasons why the study was given historical depth.

It was felt that the best possible way to study people making a decision was to live with them while they made it. Such an approach has many advantages. If the researcher is interested in covert activity, in political behaviour, it is essential to be close to the ground of the action. As Long (1962) and Burns (1961) have observed, few people will openly acknowledge their interest and involvement in political activity. Those who are politically involved usually claim that they are acting in the public interest. That is how they legitimate their behaviour. My own experience suggests that it takes many months of careful interaction before informants will discuss a package of, often, self-interested motives that went with a set of behaviours originally justified as in the public interest. As Argyris (1962, 1965) has repeatedly stressed, it is extremely difficult to develop relationships of trust, and even more difficult to maintain them. This is especially so when the researcher enters an environment where conflict is the dominant mode of interaction.

Dalton (1967: 87) finds that the intimacy of participant observation not only allows the investigator to impute motives more correctly, but also enables him to avoid pointless and abrasive questioning and to get at the best-informed respondents when he needs them later in the research. The researcher has time to build superior rapport before he asks disturbing questions; and his approach is sufficiently flexible to permit him to wait and see what the critical research questions are. In many cases, the established

[1] Those who advocate a multimethod approach acknowledge that 'not all components...should be weighted equally' (Webb *et al.*, 1966: 5).

researcher is able to gain access to sensitive material that the more peripheral investigator usually never reaches.

Several authors[1] have described the possible roles an observer could take in a field setting. In this study the participant-as-observer role was used. This is different from the purely observer role in that both field-worker and informant are aware that theirs is a field relationship. Olesen and Whittaker and also Denzin discuss the participant–observer role in terms of the symbolic interactionist perspective: 'We regard participant observation as a mutual venture in which reciprocal interpersonal exchanges[2] between the research investigator and the actor result in more or less mutually meaningful, well-understood viable social roles' (Olesen and Whittaker, 1967: 274). How the researcher makes his role in interaction with his informants is a key factor in the success of the research.

Olesen and Whittaker (1967: 274) discuss the role-making process in terms of four phases:

1. Surface encounter – the initial contacts, often between total strangers.
2. Proffering and inviting – the reciprocal definitions of self by self and others.
3. Selecting and modifying – the mutual selection of meaningful and viable portions of research roles.
4. Stabilizing and sustaining – the achievement of a tentative balance between researcher and informants.

I arrived in Michaels for the first time at the end of September 1966. My role was to follow the decision process which had just begun. I was given a desk in the section of the systems analysts' office where the team working on the computer decision was housed.

The four-phase process that Olesen and Whittaker describe took about two and a half months to work out in this case. By the end of November 1966, I had achieved tentative acceptance by the systems analysts. The initial reaction of Reilly (the systems manager) and his team was one of distrust and antagonism. Open hostility to my role was common. Ray Ashton, the senior systems analyst on the project I was interested in, used every opportunity to belittle me publicly. In one instance, when I had asked him to arrange for a

[1] Gold (1958), Lupton (1963), Olesen and Whittaker (1967), Denzin (1970).
[2] In an interesting paper, Argyris (1968) applies his theory of interpersonal behaviour to the researcher–informant relationship. His analysis is not confined to participant observation.

car-parking permit, he described me over the telephone as a 'nonentity'. Reilly was equally obnoxious. He tried on many occasions to drag me into his conflicts with Kenny[1] and to use my presence as a way of weakening Kenny's position with the directors. I found this daily abusive behaviour extremely difficult to live with. I could make few demands on the analysts in terms of information. The data collected in the first two months were poor.

The major advantage of this early period of hostility was that it quickly revealed many of the critical parts of the Management Services department's social structure which might otherwise have remained hidden. In particular, it dramatized the relationships between Reilly and Kenny and Reilly and Ashton, and offered immediate clues about the stand each of them was taking in the decision process.

In the proffering and inviting stage, the analysts communicated their expectations of what my role should be. Many of these were anti-academic. The theme was, Pettigrew may be a member of the faculty of Manchester University, he may know something about sociology, but as far as we are concerned he knows nothing about systems analysis.[2] It was made clear that my status would be that of the lowest trainee. For a time I gladly accepted this role. Part of this acceptance involved openly acknowledging my ignorance and even playing on it by applying the descriptive title of 'technical jobs' to the menial tasks I did. This became a bit of a joke in the office; people would say, 'What sort of technical job are you working on today, Andy boy?' As a group, the analysts I worked with prided themselves on their grasp of current social, political, and economic affairs. They tended to have uniformly liberal views and all but one read the *Guardian* newspaper. I refrained from using any of my 'book' knowledge when they had discussions and generally kept my presence 'low key' by keeping out of arguments. Eventually, signals of acceptance came in the form of requests for my participation in these discussions.

Acceptance of the trainee role was necessary for my early integration into the Systems department. As soon as I felt accepted I pushed myself forward into the selecting and modifying stage. This involved gaining access to the analysts on the other side of the office and also participating in various departmental and interdepartmental

[1] Head of the Management Services department, and Reilly's boss.
[2] In September 1966 this was quite true.

meetings on the computer decision. The layout of the Management Services department (excluding the OR section) was as shown below:

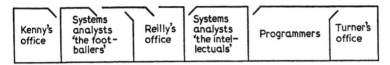

I was located with the group of analysts I term the 'intellectuals' as opposed to the 'footballers'. The footballer–intellectual distinction was my way of summing up the differences between the two groups. By chance, when I arrived in the Systems department, a trainee was transferred from the 'footballer' side of the office to the 'intellectual' side. It was the attempts by the intellectual analysts to communicate to the trainee the style of behaviour expected of him in his new environment that first made me aware of the differences between the two groups. It took much longer to discover the reasons for this division, and they will be dealt with later.

The research problem this created was that I became identified as an intellectual and found it difficult to reach informants in the footballer section. Since the two groups rarely interacted at either the social or the work level I had to widen my role so that I could move legitimately into the footballer section. I could do this only by making my research activities more visible. This had the effect of disturbing the balance of acceptability I had created earlier.

Such are the possible reactive effects of the participant–observer role. In time, however, I became accepted and was able to move with relative ease between the various sections, programming and analyst, of the Management Services department. My relationship with Reilly improved to such an extent that I began to perform a therapeutic role for him. When the strain of the intradepartment conflict became high, he would call me into his office and describe in great detail his own and others' feelings about the course of events. Presumably, as the only person in the department without a material interest in the decision process, I was the only individual he could safely turn to as a sounding-board for his innermost thoughts. In these interactions I had to be scrupulously careful both to remain neutral and to avoid communicating inadvertently either Kenny's or Turner's point of view on a particular issue in the decision process.

My relationships with Kenny and Turner were much easier. I tried to avoid being seen either talking to Kenny or going into his office, in case Reilly and Turner should think I was feeding him with information about their plans. Any contact I had with Kenny was outside Michaels. To avoid over-complicating my role, Enid Mumford did all the early interviewing of Kenny and took charge of what little face-to-face contact we had with the directors. Having two researchers operating at different points in the system is a major advantage in a decision-making study where the key participants work at different levels in the organizational hierarchy.

Between September 1966 and July 1967 I spent four days a week in Michaels talking to people, listening to conversations, attending meetings, and going out for lunch and for evening pub-drinking sessions with the computer staff. After July, and up until April 1968, my visits were rather less frequent. I was now sufficiently accepted to be able to make an appearance for key meetings or crisis situations and still pick up the detailed information I needed.

In this period I also developed a relationship with the Newton computer salesman, Allison, who kept me informed of meetings between his company and the Michaels computer people. He became, in effect, a third observer in the study.[1] Allison did not perform this role out of any idealistic belief in social science research. He was as well aware as Reilly was of my privileged position as an information source. I had access to the financial quotations of Allison's competitors. The expensive hotel lunches I had with Allison were conversationally like a war of nerves. Each of us was trying to use the other as an informant to generate as much information as possible while giving away as little as possible.[2] In this way I gathered some valuable material. Two other computer salesmen were approached but refused interviews. When their companies had finally been eliminated from the tendering process, I approached them again and they both granted interviews. These were also difficult situations to deal with. Both companies, in preparation for future attempts, wanted to know why they had lost this particular order.

[1] I was careful to check any data Allison gave me with documentary sources in Michaels, and also to interview Kenny, Reilly, and Turner about their perceptions of the meetings he described.
[2] I should like to stress that neither party divulged any company or competitor secrets.

Largely because of the sensitive nature of much of the material collected, most respondents refused to allow a tape recorder at meetings or interviews. In the early stages of the research a few of the people I talked to were reluctant to let me write down what they were saying. To overcome this difficulty, I always kept a small notebook at hand for the purpose of recording any relevant conversations I might have. After each encounter I would make as accurate a record as possible of the conversation. After a time I developed a surprising adroit memory and was able to reconstruct interviews from the short notes I had made during the day. Every evening I dictated the day's material into a tape recorder for typing.

Problems of Bias and Validity

Many authors have noted the reactive effects of observational methods.[1] Webb *et al.* (1966: 113) state: 'No matter how well integrated an observer becomes, we feel he is still an element with potential to bias the production of the crucial data substantially.' For Zelditch (1969: 13), bias is inevitable because a single observer cannot be everywhere at the same time, nor can he always define his role as widely as he would like. Vidich (1969: 71) calls attention to the possible distorting effects of selective perception and interpretation on the observer's part. Miller (1969: 87) discusses problems of 'over-rapport', of the observer 'going native', while Dalton (1967: 86) and Blau (1967: 34) raise the possibility that the observer's often marginal position may attract him to marginal men in the social structure he is studying.

Faced with all these doubts concerning the validity of observed data, a researcher may well feel demoralized. There is no doubt that from time to time my presence in the Management Services department influenced people's attitudes and behaviour. Informant bias is always possible; positional bias is, of course, an important aspect of the data. In many ways the study was seeking to demonstrate self-interested bias. While no single method is completely reliable, measures can be taken to increase the validity of data. In the present case, the use of multiple observers and multiple sources of documentary data were built-in checks, which also prevented

---

[1] Argyris (1968: 194) justifiably comments: 'The issue is not contamination versus no contamination. The issue is under what conditions can the researcher have the greatest awareness of, and control over, the degree of contamination?'

over-identification with the views of particular informants and widened the range of data collected. The major check on the reporting of events and on the positions individuals took on issues came from the analysis of documentary material of various kinds.

Analysis of Documentary Data

Access was given to the following sources of data:

1. All reports, from whatever section of the Management Services department, to the directors.
2. All internal memos in Kenny's files[1] relating to the computer decision. These included memos to and from his subordinates and to and from the directors.
3. Minutes of internal departmental meetings and of meetings between Kenny, Reilly, Turner, and the directors.[2]
4. The report written by the consultants who were called in to evaluate the first set of manufacturer proposals.
5. All correspondence in Kenny's files between the computer manufacturers and his department. These included letters to and from the manufacturers from 1964 up to and throughout the decision process. The directors did not encourage direct contact between themselves and the manufacturers, so copies of letters sent to the directors invariably ended up in Kenny's file.

As Webb *et al.* (1966) note, there are problems associated with the analysis of documentary material. These relate particularly to two sources of bias, namely selective deposit and selective survival. Because, in this case, the material examined was not very old, it is doubtful if selective deposit and survival constituted a real threat to validity. The willingness of Kenny to let me inspect the documents before he could remove any threatening items also helped to eliminate bias.

---

[1] Reilly refused outright to let me analyse his file material. When I asked Turner about his files he pointed to the wastepaper basket and then demonstrated that his filing cabinets were empty. Reilly's refusal meant no great loss of data. Most of his memos were in Kenny's file and I was able to read them there. Kenny was the key to the information flow in the Management Services department.

[2] Memos and minutes of meetings were the main sources of data on the directors' attitudes to the computer decision. Interviews with Kenny, Reilly, and Turner after board meetings also produced useful data.

The documents were used both to check verbal statements and to find out whether positional biases made verbally were actually transferred on paper to the directors, the ultimate decision-making body. The pattern of analysis was suggested by Budd, Thorp, and Donohew (1967). Statements were content-analysed into positive, negative, and neutral categories. A positive statement would be 'Newton have never let us down'; a neutral one, a descriptive statement like 'the Wilson Electric reading machine was tested last week'.

The letters to and from the computer manufacturers were an invaluable source of data on a number of issues. The style of address, the mode of presentation, the topics covered, and the frequency of writing – all are revealing in terms of one person's perception of another. The way the above factors were represented in the letters offered fascinating evidence as to whether there was a developed or special relationship between Kenny and any of the manufacturers. In this sense the letters complemented the observational and interview data on how Kenny and his subordinates saw and reacted to the manufacturers and how the manufacturers behaved towards them.[1] Another indicator of the nature of the relationship between Kenny and the manufacturers was the status of his correspondents. With some companies, Kenny invariably communicated to and received letters from directors; in other cases all his contacts were with salesmen. The relative number of times Kenny accepted golfing and other social invitations was a further unobtrusive measure of whether he had any special relationships.

Operationalizing Power

Dahl (1957, 1961, 1968) has repeatedly lamented the problems of operationalizing power. He has noted the gap between concept and operational definition, the lack of correlation between different operational measures, and the controversy over the reliability of those measures (1968: 414-15). In its simplest form, his argument rests on a distinction between rigour and relevance: 'Attempts to meet high standards of logical rigor or empirical verification have produced some intriguing experiments', he declares, 'but not

[1] Unlike historians and literary critics, sociologists have been prone to ignore the letter as a source of data. Notable exceptions are a study of the Polish peasant by Thomas and Znaniecki (1927) and the suicide studies of Garfinkel (1967).

F

rounded and well verified explanations of complex political systems in the real world. Conversely, attempts to arrive at a better under-standing of the more concrete phenomena of political life and institutions often sacrifice a great deal in rigor of logic and verifica-tion in order to provide more useful and reliable guides to the real world' (p. 410). In an earlier work, Dahl (1961: 330) has stated that, no matter how assiduous the researcher, the study of power 'requires the use of operational measures that are at best somewhat unsatisfactory'. Although such a view may seem unduly pessimistic, the caution it reflects is valuable. Where there are problems and no easy solutions, it is at least useful to be fully aware of the difficulties.

Dahl's way of handling the operationalization problem is both pragmatic and optimistic: 'One way to compensate for the unsatis-factory character of all existing operational measures is to be eclectic. In this study, an eclectic approach was adopted deliberately, not only to avoid putting all our eggs in one methodological basket but also in order to take advantage of the existence of a very wide assortment of data' (1961: 330-1). The present approach has sought to be equally eclectic.

The main research problem was to identify the power resources felt to be critical by the participants in the Michaels computer environment. Control of information flow, assessed stature, extent of role set, and relative possession of technical knowledge turned out to be critical factors. They were identified by observation and extensive open-ended interviewing. Questionnaires were used to obtain information on the relative amount of computer experience and training possessed by the programming and systems groups. Data on the extent of the key participants' role sets were gathered by interviewing, observation, and diary-keeping. Kenny, Reilly, and Turner each agreed to keep a diary on a prepared sheet with spaces for telephone calls and face-to-face contacts. The diaries were kept for one week. The three managers were interviewed at the end of each day in order to refresh their memories about their interactions for that day.

Since Kenny was the key gate-keeper[1] in the information flow to and from and within the Management Services department, his files were extensively analysed. The main data sources were reports, memos, minutes of meetings, and letters. Use of resources is probably more important than mere possession of them. The analysis of

[1] See Lewin (1951: 176-8) and Easton (1965).

documents was obviously a principal way of discovering how Kenny used his control over information. Interviewing and, in particular, direct observation were the main ways of collecting data on strategies of resource use.

Summary of Methods and Sources Used to Study the Decision Process

The triangulated research strategy employed in this part of the project can be summarized as follows:

Multiple methods:
1. Direct observation over time
2. Interviewing
3. Content analysis of documents
4. Diary-keeping
5. Questionnaires
6. Unobtrusive measures

Multiple sources of documentary data:
1. Departmental reports
2. Internal memos
3. Minutes of meetings
4. Letters

Multiple observers:
1. Myself
2. Enid Mumford
3. Allison, computer salesman.

THE HISTORICAL STUDY

A comment made some years ago by E. G. Boring will serve to introduce this section: 'The best fact is one that is set in a context, that is, known in relation to other facts, that is, perceived in part in the context of its past, that comes into understanding as an event which acquires significance because it belongs in a continuous dynamic sequence. . .' (1963: 5). As data were being gathered on the decision process, it became increasingly clear that the behaviour observed could not be adequately explained without reference to the past. The theories of decision-making, conflict, and power being examined required further development in their processual form.

Therefore the original longitudinal research design was extended to include historical data covering the period 1957-66.

The fact that Kenny, Reilly, and Turner lived through most of the history of computer activities in Brian Michaels was an important, though not a sufficient, reason for acquiring historical data. Technological changes, together with the rise of a new occupational group called systems analysts, which disturbed the patterns of occupational interdependence in Michaels and ultimately status and power relations, were not peculiar to Michaels. At least, that was the hypothesis. The problem was to find a way of testing it. While that issue was being considered, information was collected on the changing patterns of relations in Michaels.

Historical Data: Problems of Internal and External Validity

'Although the logic and approach of science can and should be used in historical sociology,' writes Lipset (1968: 52), 'it is obvious that work in this field cannot validate hypotheses with the rigor normally associated with the concept of a science. That this is so should only highlight the challenge. No discipline can select its research problems solely from those which are easy to study with extant methods.' It is important to say that uncertainty over methodology should not prevent social scientists from attacking significant problems. It is equally important to be aware of how methodological difficulties might impinge on the collection of valid data.

Historians have traditionally been conscious that the reality they study can 'only be an image or hypothetical conception of the actual past' (Berkhofer, 1969: 12). This is particularly so when the subject of their interest is in the distant past and documents are the only available data source (Webb *et al.*, 1966: 178). The present research, however, involved collecting data on experiences within the lifetime of respondents. Berkhofer claims that in this respect the social scientist has a considerable advantage: 'The historian, unlike the social scientist, can never[1] check his conclusions against a personally inspected, complex living reality, only against the fragmentary remains of that once living reality' (1969: 12).

If the historical researcher is interested in the internal validity[2]

[1] In fact, biographers frequently meet their subject and many of his contemporaries. For an excellent example of the careful use of the interview by a historian, see Williams (1969).
[2] For a full discussion of internal and external validity, see Webb *et al.* (1966), Campbell and Stanley (1963), and Campbell (1969).

of his findings (whether real differences exist in the comparisons he is making), he is likely to be faced with problems of data collection. Weiss and Dawis (1960: 384) hold that 'it is indefensible to assume the validity of purportedly factual data obtained by interview'. With historical interviews there is the problem of differentially accurate recall: 'A testimony is stamped by his personality, coloured by his private interests, and set within the framework of reference provided by the cultural values of the society he belongs to' (Vansina, 1965: 76). Informants who have long since left the environment they are discussing may have acquired a 'foreign mentality' which will profoundly distort their testimonies (Vansina, 1965: 191).

The present study has tried to reduce some of these biases. First, data were collected from primary sources only – eye-witnesses. Second, where the interest was factual, interview data were checked with documentary material, for example, company reports, correspondence, and internal memos. Testimonies were internally checked for internal contradictions, and externally checked against facts established from other sources. For the most part, however, the focus of interest was not detailed factual information.[1] Rather, interest was in comparing the changes in the attitudes of one group to another over time. Here the distortions or biases of one group in respect of another were important data in themselves.

A researcher is in a stronger position to interpret historical material if his data collection and analysis are undertaken after he has acquired a thorough knowledge of the present-day culture of the society he is studying. Southall (1954: 139), quoting an anthropological example, argues that before interpreting tradition 'it is essential to know the general social structure of a people, the age, education, and social status of informants and the exact social groups and loyalties from which they come'. The two years I spent observing and interviewing in Michaels helped not only in interpreting the historical data but also in throwing up research questions. I made every effort to communicate my familiarity with Michaels before starting an interview in an attempt to reduce respondent desire to give invalid information. Creating the impres-

---

[1] The fact that the NTL 200 arrived in Michaels on Maundy Thursday 1962 is irrelevant to the main issue, which was, why did Michaels buy the NTL at all?

sion of a 'non-naïve' observer did not, of course, go as far as prompting (Kahn and Cannell, 1962).

'When a sociologist carefully randomizes the selection of respondents so that his sample represents a large population, representativeness or external validity is involved' (Webb *et al.*, 1966: 11). Some attempt was made to deal with the issue of choice of respondents for the historical interviews, but the eventual sample was not ideal. Because the personnel records were chaotic and incomplete in many cases, it proved difficult to identify, let alone trace, the programmers and O & M officers who had left Michaels between 1957 and 1966. Faced with this difficulty and with the additional validity constraint of having to choose informants whose status was such as to have equipped them with the requisite kind of information, I decided to satisfy the latter constraint first. Seven of the eight people who had occupied managerial positions in programming or O & M between 1957 and 1966 were traced and interviewed. Ten programmers were interviewed; all ten had been in Michaels during the period 1957-61, and six of them had been there during both the 1957-61 and the 1962-6 periods.[1] Nine O & M officers were interviewed, seven for the 1957-61 period and eight for the 1962-6 period.[2] Since about twenty-six programmers and twelve O & M officers had left the firm between 1957 and 1966, the above samples are small. Nevertheless, because my familiarity with the Michaels structure enabled me to choose 'critical' informants, and because, moreover, I had an almost 100 per cent success in interviewing those informants, I am confident that the data are valid.

Like the documents, the interview material was content-analysed into positive, negative, and neutral categories following the pattern recommended by Budd *et al.* (1967). The inter-coder reliability score was calculated from the formula given by North *et al.* (1963: 49). An inter-coder reliability score of ·91 was obtained, which suggests that the coding procedures and therefore the data can be looked at with some confidence. Details of the calculation are as follows:

---

[1] For an explanation of the two time periods, 1957-61 and 1962-6, for which the historical data are presented, see p. 83n.
[2] Five of the programmers and four of the O & M officers/systems analysts interviewed were still working at Michaels. In addition, three of the current senior stock-control staff were interviewed for their perceptions of the early programmers and O & M officers.

$$\text{Reliability} = \frac{2(C_{1,2})}{C_1 + C_2} = \frac{\text{No. of category assignments on which all coders agree}}{\text{Sum of all category assignments by all coders}} \quad .$$

In this case the figures taken from a sizeable sample of interviews were:

$$\text{Reliability} = \frac{2(C_{1,2})}{C_1 + C_2}$$

$$= \frac{2(174)}{188 + 194}$$

$$= \frac{348}{382}$$

$$= \cdot 91.$$

Operationalizing Changes in Status and Power over Time

Earlier it was hypothesized that the programmers' status was declining over time because of the dual impact of technological change and the need for and rise of a new occupational group – systems analysts. I suspected, further, that the Michaels programmers had not declined in status, relative to the Michaels analysts, as much as the general trend in the industry would have suggested. The ready explanation of this seemed to be the success of the Michaels programmers' power-maintenance strategies. Testing these suppositions required:

1. Some way of operationalizing status changes in Michaels over time.
2. Some way of operationalizing status changes in the computer industry over time.
3. A way of demonstrating the industry-wide rise of systems analysts.
4. Details of the technological changes, and data on why and how they were affecting the occupational structure of the industry,
5. Data on the power strategies of the Michaels programmers and analysts.

Following Thompson (1961: 491-2), two main indicators of status were used – relative salary and educational level. Data were collected on these from an analysis of the Michaels personnel files. As noted earlier, these files were often incomplete, and this was particularly so with regard to salary, but enough data were obtained to yield meaningful comparisons between the programmers and the O & M officers/systems analysts. Methods of payment, the differential laxity with which bureaucratic rules were applied to the two groups, and various perks were also used as indicators of status differences. This material was gathered in the history interviews.

It was thought that an analysis of advertisements would give corresponding data on salary and educational levels for the computer industry in general, and would also indicate, to some degree, the rise in the demand for systems analysts.[1] The problem was to find a valid source of job advertisements. The first inclination was to go to the *Computer Bulletin*.[2] This was rejected because of the paucity and esoteric nature of the jobs advertised. A further idea that came to mind to show the rise of systems analysts was to content-analyse the titles of the articles in the *Computer Bulletin*, looking for an increase in the number of articles with 'system' in the title as against 'program'. Since neither those words nor their derivatives were often used, this idea was squashed. I then tried looking for trends in articles about programmers and systems analysts in the *Computer Bulletin*. Again the idea was dropped beccause of the lack of data from which useful comparisons could be made.

Eventually I decided to look at the British national newspapers. A Sunday newspaper was chosen for two main reasons:

1. There appeared to be concentrations of job advertisements in the weekend editions.
2. Taking the whole population of Sundays, i.e. all editions between 1 January 1957 and 30 December 1968, would be easier than taking the complete population of dailies. Exhausting the universe is a near complete answer to questions about external validity.

Three British Sunday national newspapers were available on microfilm at the Yale University Library – the *Sunday Telegraph*, the *Sunday Times*, and the *Observer*. Selections of each newspaper,

---

[1] There are no published national data on the salary and educational levels of British computer people.
[2] The journal of the British Computer Society.

at different times, were inspected for any systematic bias. The *Sunday Telegraph* was excluded because its advertisements appeared to be focused on clerical and lower managerial jobs. The other two newspapers attracted many advertisements for technical and managerial posts. Either would have done. The *Observer* was chosen because, in comparison with the *Sunday Times,* the type-set was clearer on microfilm and the advertisement sections were more distinctly laid out.

  The question then arose of having some sort of relevant national norm with which to compare the salary data obtained from the advertisements. Of the statistical salary indexes available, the one that covered groups nearest to the technical groups studied here was the Index of Average Earnings – Administrative, Technical and

FIGURE 1 *Comparison of Retail Price Index and Index of Average Earnings: 1957-68*

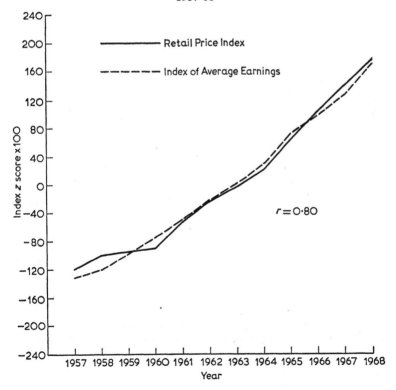

Clerical Employees, Male and Female, All Industries and Services.[1]
This was not exactly what I was looking for, however, and I decided
that the Retail Price Index[2] would be a more appropriate comparative measure. As it turned out, when the two indexes were reduced
to standardized scores and compared, a correlation of ·80 was found
(see *Figure 1*). The Retail Price Index (RPI) was therefore selected
for use, but it is clear that it would have made very little difference
to the findings which of the two indexes had been used.

The data on educational qualifications in the advertisements were
coded into mutually exclusive categories, and a percentage score
was calculated for each category per year over the twelve-year
period.

The same procedure was followed with the salary data.[3] However,
because the salary data were on a different scale from the RPI, for
comparative purposes the two scales had to be reduced to standardized scores. Hays (1963: 186) gives the formula for standardized
scores:

$$z = \frac{X - M}{s}$$

where X is the original measurement, M is the mean of the distribution of which X is a unit, and s is the standard deviation of the
distribution. Following the calculation through, in this case for five
distributions, involves these steps:

– finding the mean of the distributions
– finding the common standard deviation of the distributions
– then calculating the z scores for each distribution individually.

When the z scores are calculated in this way, the only relationship
implied between the distributions is height. By computing the
standard deviation of each distribution independently instead of
collectively, it is possible to calculate how each distribution relates

[1] Source: *Employment and Productivity Gazette*, December 1969, pp.
1156-7 (London: HMSO).
[2] Source: *Statistics on Incomes, Prices, Employment and Production*, No.
29, Department of Employment and Productivity, June 1969 (London:
HMSO).
[3] Given the lack of ambiguity, it was felt unnecessary to have a reliability
check on the coding of the advertisement data. If an advertisement said
programmer, it was coded such; if it quoted £1500 as a salary, likewise.

to each of the others around the mean.[1] The extent of the relationship can then be calculated by means of the product-moment correlation coefficient. The formula[2] used for computing the correlation coefficient of z scores was:

$$r_{xy} = \frac{\Sigma z_x z_y}{n} .$$

The next stage in the analysis was to look for trends in the data. Several authors, while trying to encourage the use of longitudinal data, have warned of threats to validity in making a trend analysis. Holtzman (1963: 202) asks the question: 'How does one distinguish between a long-term trend and an oscillation, without being arbitrary? What may appear like a trend may indeed be an oscillation about a still more stable trend if the time span were greatly lengthened.' Webb *et al.* (1966: 82) make the general point that 'all the extraneous events of history are at work to threaten valid research comparisons'. They recommend (p. 46) that the researcher ask himself: 'Are there any corrections which may be applied to remove extraneous sources of variance and improve the validity of comparisons?' Campbell (1969: 411-14) notes that all time series are unstable; care must be taken, therefore, that instabilities do not exceed the causal effect the researcher is claiming. Above all, Campbell cautions against the use of monocausal explanations with time-series data. His generalized strategy is to do supplementary research to back up plausible rival hypotheses.

All these threats to internal validity were present to a greater or lesser degree in this study. However, since data were collected to exhaust the historical time series (from 1957 to 1968),[3] and since the trends generally showed few signs of instability, the problems associated with oscillation and instability could largely be ignored.

Dealing with the issue of monocausal explanations in this case required evidence concerning the technological changes that hit the computer industry, and data on why and to what extent the rise of systems analysts was a status threat to programmers. Both were

---

[1] I am grateful to Professor Ben Schneider for this idea.
[2] Taken from McNemar (1963).
[3] In 1957 the numbers of advertisements for programmers, O & M officers, and systems analysts were twelve, one, and one, respectively. It is doubtful if there were many advertisements for any of the groups before that year.

supplied. Evidence for the technological changes was obtained from published material and from the perceptions of the Michaels computer groups. Information on the rise of analysts was gathered by counting the advertisements for the 1957-68 period.

The point that Webb *et al.* (1966) make about extraneous events over time threatening valid research comparisons is a more difficult objection to deal with. They cite (p. 97) as an example that the frequency of advertisements for engineers and scientists in the United States was greatly influenced by Defense Department cuts in 1964. One unexpected finding in this study may have been caused by such an extraneous factor. This was a consistent drop in the frequency of advertisements for both systems analysts and programmers after a joint peak in 1965.[1] While this finding did not disturb the clarity and consistency of the predicted trends, it does serve as a cautionary note in interpreting time-series data of this kind.

A further topic of theoretical interest was power. In particular, the analysis sought to show how the power of the programmers and analysts changed over time, and the consequence of this for the distribution of status in Michaels. Again, the emphasis was on operationalizing power through the identification of resources, together with individual perceptions of how these resources were used. In the lengthy history interviews,[2] most respondents were prepared to discuss strategic behaviour. The interviews were checked internally for contradictions and externally by cross-interviewing.

Since the loss of key personnel and the control of recruitment and learning processes for an occupation may respectively diminish and protect a group's power, the company personnel records were analysed for labour turnover and the experience and training of past staff. Questionnaires[3] given to the analysts and programmers employed in 1967 and 1968 offered comparable data on the experience and training of current staff.

---

[1] The finding is discussed more fully in Chapter 6.
[2] One interview extended from 10 a.m. to midnight. We went from office to lunch, back to office, to pub, to dinner, and thence to a club. Several interviews lasted from four to six hours. The interviews were recorded in my own version of shorthand, and rewritten fully as soon as possible thereafter.
[3] These questionnaires were given as part of a multi-form study of programmers and analysts. I am grateful to Enid Mumford for permission to use these data here.

Summary of Methods and Sources Used in the Historical Study

As in the study of the ongoing decision process, the general strategy was to use multiple methods and data sources in an attempt to overcome the different threats to validity posed by the different data-gathering instruments. Interviews, questionnaires, documents, and newspaper advertisements were included. Data were gathered from multiple points in the system to check a variety of perspectives.[1] The documents analysed included personnel records, correspondence, company reports, and internal memos. Special attention was given also to the particular problems of historical investigation and time-series analysis. History, however, 'is no more than a calculation of probabilities' (Vansina, 1965: 185).

---

[1] Unlike the observational part of the study, the historical investigation had to rely entirely on secondary data on the directors' perceptions. This is an unavoidable weakness.

CHAPTER 5

Specialization as an Emergent Process: Phase One

A major theoretical assumption that informs this chapter is that existing cleavages are of extreme importance in predisposing a group to action. The aim of this chapter, and the following one, is to demonstrate how historical data might be used to predict where a group might pull apart on a particular issue, and why.

The computer decision at Brian Michaels can be understood as a social drama. Turner (1957: 93) defines a social drama as 'a limited area of transparency on the otherwise opaque surface of regular, uneventful social life'. These social dramas have a processual form. They may be formulated as (1) breach; (2) crisis; (3) redressive action; (4) reintegration (Turner, 1957: 92). The present concern, however, is less with the intra-processual form of a social drama than with the analysis of a sequence of dramas over time. Turner was also aware of the potential of this analytical approach: 'If we examine a sequence of social dramas arising within the same social unit, each one affords us a glimpse, as it were, of the contemporary stage of maturation or decay of the social structure of that unit' (p. 93).

Our interest, like Turner's, is in relating past social dramas to present ones; in this case, previous computer decisions to the present one. Turner, however, was studying a rather different social system from this one. While it may have been possible for him to characterize the periods between dramas in Ndembu village life as 'opaque', 'regular', and 'uneventful' (1957: 93), there were no such periods in the sequence of computer activities in Brian Michaels. As the two studies differ on the static–dynamic dimension, so the two social systems diverge in their degree of openness to the environment in which they operate. Between 1950 and 1954, when Turner's field-work was carried out, Ndembu village life was experiencing pressures for change from a variety of 'Westernizing influences'. Neither the extent of nor the pressures for change in that context can be compared with the large-scale changes that took place between 1957 and 1969 in computer technology. Michaels was just one of many companies that, having committed themselves to computers, were obliged to keep themselves open to further changes. The pressures came from both the marketing strategies of the computer manufacturers and the computer specialists themselves. To some extent the computer specialists' careers were dependent on their ability to keep up with the latest piece of electronic gadgetry or the newest programming language. It was in their interests to push for change, even when, from the company's point of view, it was economically unjustifiable. The computer specialists' slogan became 'if it works it's obsolescent'.

Studies carried out in Britain by Mumford and Banks (1967) and in the United States by Myers (1967) have revealed some of the, from the company's viewpoint, dysfunctional consequences of this process. However, the irony of the matter is that, as fast as the computer specialists have altered others' tasks through technological changes, so their own jobs have had to accommodate to the same technological changes. The present interest is to show how this process of accommodation took place in the emergence of the two main occupational specialties in the computer industry – programmers and systems analysts.

Such an analysis has immediate relevance to the wider concern with decision-making as a political process. The meaning that career progression might have for individual behaviour in decision-making situations has already been stressed. Likewise the potential for conflict of a political nature in a non-programmed innovative decision. The Brian Michaels 1966-8 computer decision was dominated by conflict. Throughout the process there was little agreement between the technical specialists or between the specialists and the company directors. Of particular significance for both theories of conflict and theories of decision-making was the speed with which Kenny, Reilly, and Turner identified with the products of specific manufacturers. A pertinent research question at this point would seem to be: What are the bases from which people respond in a conflict situation? As Coleman (1957: 6) suggests, these bases may have less to do with the particular issue in focus at the time than with existing antagonisms between individuals and groups: 'In such disputes, the particular issue involved can hardly be considered a unit in itself, it is only part of a continuing conflict, periodically active, the rest of the time languishing.' Given this assumption, the fruitful research question is not: What was the precipitating event?, but rather: What were the existing networks of social relations, likes, dislikes, and organizational attachments prior to the dispute? The initial hostilities, at least, might then be profitably related to the variety of pre-existing attachments that pull people apart. Thus the way in which Kenny, Reilly, and Turner rushed to the support of particular manufacturers may be understood in terms of existing antagonisms leading people to take sides quickly. It may be a matter of 'I'm against it because he's for it'.

Coleman is not the only writer to argue that existing antagonisms can predispose a group to action. Nadel (1957: 113), in criticizing the experimental findings of Robert F. Bales, observes: 'We must not forget that in "real" situations role-relationships have a significant prehistory; they are not created *ex novo* in the contexts in which they are observed to operate.' Williams (1947: 41) considers that 'the factor of historical tradition must be accorded the status of a variable'. He notes that 'old rivalries, conflicts and traumas are remembered and traditional prejudices may tend to be perpetuated, well beyond the point at which they cease to have any intrinsic relevance to current situations'. Sherif (1966), in a chapter entitled 'When the Past becomes a Heavy Hand', makes the general point that 'the comprehension of here-and-present actions in many inter-group encounters requires considerable knowledge of past events and future designs. . . . So long as we ignore the guiding perspective provided by past intergroup relations, formulations on intergroup attitudes will remain contradictory and in some cases erroneous' (pp. 20, 22). Sherif was also aware of the potential of historical investigation for analysing the *process* of stereotype formation. In line with his processual view, he is careful to argue that 'group stereotypes are products, not *initial causes* of rivalry, hostility and conflicts between peoples'.

Just as it is unrealistic to make causal statements about conflict behaviour without time-based data, so it is to make causal statements about power structures. Conflict behaviour may evolve around the distribution of power in a social system. As each social drama is concluded a new balance of power may be created. The importance of a power structure should not deflect attention from the details of processes by which the power structure is sustained, replenished, and changed. At the level of individual strategy, past successes with a particular power play under given circumstances may encourage repetition. Defeat may result either because the individual has failed to perceive that circumstances have changed or because an opponent now familiar with historical precedent has anticipated his move and responded accordingly. The resources upon which an individual's or a group's power is based may change over time. In this case, data on the emergence and maintenance of status systems are relevant to a theory of power because of the role that status and reputation play in the circulation of power. Time reveals the instability and imbalance in power relations. Power cannot be satisfactorily operationalized in static terms. Explaining a decisional outcome in terms of power requires both information on past fluctuations of power and data on the current use of power. Both are supplied in the present study.

The generalized assumption is 'that the past affects the very way in which the future comes into being' (Homans, 1967: 92). The organization is viewed as an ongoing system with a past, a present, and a future. This quality implies that sound theory must take into account the history and the future of the system and relate them to the present.

A NOTE ON HISTORICAL EXPLANATION

The neglect by sociologists of the study of social process has already been noted. Some of this neglect may be attributed to sociologists' lack of concern with history. Speaking of the so-called structural–functional school of social theorists, Banks and Banks (1964: 549) observe: 'They have been more interested in the history of sociology than in the sociology of history. With a few exceptions, they have preferred to gather data from contemporary society or to rely on the work of historians, rather than to conduct their own researches into the past.' Cohen (1965: 9) suggests that such a neglect can have theoretical consequences: 'Until recently . . . the dominant bias in American sociology has been toward formulating theory in terms of variables that describe initial states, on the one hand, and outcomes, on the other, rather than in terms of processes whereby acts and complex structures of action are built, elaborated, and transformed.' Historians have been quick to note this gap in social science thinking: 'Social scientists in general have shown

G

little awareness of the rich field of exploration that recorded history offers them, and have in many instances signally failed to grapple with the analysis of temporal processes' (Cochran *et al.*, 1954).

Unfortunately, productive contacts between historians and social scientists have not yet materialized. Berkhofer (1969), in trying to generate the theoretical and analytical base for such contacts, has noted that already there is evidence of misrepresentations and misperceptions by one group of the other on critical matters. The sociologists' conception of historical explanation would seem to be one theme that cannot be ignored.

One consequence of intergroup conflict that has received detailed attention in the literature is the tendency of competing groups to polarize issues. Berkhofer (1969: 245-6) gives the historian–social scientist relationship as an example. The historian is supposed to be concerned with the particular, the concrete, and the unique, while the social scientist is interested in the general, the abstract, and the repetitive. Philosophers of science have clothed this distinction in the convenient dichotomy between idiographic and nomothetic disciplines. As with most dichotomies it conceals as much as it illuminates.

Sylvia Thrupp (1957: 12), a historian, has described the dichotomy as a 'classic distortion'. Becker (1958: 490) tries to avoid the issue by seeing idiographic and nomothetic as a continuum. Malinowski (1944: 7) gets to the heart of the matter: 'The hackneyed distinction between nomothetic and idiographic disciplines is a philosophical red herring which a simple consideration of what it means to observe, to reconstruct or to state an historical fact ought to have annihilated long ago.' More recently (Brown, 1963), there has been a greater awareness of the necessary interpenetration and interdependence of both generalizing and descriptive activity. The particular possesses significance only in the context of the general. Description and analysis are reciprocal in practice. Danto (1965: 218), for example, affirms: 'Phenomena as such are not explained. It is only phenomena as covered by description which are capable of explanation, and when we speak of explaining them, it must be with reference to that description.' Mere evocation or the recounting of what happened does not constitute explanation. To the sociologist, a chronicle may give information, a necessary prerequisite to explanation, but it cannot give understanding. For the latter, one must discover the ways in which events are interrelated beyond their relations of temporal sequence or coincidence. As McIver (1964: 129) points out, 'the causation of events ... must be sought for not mainly in prior events but in the processes of which they are manifestations'.

Explaining historical material requires the use of abstractions which delve into the patterns of continuity and change in social life. The present analysis seeks to show how changes in the task environment of two occupational groups over time had consequences for the groups' relative power and status. In this case, the link between the sociological and historical approaches involves looking at the changes in the patterns of relationships between the two groups and considering the consequences of these changes for the social system of which they were a part.

THE TASK ENVIRONMENT OF SYSTEMS ANALYSTS AND PROGRAMMERS

Historically, there has been great confusion and uncertainty regarding the interface between systems analysis and programming functions. This is to be expected when the occupations have arisen quickly from a technology which itself is continually undergoing change. Today the professional computer journals on both sides of the Atlantic are dotted with papers setting down what the two occupations *ought* to be doing. Naturally enough, the articles appear somewhat partisan. Robinson (1968), for example, describes the systems analyst's role in such complete terms that all the programmer is left to do is code. Constantine (1968) is equally anxious that programmers should fight attempts to make them into 'clerical coders' when their skills qualify them for the title of 'software engineers'.

One way of trying to map out the task environment of analysts and programmers is to consider what is involved in a computer project. Robinson (1968) suggests that such projects comprise the following phases:

1. Application selection
2. Feasibility study and proposal for new hardware
3. Data-gathering and analysis
4. System design and specification
5. Programming
6. System-testing

7. Changeover
8. Operation, including system maintenance.

He notes that from his experience 'the analyst is often responsible for the *control* of all these phases except the last and, almost invariably, is concerned in all the phases' (Robinson, 1968: 228). From this formulation the analytic portion of the skills of the systems analyst, though important, is a minor part of his role. Mumford and Ward (1968b: 48-9) draw attention to the implementation function of analysts: 'They are not required merely to design new systems. They must also get them into effective operation. This requires a whole range of skills, including selling ability, an appreciation of the factors influencing people's behaviour at work and a sound knowledge of the internal politics of the firm.' Such skills in relations with company management and user departments are likely to be particularly useful at phases 1, 2, 3, 7, and 8 of any project.

While some programmers consider that they should be, and indeed have been, involved in all eight phases of a project, their interdependence with analysts is usually greatest at phases 4, 5, and 6. The issue at this point is often simply how detailed a systems specification the analysts should give the programmers. A programmer might accept the analyst's competence and right to design the full procedure and document flows for off-machine activities, including outputs relevant to the needs of all recipients. If, however, an analyst defines the systems specification to include details of the file structure and the sequencing of runs in the computer, the programmer may feel that all he has to do is to code these operational steps into a language the computer can accept.

Stated simply, the main issue in the task environment of analysts and programmers is: How near the computer are the analysts going to get? The closer the analysts get, the more the programmers' role is diluted. While each party might have developed certain expectations about the nature of the interdependence of the two groups, the exact nature of that interdependence is likely to vary from situation to situation: 'At each institutional locale . . . the jurisdictional areas of each specialist group have to be adjudicated and negotiated. The division of labor cannot be legislated; it must be worked out at each locale' (Strauss *et al.*, 1964: 5). Such negotitation is an ongoing process. Most specialties are anything but stable entities with relatively fixed boundaries and tasks. The present concern is to show, first, how the specialties of programming and systems analysis emerged in Brian Michaels and, ultimately, the impact this process had on the patterns of relationship during the 1966-8 decision process.

COMPUTER ACTIVITIES IN MICHAELS 1957-61: [1] THE PROGRAMMERS IN CONTROL

The Computer Department
As soon as Harry Bell and Ted Morgan had convinced the Michaels directors that they should buy the SE 100 computer they began looking for programmers. Morgan takes up the story:

> 'When we originally recruited programmers we asked for experience and a first-class honours degree in mathematics. We got three, Gerald Lane, Pete Taft, and John Harker.'

This was late 1956. By September 1958 Bell was managing a staff of eight senior programmers, two junior programmers, two O & M officers, and two liaison officers with the user departments, in addition to computer operators. Morgan was assumed to be Bell's deputy, but he had no title. Bill Reilly, who had been recruited in 1957 from the company's Work Study department to help Bell and Morgan, had no title either. He later quipped: 'If you weren't a programmer, nobody knew what to call you in those days.'

The programmers were equally vague about the formal structure of the department:

> 'Well, what I mean is that there were very few official titles at that time. People were senior to others in the programming section but this was sort of understood.'

This ambiguity of place was not confined to the Computer department. Bell later commented:

> 'The management didn't understand what was going on. They didn't even know what to call me. At one time it was suggested that I should be called "consultant to Michaels"!'

[1] Data are presented in this and the following chapter for two time periods, 1957-61 and 1962-6. The year 1962 was chosen as the cut-off point because the computer industry was changing at that time from first- to second-generation computers. This change was reflected in Michaels in the purchase of the NTL 200.

From the programmers' point of view this ambiguity of place was compounded by ambiguity of function. They were clear about their task, to design a computer system for the Stock Control department of the clothing division and to program and implement it. They were much less clear about the roles to be played by other people in the Computer department. Morgan's dual role as Bell's 'number one man' and supervisor of the punch-room staff seemed acceptable. After all, 'data preparation was a rather routine clerical job'. The problem for the programmers was trying to justify the appearance of Bill Reilly and Tim Philby, the two recruits from the Work Study department. Bell and Morgan were much clearer about the role of these two gentlemen. Morgan remarked:

'Wilson [a company director] was most anxious we should recruit a couple of people into the team with specialist knowledge of the affected departments. In this way we came across Reilly and Philby. Both of them were more or less spies for Wilson.'

Bell seemed equally sure:

'In fact Reilly and Philby were sent to spy on us. Philby used to report what we were doing to his old boss in the Work Study department. However, he was a great "detail" man and got so bogged down in detail that he could never see the wood for the trees. Also, Reilly's job was to police us, querying everything we did with the management.'

Reilly's way of discussing this issue is significant. He says:

'Bell and Morgan were recruited from the furniture side of the business. Two of us were appointed from the clothing side, Tim Philby and myself. Then started what, in some respects, was a part of my working life that I could do well with forgetting. At that time Mills was in charge of the furniture division and we were working for Wilson. Really it was a typical Brian Michaels situation. Philby was a real Wilson man, everybody knew it at the time. Wilson expected Philby and myself to report exactly what Bell and Morgan were finding out and telling Mills. Really it was a terrible predicament to be in. I'd rather forget about it altogether.'

The spying episode clearly indicates competition at board level between the two divisions of the company. It also reveals one of the ways in which Michaels directors operate. Wilson was using 'his men' to check on the activities of two other men from another division of the company. In addition, the case illuminates the strategy used by a Michaels director to monitor the behaviour of a strange new breed of men working with a mysterious piece of technology. The strategies employed by the Michaels board to try to control the computer technologists are a topic we shall return to later. For the present, it is significant to note that Reilly, in describing this episode eleven years later, calls it 'a typical Brian Michaels situation'.

In this environment the Computer department was formed and the first batch of programmers appeared with their honours degrees in mathematics.

The Programmers

The arrival of programmers in Brian Michaels produced a culture shock of some magnitude. Many Michaels employees have never got over the experience. The programmers who were interviewed in the course of this study have equally vivid memories. Bell has described Michaels as:

'a quill-pen firm . . . which traditionally has employed low-quality people to do low-quality work. The result is that it's the hardest of all firms to introduce change into.'

While fear of what they represented may have been a major factor in explaining some of the extreme reactions towards the programmers, there were other equally pertinent reasons.

In the first place, the programmers appeared to be aliens with no interest in the firm of Brian Michaels. Like many other specialist groups, they were driven by the immediate challenge of their work. One programmer commented:

'In the early days we motivated ourselves. Getting the job on the computer was everything. The integration of the department in the company was very small indeed. As a group of people we were very independent. We had no sense of involvement in company affairs.'

Another said:

'As a team we worked for an academic rather than a business

interest. This was certainly true of the technical people. We were all back-room boys.'

This lack of involvement even excluded interest in long-term policy matters in their own department:

'Bell never went beyond the short-term objectives. This was quite sufficient incentive for us. The major motivation was that this was a pioneering job. The problems of getting to the short-term objectives were fascinating enough.'

Bell's rather closed managerial style brought praise from the programmers:

'Harry really put up the drawbridge. He kept the wolves from the door and allowed the boys to get on with the job.'

Even with Bell's style and their different work patterns, the programmers could not totally isolate themselves. In fact, their strange work timetable and casual dress attracted criticism. The computer operators were the first group to pick up this ill feeling. One operator, now a senior programmer, said:

'It started off with the operators; they were the first people in the company to work odd hours. They had beards, used to dress roughly, and were going home at 8.30 in the morning when everybody else was arriving. One day one of the personnel people came up and told me off for wearing a roll-collar sweater. He said to me, "You're supposed to be a young executive, you should dress accordingly".'

The programmers also disrupted the company rules about clocking on and off. This, together with the rewards their market position afforded them at such a comparatively young age, created problems with the company status system. Since the Personnel department had to deal with these issues it was the focus of a lot of the pro-grammers' discontent. The Personnel department had a terrible reputation for being ruthless and inconsiderate. One senior pro-grammer referred to its staff as the 'gestapo'. An operator commented:

'They were always asking us why we were late. They didn't realize we'd probably been working half the previous night. We were on overtime – some of us were earning £1200 with a base of

£800, at that time a good deal more than their young executives! The fact was they tried to, but couldn't, control us in the same way as the little girls. They had a standard 8-5 attitude to everybody. We answered back. This had never happened to them before.'

The programmers were clearly a group apart from the rest of the company. As Gerald Lane said: 'There wasn't a graduate in the company. We must have stood out.' They differed in education, values, work patterns, dress, and rewards from the rest of Michaels employees. While it is understandable that a stock controller might refer to them as 'long-haired, highly paid yobos', it is less clear that the conflict between the programmers and user departments was just over value differences. As Mumford and Banks (1967) have pointed out, when a man is faced with change, the first question he is likely to ask is: How will it affect me?

The Programmers and the User Departments

To the programmers, the Personnel department embodied all they disliked about their work situation. For the stock controllers, the computer represented a similar threat. They had no wish to become the victims of a change apparently imposed on them by a group of outsiders who knew little of their work. A stock controller, later to join the Computer department, recalled:

'I was very loath to join the computer set-up at first. There was a great deal of anti-feeling towards the programmers which was heartily reciprocated. They called the stock controllers idiots and took the attitude that it was the programmers' job to tell them what to do. The user departments used to say *the* computer when referring to the Computer department.

I remember Kahn, who was head of stock control at that time, going into a tirade about computers when I had to see him as part of my induction course. He used to say: "These people coming into the business with the machine aren't going to tell me how to run my department." I had scars on my memory about computers before I even got near them.'

Harry Bell was later asked how he got on with the stock controllers:

'I had enormous problems. Kahn was opposed to the whole system. Also, individual stock controllers were opposed to it. One

man said to me: "It's taken all the interest out of the job."
Another said: " Before the computer I was so overworked people
would tolerate my mistakes. Now everyone expects me to be
right." We were tightening the controls over these people.'

Although they were being asked to accept output from people
who symbolized a machine they did not trust, the stock controllers
were still responsible for making the kinds of decision they had
made in the past. One stock controller expressed their feelings like
this:

'We put so many obstacles in its way in the form of nervous
argument. We didn't believe it could give us all the things we
needed. We were frightened the computer would wrongly calculate something for us and we wouldn't notice this.'

Essentially the stock controllers felt that if they did not lose their
jobs altogether, their skills would be diluted and their livelihood
threatened. None of these things happened. In fact, the very opposite
occurred. The computer eventually took much of the routine from
their work and allowed them to utilize their merchandising skills
more effectively. The status of the department has considerably
improved since this time. Today the head stock controller acknowledges the changes in his department's fortunes but insists that in
1958-9 'it wasn't obvious that this was going to happen'.

Many people in the company attribute the user departments' early
fears to the programmers' style of operating. The programmers were
said to be 'domineering', 'arrogant', and 'outside the situation of the
ordinary stock controller'. Even when they organized lecture courses
for the stock controllers, the latter could not understand what was
going on. A stock controller said:

'In the early days the programmers would give us lectures on
mathematics. What we really wanted to know was what the
machine could do for us and *not* the mathematical formulas
behind the operations!'

What eventually happened is well characterized in the following
quote:

'If someone comes along from outside and just walks in without
consulting people in the department, then it's only natural that
staff begin to pull down the blinds.'

Early in 1959, then, the programmers had mastered what was for them at that time technically an extremely complex and challenging task. They were now producing computer output for the Stock Control department. The only problem was that the stock controllers refused to accept it. A very expensive piece of machinery was producing, from the company's point of view, irrelevant information. In this situation Jim Kenny arrived to set up an O & M department.

The Programmers and the O & M Officers

Kenny was brought into Michaels with the encouragement of the chief personnel officer and Brian Michael himself. Somebody had to act as a link between the programmers and the stock controllers. Someone had to translate the company's needs into computer terms. O & M officers at that time were generally involved in redesigning clerical procedures. It was felt that eventually they could redefine the system of work in the Stock Control department, set it out in the form of flow charts and reports, and then leave the programmers to translate these flow charts into a form acceptable to the computer.

Bill Reilly and two liaison officers, Tom Reagan and Harvey Peters, considered that they had been trying to do just that from within the Computer department. They found it very difficult to convince the programmers of the value of their approach. I asked Tom Reagan how he and Bill Reilly got on with the programmers:

'Not too well. The programmers wanted to go their way. They regarded Bill's work as trivial and time-wasting. They more or less dismissed his O & M work.'

Harvey Peter's attitude was part admiration, part contempt:

'As a group they were highly individualistic, and at the time they struck me as being brilliant, though I wouldn't think that so much now . . . they had a tremendously selfish attitude. Anybody who was not a programmer was less than human. They were so involved in their work. I suppose it was so demanding, they had to look down a very narrow path.'

Reilly described the situation in 1957-9 as follows:

'The whole thing was a bit of a melting-pot. The only real distinction between us and the programmers was that they had no knowledge of commerce. . . . There was no doubt their mathematical training helped their logical abilities. . . . I suppose you'd expect differences between the two groups for they were down in London all the time. We were only down every other week. When they eventually came up to Wolverhampton, we had to shield them from the management.'

The programmers who were interviewed did not take such an extreme stand towards Reilly, Peters, and Reagan as the latter thought that they did. The programmers' attitude was more a matter of: *we* have the skills, what is all the fuss about? Pete Taft, a senior programmer, commented:

'There was a bit of friction, but not because we couldn't talk each other's language. We were the systems analysts working with the O & M boys. The only real friction came when what we wanted and what they wanted in systems terms differed. There were no real technical arguments because we were involved in the actual systems design. They weren't in a position to argue over technical points anyway.'

The analytical training the programmers had was important to them, as was the lack of this training in some of their co-workers:

'Reilly didn't have this and was therefore much less objective in problem-solving than we were.'

Gerald Lane expressed a similar view:

'Reilly was nothing exceptional. He was persistent and keen, but when Bell left Reilly moved over to Jim Kenny's new O & M outfit.'

In spite of these differences in background, training, and work orientation, both groups in the Computer department talked of a distinct feeling of group solidarity. Much of this was due to high involvement in their work. In 1957-8 there were only about a dozen computers on order in Britain. Michaels purchased the first SE 100. The members of the Computer department felt like pioneers. They were. A programmer remarked:

'In the main, relations in the Computer department were very good. Morale was very high when we were really trying to get the system going. I can't remember a group with such high morale or of such high calibre since. They were the pioneers.'

Reagan, after accusing the programmers of arrogance, noted:

> 'There were these differences but not enough friction to really divide the department. There was an air of enthusiasm to get things through that meant there was no real split.'

Harvey Peters, the other liaison officer, pointed out the existence of an outside threat to the department which united everybody. Neil Turner, at that time a senior programmer, agreed:

> 'As I've said, we were very much a group. There was a slight split between the programmers and Ted Morgan's laddies but no real friction. Nobody else in the business was obviously backing computers. We were the only group interested in proving they were worthwhile. We were bound to be a close-knit group.'

This feeling of group cohesiveness was well dramatized in their out-of-work activities. Reilly described the formation of a pub drinking club christened 'The Fluids Society'. When the team started to break up in 1960-1, quite a few went to the London area and a 'London Fluids Society' was formed. There was a tendency for members of the team, when it disbanded, to join each other in a small number of firms. Six moved to two companies in the south of England.

The Organization and Methods Department 1959-61

Jim Kenny arrived in Michaels in March 1959. He recruited his first four O & M officers from within the company and then offered jobs (in 1960) to Bill Reilly and Tom Reagan. They both accepted the offers. The O & M department was situated in the company's head office in Birmingham. The stock controllers were in the same building. The Computer department was twenty miles away in Wolverhampton.

Kenny was not impressed with the job the programmers had done:

> 'The computer was doing nothing but printing out some simple information. My first step was to say "let's have a look what the stock-control problem really is". Before I joined Michaels the only people who had contacted the Stock Control department were programmers. I put in a systems team.'

Kenny's early contact with the stock controllers was not trouble-free. He blamed this on the backlog of discontent that had built up between the Computer department and the stock controllers:

> 'Any hostility was due to the way they (the Computer department) did things. They did them over the stock controllers' heads. Also, the stock controllers were afraid to let the records go. I remember Kahn telling me that the stock controllers used to hide on a Friday afternoon. The department was cutting down staff and they were afraid they'd be fired if they were seen by the management. The stock controllers regarded all their records as, if you like, acquiring evidence for the inquest.'

However, the present head of stock control recalls a certain amount of ambivalence towards Kenny's own activities:

> 'So the first thing that happened was that Mr Kenny came in and decided he would do a complete study of stock control and determine what we really wanted and what we didn't. This is where the main arguments came.'

The stock controllers were still very concerned about the restricted amount of information the computer was putting out compared with the manual system. There was also the issue that the output was in a different form and language from what they were accustomed to. Slowly they began to appreciate Kenny's style of operating. They began to draw comparisons with Bell's behaviour:

> 'Bell and Co. really didn't know about stock control and they had no time to study it. But Mr Kenny came and really studied stock control and we sat beside him and his team while they did this.'

> 'I think the O & M team were rather lenient here because what they did was to slowly but surely take away from us the informa- we thought was required but ultimately didn't require.'

By the end of 1960 the computer system was, from everybody's point of view, an acknowledged success. A week's stock had been saved. The stock controllers now had the information they needed in time to start making decisions about future stock levels. Their job increased in status. They were relieved of much of the clerical drudgery and could now act like merchandisers. The chief stock controller recalled:

'I had always felt that the original system was like a man walking around in a street without really being able to see what was going on around him in other areas. Now with the new system it was like a man in a helicopter who had an enormous range of vision and could see for miles around.'

The main task the O & M department performed in making the SE 100 computer system a viable one was to act as an intermediary between the Computer department and the stock controllers. Between 1959 and 1961 the O & M department had only minimal contact with the Computer department. This was largely because the programmers were still heavily committed on the technical problems of systems design and programming for the clothing stock-control operation. In addition, at the end of 1959, the programmers had begun a new project, computerizing the stock-control function of the furniture division. The head of the programming section recalled the heavy commitments of that period:

'The Computer department looked after clothing and furniture stock control. There was no time to do anything else. Up until 1959 we were trying to get something working. From 1959-60 we tried to make it operationally robust and from 1961 onwards we were trying to cut it down to size. It was a full-time job in 1959-60 just trying to get the thing going.'

Summary of Programmer–O & M Officer Relations 1957-61[1]

A content analysis was made of the history interviews with programmers and O & M officers. As noted in the previous chapter, statements were coded into three categories, positive, negative, and neutral, and the inter-coder reliability score for the data was ·91.

Table 1 substantiates the earlier conclusion about the ultimate balancing of attitudes between the two groups in time period 1957-61. Each group made nearly the same number of neutral comments about the other, twenty-seven as against twenty-six. As might be expected from the quotations given above, the groups showed consistently strong negative attitudes towards each other. The

1 Note that the summary data are presented for programmers versus O & M officers and not for Computer department versus O & M department. The implication is that people like Reilly, Reagan, and Morgan were seen to be, and accepted that they were, doing O & M-type work within the Computer department prior to the creation of the O & M department.

TABLE 1 *Comparison of attitudes: O & M officers to programmers and programmers to O & M officers: 1957–61*

	Positive	Negative	Neutral
O & M officers	20	36	27
Programmers	14	29	26

No significant differences: positive–negative cells only.

interesting point is that the ratio of negative to positive comments is nearly the same for each group. For the O & M officers the ratio is 1·8: 1, and for the programmers it is 2·1: 1. There is only the slightest indication that the programmers felt more negatively towards the O & M officers than vice versa. A χ^2 test revealed no significant differences in the direction of the attitudes. Clearly, the feeling of solidarity that had arisen between the two groups while they lived side by side in the Computer department had watered down somewhat when the O & M officers moved into their own department. The important point to note at this stage is the similarity of the ratio of negative to positive statements for the two occupational categories. This ratio was soon to change radically for reasons that will presently be discussed.

While the two groups were alike in the proportion of negative attitudes they expressed towards one another, their negative feelings about Brian Michaels, its management, and user departments were not so balanced (see *Table 2*).

TABLE 2 *Comparison of O & M officers' and programmers' perceptions of Michaels, its management, and user departments: 1957–61*

	Positive	Negative	Neutral
O & M officers	38	71	46
Programmers	10	74	38

Significant beyond ·001 level with 1 degree of freedom: positive–negative cells only.

Given the comments that the programmers and the user departments made about one another, it is hardly surprising that the accumulated feeling of the programmers is negative. It is a little more surprising that the O & M officers should also have negative things to say about Michaels, its management, and the user departments. This is especially so since the great majority of the early O & M officers were recruited from the Michaels Work Study or Stock Control departments. Some of the ill feeling expressed by the O & M officers was directed specifically at the company. These feelings would not have been echoed by everyone in the company. But one O & M officer said:

> 'Michaels is a funny place. The previous ten years had seen all sorts of purges and passions. It wasn't the sort of place where people felt secure.'

Another commented:

> 'Michaels isn't the sort of place you'd want to retire into! '

The day-to-day contacts the O & M officers had with the stock controllers brought home to them the stresses of being change agents. Reilly talked of his frequent encounters with the head stock controller, Kahn, in the following way:

> 'Kahn was one of the biggest cursers I've ever come across. I wouldn't like to repeat any of it now; but his general approach was, "How are you going to do it?" He'd pick a difficult one like rainwear or swimsuits and say, "Tell us the answers". We'd say: "You tell us how you do it and we'll work out how to do it on the computer." We knew he didn't know how he got his figures. They were just based on experienced hunches but he wouldn't admit it. He refused to cooperate. Kahn was afraid of his position. He was afraid the computer would affect his position.'

Eventually, the Michaels directors forced Kahn to cooperate – an early signal to the user departments of where the board's allegiancies lay.

The most notable finding shown in *Table 2* is the significant difference ($p > \cdot001$) in the proportions of negative responses given by the two groups. The programmers clearly felt much worse about Michaels than did the O & M officers. The ratios of negative to positive responses are 1·8 : 1 and 7·4 : 1 for O & M officers and programmers, respectively.

Several factors could account for this result. The programmers saw themselves, and were seen, as an alien group in the Michaels environment. To many Michaels employees the programmers symbolized their fear of the computer. In this respect the programmers and O & M officers were quickly perceived to have an identity of interest. However, the two groups differed on several items that made the programmers misfits and outsiders. First, the programmers were recruited from outside the company. Generally speaking, the O & M people were not. Second, the programmers had degrees and were rewarded at a level well above the company norm for people of their age. Evidence would also seem to suggest that they were paid more than the O & M officers were.[1] Third, the programmers' and operators' work patterns were unlike anything the company had seen before; a consequence of these strange work patterns was that the company had to make compromises in the way it rewarded and disciplined the programmers. The O & M officers worked a normal 8.30 to 5.00 day; they were not yet part of a seller's market for labour. Finally, the O & M department was located in the company's head office, in rooms practically adjoining the Stock Control department. The Computer department was twenty miles away in Wolverhampton.

CONCLUSION: PHASE ONE

The period 1957-61 was a turbulent one in Brian Michaels for everyone involved with computers. The company management and stock controllers were mistrustful and antagonistic towards the Computer department. The Computer department reciprocated in kind. Meanwhile an O & M department was formed. The early competitive relationship between the O & M officers and the programmers thus became institutionalized in the company structure. There was still no question, however, that the programmers were in control of computer activities.

Reference has been made to Robinson's (1968) eight phases in a computer project. If this is used as a guideline, the Computer

---

[1] Further information concerning the differences between the two groups in terms of education and and rewards is presented in later chapters.

department alone handled seven of the eight phases. The seventh phase, 'changeover', was the only one in which the O & M department had any influence. An O & M officer described his department's involvement with computers like this:

'The clothing stock-control system was designed by the Computer department. The initiative always lay with the programmers because that's where computers started. The O & M people just concerned themselves with the manual changeover.'

The important research question is not, however, which group controlled the use of the early computers, but why it did so. To answer that question one must look at the state of computer technology in 1957-9 and the skills that were required to apply it.

In 1957 there was no micro-electronic circuitry, no instant computer packages, and no computer languages. Computers were only just beginning to be employed for commercial purposes. The companies that bought them committed themselves to a very risky experiment. The machines were slow, bulky, and unreliable. Michaels had to employ eleven maintenance engineers to keep the SE 100 in operation during the three shifts of the normal machine cycle. By the time both the clothing and furniture applications were on the SE 100, the computer was practically in use for 168 hours a week.

The biggest problems with the early computers were in systems design and programming. Bowden (1970:44) has acknowledged the difficulties of unreliability and lack of storage capacity. He continues: 'Worst of all, it took so long for the mathematicians to get the program right that it was usually quicker (and cheaper) to get the calculation done by clerks.' (This is taken from a paper in praise of mathematical programmers.) Clearly the Michaels programmers would not go that far in self-denigration. After all, they did overcome many of the technical problems that beset them. As Pete Taft observed:

'... the programming team had virtually no help from the manufacturers. Scientific computers had been in use for a little while but the art of writing programs for commercial applications, using machine languages, was more or less in its infancy. We more or less had to do the job ourselves and we had no experience to draw on except our scientific computing background. It wasn't just programming either – the whole concept of EDP was pioneered in Michaels. Data preparation and transmission all had to be done from square one.'

Another programmer said:

'Compared with modern computers it was a real chewing gum and string thing. The input and output facilities were terribly naïve; but it had good storage and this was a good thing for a commercial application. But the thing worked because the system was designed to suit the hardware.'

The systems design and programs had to be tied to the particular technical constraints imposed by the computer and its input and output facilities. Each type of computer had its own machine language. Each computer system had to be designed with the technical restrictions in mind rather than the needs of the user departments. In this situation, those who had the appropriate technical skills controlled the computer. The programmers had these skills, the O & M officers did not.

The large power differential between programmers and O & M officers was soon to change. A new generation of equipment appeared which offered faster, cheaper, and more reliable service. Research was going on all the time to simplify programming. A new occupational group appeared called systems analysts, who claimed an area of task jurisdiction and a body of skills. All these factors were to affect the level of perceived hostility and the distribution of power and status among those concerned with computers in Brian Michaels. It must have been difficult for Jim Kenny to foresee all these changes and their implications in 1961. His recollection of how he felt about the programmers at that time gives a clear indication of his future strategy towards them:

'They were like a bunch of sixth-formers, sixth-form mathematicians. They were slick, witty in a sarcastic sort of way. They hid behind their technology. Trying to get to grips with them was extremely difficult. They were regarded as a lot of eggheads who lived in their own little world. The programmers were contemptuous of everybody in the business. Everybody had a nickname. They had their own language and all this was reflected in their out-of-work group they called The Fluids. They asked me to go out drinking with them but I refused. The whole thing was bloody infantile. I've no time for that sort of thing. I suppose a lot of their behaviour was partly defensive. They were an odd group. They had to protect themselves.

They were a little "in" group. They larked around at Wolverhampton like a bunch of school kids. I thought, I must get control of them.'

CHAPTER 6

Specialization as an Emergent Process: Phase Two

By the end of 1961 the programming and O & M functions in Brian Michaels were fairly well established. Each of the groups concerned had begun to stake out claims to a share in the handling of computer activities and was defining its identity *vis-à-vis* those activities. Following Becker and Carper (1956), Strauss *et al.* (1964), and Bucher (1970), occupational identity involves the following components:

1. A definition of the field with which the occupation is identified – its boundaries, its major body of knowledge, and associated methods.
2. A mission that the field serves – the value system that justifies and sustains the occupation.
3. The activities that are proper to the field.
4. The relationships that should obtain both between members of the field and with persons in other fields.

The programmers were rather surer of their occupational identity. In the particular locale of Brian Michaels, they had been the first to carve out their area of expertise. They were able to sustain this early definition of their proper field of activities because of their control over computer technology. Like the technical engineer in Crozier's (1964) study, the programmers had control over the dominant source of uncertainty in their task environment. Their power was bolstered by a value system that defined issues in technical terms and required solutions of an equally technically specific nature. Designing and programming a computer system was a mathematical problem which, of course, could be handled only by trained mathematicians.

To the O & M officers, the Achilles heel of the programmers was their lack of knowledge of, and lack of interest in, company business systems. This had implications at the design and implementation phases of the computer system. The O & M officers, backed by the company management and the user departments, tried to define their proper field of activities in those two areas. By the end of 1961 they had been fairly successful at the implementation phase but had done no real work in systems design. They too had a value system. As the weaker group, they often expressed it in such a way as to differentiate themselves from the programmers *and* to explain what they had to offer. A quotation from an interview with Reilly offers a good example:

'The programming characters were completely different from us. They knew a lot about maths and how to handle the first-generation "beasts". They hadn't the faintest idea of the commercial work involved. There were the people who couldn't speak the commercial language and us who knew a bit about programming and the local systems in detail. There was therefore a process of mutual education.'

In the period 1962-5 the O & M officers sought to expand, and the programmers to maintain, their respective spheres of activity. Issues surrounding 'the reality of interdependence' (Thompson, 1961) were expressed in conflicts over power. Changes in computer technology modified the relative status of the two groups. These changes in status fed back into the power conflicts. The aim of this chapter is to describe and explain the determinants of these conflicts and to explore how and why the changes in the task environment of the two groups impinged on their relative status.

COMPUTER ACTIVITIES IN MICHAELS 1962-4

The Decision to Buy the NTL 200: Drama No. 1

Jim Kenny's frustration with the programmers and his desire to control them would have to wait; at the end of 1961 he resigned:

'In 1961 I resigned. Eventually I was persuaded by Brian Michael to stay on. He had hired me in the first place; he interviewed me personally, a pretty unusual thing. In the meantime, they appointed Ramsbottom. In the selection procedures that went on I selected somebody else. Ramsbottom was well down the list. Ramsbottom was given an impossible task. I was given a job of looking at management development in the company.'

No sooner had Ramsbottom arrived as head of the O & M department than he was asked to do a feasibility study for a new computer. Mills, a director of the furniture division, had persuaded Brian Michael that another computer was required to automate the furniture stock-control and accounting functions. Since the SE 100 was fully occupied dealing with clothing stock control and part of furniture stock control, an additional computer was necessary. Ramsbottom takes up the story:

> 'I did the feasibility study for a furniture application and worked out a system where the computer would generate its own orders and suppliers' invoices as a result of the stock-control system. This was quite a detailed study. It involved seeing a lot of suppliers and getting them to accept the invoice . . .
>
> From this we sent out a complete specification to about a dozen computer suppliers. Most replied with a quote and from these we shortlisted three: BCD, IDM, and NTL. Most of those ruled out were because of price factors or because they didn't have random access at that time. In the end it got down to a price wrangle. BCD as usual wouldn't budge on their price and they opted out. Meanwhile NTL were showing themselves amenable to price cuts; I think largely because if they got the order it would be their first sale of the 200 in this country. Finally they knocked £100,000 off. In my evaluative report to the management, I said that of the three shortlisted any one technically could do the job. The management decided that price and the NTL random-access device, which Mills was attracted to, were the key factors and chose NTL.'

I asked Ramsbottom what part the Computer department played in the decision:

> 'They played no part at all in the systems specification sent to the suppliers and only played a minor part in the whole process, except for when replies came back from the computer suppliers, and they evaluated those technical proposals. We used their services because they were there but I don't think they were absolutely necessary from a technical point of view. In the end they backed my statement that any of the three could do the job. Really if they had had more experience they should have been able to specify in detail why one was better than the other. In

certain respects they tended to be offering opinions in the same way I was, and I could only really do this from the information that the suppliers gave me.'

Mills also asked the Computer department which machine they would recommend. Neil Turner, chief programmer at the time, had a rather different version of what happened:

'There was no real feasibility study, not by us anyway. Ramsbottom did a smallish study on timing and throughput which took about two months ... We came out on the side of BCD because we considered the random access on the NTL wouldn't work. Mills also asked Ramsbottom to come to some sort of decision on the manufacturer, but all he did was to ask us what we thought and then go back to Mills with our recommendation.'

I asked Turner if there had been any further contact between the two departments:

'There was no friction, if that's what you mean, but then there wasn't really any relationship at all. We thought it was stupid of Mills to ask Ramsbottom; he knew nothing about computers. Effectively, the decision was made by Mills. He had some sort of relationship with NTL. His son worked there.'

Brian Michaels seemed to be about to take another very risky decision. NTL had sold very few computers in Britain. The random-access device it was recommending was not yet operational in the United States. Ted Morgan described how Michaels cleverly tried to reduce as much of the uncertainty as possible in this part of the task environment:

'Yes, it was a pretty risky decision. We tried to reduce it the best way we could by looking for resources on our side. We had about £6-8 million of NTL office equipment – we were a very big customer of theirs and the relation between the two companies at board level was pretty sharp. At the technical level we also had good contacts with them, mainly because of their association with Scientific Electronics. We had no real ties with BCD. I recommended going for the NTL machine as long as we got assurance from the NTL board that the installation was a *joint venture*. We took a chance but we hedged on every aspect we could. We made them put in a spare random-access unit, got them to use our installation as a field engineering test to which they would be expected to bring customers, and got Maynes to provide engineering support from the States.

It took me several months to work out the NTL contract. We finally got them to agree that we could return the contract and get our money back if in the first six months, in our opinion, the equipment was unsuitable. In the end we were in a very strong position: if we threw the computer out the news would get around very quickly; they had to back us up.'

This episode is a very clear example of what Thompson (1967) calls 'managing dependency'. He notes that 'when support capacity is concentrated in the task environment, organizations seek power relative to those on whom they are dependent' (p. 38). He continues: 'In the management of this interdependence, organizations employ cooperative strategies. . . . Under cooperative strategies, the effective achievement of power rests on the exchange of commitments, the reduction of potential uncertainty for both parties' (pp. 34-5).

Given that it had to make a high-risk decision, Michaels chose the supplier with whom it could manage the dependency most effectively. NTL and Michaels had ties at board and technical levels. Michaels was one of the biggest purchasers of NTL office equipment. These were the standing resources that Michaels could use to reduce its dependency on NTL. Once negotiations started between the two companies, two further strategies were used: contracting and coalescing. The latter is defined by Thompson (1967: 35) as 'a combination or joint venture with another organization or organizations in the environment'. Clearly this is what Morgan was describing when he talked of getting NTL 'to use our installation as a field engineering test to which they would be expected to bring customers' and of getting 'Maynes to provide engineering support from the States'.

The board of Brian Michaels noted the apparent success of these cooperative strategies. They were to play an important part, though in a different form, in future computer decisions.

O & M Officer–Programmer Relations: A New Interdependence

The main outcome of the NTL 200 decision was to disturb the existing balance of interdependence of the programmers and O & M officers. A programmer said:

'Once we had ordered the NTL we started to have a real relationship with O & M for the first time, because somebody had to specify the job we were doing in detail. We knew the system would be roughly the same as the clothing stock-control job but we didn't know in enough detail the system of payments and stock-control operation in the furniture division. This is where the O & M department came in.'

An O & M officer described the change in relations between the two groups like this:

'Yes, we started to take the initiative in some areas. For example, in furniture we produced specifications from which the programmers had to write their programs. They had to write programs for the jobs we told them to. Ramsbottom started the furniture payments in 1962 and the computer people were forced to work with him even though they thought he was stupid!'

My response to this answer was, 'There was some move into programming activities then?' I received a reply that was suggestive of strategic behaviour:

'Yes. This was partly because we were involved in the NTL 200 decision. Mills made the decision, but Ramsbottom was responsible for making the recommendations. It was a conscious move to get in on the specifications. The problems were in taking away some of the Computer department's activities and finding the staff at our end who could do that work.'

Ted Morgan gave the most succinct description of the O & M department's activities on the NTL 200 installation:

'On the 200 the O & M group put out the specifications to the manufacturers, they were mainly concerned with the proposal end. They did an enormous amount of work on the general systems design and then withdrew into forms design and output plus the selling of the accountancy changes to the suppliers. They were deeply committed on the user side but didn't really have the strength on the technical side of computing.'

A comparison of the activities of the programming and O & M groups on the SE 100 and NTL 200 installations shows clearly that, when the NTL 200 was installed, the O & M people made apprec-

iable inroads into what had been the programmers' spheres of
activity on the earlier occasion (see *Table 3*).

TABLE 3 *Comparison of activities of programmers and O & M
officers on the SE 100 and NTL 200 computer installations*

Phases of a computer project[a]	SE 100	NTL 200
1. Application selection	Michaels board/ programmers	Michaels board/ O & M officers
2. Feasibility study and proposal for new hardware	Programmers	O & M officers/ programmers
3. Data-gathering and analysis	Programmers	O & M officers
4. System design and specification	Programmers	O & M officers/ programmers
5. Programming	Programmers	Programmers
6. System-testing	Programmers	Programmers/ O & M officers
7. Changeover	Programmers/ O & M officers	O & M officers
8. Operation, including system maintenance	Programmers/ O & M officers	Programmers/ O & M officers

[a] Taken from Robinson (1968: 228).

Whereas the programmers had effectively controlled the first four
phases on the SE 100, they now played a part in only two of those
phases –a minor part in phase 2 and a more extensive part in phase
4. Later conflicts were, in fact, to centre on the system design and
specification stage. For the time being, like the purchasing agents in
Strauss's (1964) study, the programmers were starting to realize
some of the problems of being at the end-point of a workflow:

'It's a farce; they sort out the general systems and leave us to
sort out all the mess-ups. People see the mistakes at the programming stage, though it may be a systems fault.'

Goode (1960b), using data from psychologists, sociologists, and
medical personnel, has noted that emerging occupational groups are
frequently accused of encroachment and charlatanism. A specific
way of making this charge is to question the emerging group's
competence. The Michaels programmers were very free with such
accusations:

'Some individuals weren't too bad. The trouble was they knew nothing about computers. Some of them had never even seen one, never mind been on a course. This meant they couldn't ask the right questions, and this used to annoy us.'

Neil Turner recalled:

'When the 200 came in it went through Ramsbottom, though we ran the show with plenty of friction between the two departments. . . . The big problem was they knew so little about computers. It stemmed from them being unwilling to admit their ignorance. We knew it wouldn't work. People trying to tell programmers what to do – they knew nothing about computers. . . . The programmers felt that in time they could easily do the O & M officers' jobs and that the officers had no knowledge of the equipment they were trying to use. The second was the more important factor. We objected to suggestions from people who didn't know what they were talking about. This was particularly so with Ramsbottom, who tried to dictate what we did.'

Ramsbottom was well aware of the ill feeling:

'I suppose there was a bit of difficulty, you might call it resentment. The Computer department had to argue that we didn't know what we were talking about when it came to computers.'

His counter-reaction was to downgrade the work of the Computer department by attacking the programmers' weak point, and to bring the directors into the picture to show where their allegiances lay:

'Previously the directors had tended to ask the programmers if they were thinking of computerizing an area of the business. Now the O & M department would do this. The directors tended to regard the programmers as superior mathematical geniuses who knew nothing except maths. They knew the programmers had no business-systems knowledge and were dissatisfied with the programmers extra-programming efforts. They were glad when we took charge of feasibility studies.'

There are strong resemblances between the developing pattern of computer group relations in Michaels and some of the typical situations described in the experimental literature on intergroup conflict. Sherif *et al.* (1961) note that in competitive situations each group begins to see the other as the enemy, rather than merely as a neutral object. Distortions of perception develop whereby each group emphasizes its own strengths and the other group's weaknesses. Thus to the O & M officers the programmers were 'superior mathematical geniuses who knew nothing except maths' or 'were the people who couldn't speak the commercial language' while we 'knew a bit about programming and the local systems in detail'. From the other side: 'the programmers felt that in time they could easily do the O & M officers' jobs' and that 'the officers had no knowledge of the equipment they were trying to use'. In fact, these attitudes do not have to be based on distorted perceptions. Largely because of the recruitment and training policies of Michaels, the programmers had very little knowledge of company systems and the O & M people had little experience with computer hardware.

Blake, Shepard, and Mouton (1964) go further than this negative stereotyping approach in suggesting that mutual negative attitudes and actions feed upon each other: 'The consequence of provocation tends to be counter provocation. This, in turn, leads to the further intensification of conflict. The end result is erosion of mutual respect and confidence in the constructiveness of the other's intentions' (p. 24). Thus a programmer's likely reaction in a situation where an O & M officer points out his weaknesses is to emphasize his strengths. This response is likely to be perceived by the O & M officer as an attack on his weak point, his lack of technical expertise. The result is that one group's defensive behaviour becomes the other group's threat. This feedback–cyclical process helps to compound the existing conflict behaviour.

Another point made by Blake *et al.* (1964: 25) is that in these competitive exchanges group members tend to select as their representative an individual who is seen as 'strong'. It is not usually possible in non-laboratory situations for group members to choose their representative. This can lead to discontent when the leader performs badly in intergroup encounters. Such was the case with Fred Ramsbottom. What is of particular interest in his case is that he became both a significant source and a significant focus of conflict for both groups.

Ramsbottom as the Bureaucratic Successor

There are many interesting parallels between Ramsbottom's predicament and the situation of Peele as described in Gouldner's books

Patterns of Industrial Bureaucracy (1964) and *Wildcat Strike* (1965a). The main difference between the two cases is that, whereas in the Gouldner example 'Old Doug' died, Ramsbottom had to carry on living with his predecessor. As Kenny, the predecessor, later admitted: 'Ramsbottom was given an impossible task.'

People in Michaels responded to Ramsbottom in much the same way as the workers in the gypsum plant did to Peele: they attacked his personality. One O & M officer commented: 'His personality wasn't very good. He was very bureaucratic.' Like Gouldner, we will not be content to explain Ramsbottom's behaviour just by reference to his personality: 'Instead of examining Peele's personality, let us begin by identifying the kinds of pressures and problems which beset him because of his role. In what ways does the role of successor conduce to increasing bureaucratization?' (Gouldner, 1964: 70-1.)

Gouldner described four main pressures on Peele. First, there had been a tradition of recruiting the plant manager from inside the plant. Second, 'Old Doug' had been very popular; he symbolized the indulgency pattern in the factory. Third, Peele came in, with the backing of an outside authority group, to tighten up the plant in the hope of increasing productivity. Finally, because he was an outsider and was not bound into the 'connective tissue' of the plant, he could not operate through the informal mechanisms that 'Old Doug' had used; he had to rely on a bureaucratic approach. This use of bureaucratic rules raised the tension in the plant still further, and strengthened Peele's allegiance both to his efficiency goals and to the use of formal mechanisms to achieve those goals.

Like Peele, Ramsbottom faced a certain amount of resentment because his predecessor had been popular. One O & M officer said:

'They [the programmers] did have a genuine respect for one or two members of our department. They liked Jim,[1] but regarded Ramsbottom as an ignorant peasant.'

A programmer said of Kenny:

'Most people respected Jim's ability, he was a visionary. What a good thing his arrival was, like a breath of fresh air. He fell off

[1] The relative acceptability of Kenny and Ramsbottom may be gauged by the frequency with which each is mentioned by respondents by his first name. Kenny is nearly always referred to as Jim.

his pinnacle somewhat, but you could get things done with him around.'

There is also some evidence that Ramsbottom was asked by the management, who were earlier described by both groups as 'the common enemy', to tighten things up. His own description of his goal was:

'To straighten out the clothing stock-control mess and introduce some accounting procedures.'

By 1961, when Ramsbottom arrived, the clothing stock-control 'mess' was, of course, very much the joint creation of the O & M and Computer departments. The attitude Ramsbottom took may give some clue as to why both groups disliked him. The pioneers from both departments were closely identified with the SE 100. They did not like to hear their work being discussed critically, especially by an outsider.

Like Peele, Ramsbottom not only represented the goals of an external source of authority but also identified with that authority group. He affirmed:

'The O & M department was looked upon as the prerogative of the directors – the mouthpiece, even the darling boys of the directors. People in the company used to think that what the O & M department thought was what the directors thought.'

While it is significant that Ramsbottom held this view of his department's relations with the directors, it is also important to note that nobody else did. His later sense of isolation from both the O & M and the computer groups may have driven him to identify with an 'out' group.

Given these pressures, Ramsbottom's behaviour turned out to be very similar to Peele's:

'When I came and formalized the control of the O & M department over the programmers they didn't take to this at all. I specified everything in chart form. There was no open warfare – it was just that I realized that the previous loose arrangement, where nobody was sure who could give whom instructions, was no good when we started to get into key areas of the business, like accounting.'

But Ramsbottom had two additional pressures to cope with that Peele did not have. First, he had to exist with his predecessor and, second, he was expected to be a strong group representative in dealings with the Computer department. On both counts he was found wanting.

Although Jim Kenny had been given a vague assignment in management development to keep him occupied, his office was still with the O & M group. Bill Reilly commented perceptively on the conflict between Kenny and Ramsbottom:

> 'Jim and Ramsbottom would hardly speak to each other. Ramsbottom resorted to highly formal methods of communication, partly because he was a bureaucratic type, but also as a defence against Jim who tended to do things informally by bypassing Ramsbottom.'

Whereas Kenny was clearly well woven into the connective tissue of relations in Brian Michaels, Ramsbottom was not, therefore he had to resort to formal means of gathering and disseminating information. This rivalry between Kenny and his successor created confusion among the O & M officers. One said:

> 'Ramsbottom would go to the directors and then Jim would go and carry on parallel discussions. You could never tell what was said. They used to come out of some meetings with entirely different stories.'

The rivalry also weakened Ramsbottom's position with the Computer department. Gerald Lane, head of the programming group at that time, did not accept Ramsbottom as the effective representative of the O & M department:

> 'Ramsbottom was nice enough to start with but went a bit sour. Jim didn't get on with him. I reflected a bit from that. Ramsbottom never made his mark because Jim was still around. There was no point in arranging anything with him because what he said didn't go.'

The O & M officers were aware of Ramsbottom's inability to represent their interests with the programmers. Ray Ashton, for example, said:

> 'As you know, I have always been fairly sympathetic to Ramsbottom, particularly for the position he was put in when he

I

arrived, but I had no respect at all for his ability. He wasn't in the innovation league at all.'

This last quotation and the one that follows, by Reilly, demonstrate the O & M officers' concern for their lack of technical competence. Clearly the worst possible leader they could have had to deal with the programmers on their behalf was somebody they considered both organizationally 'isolated' and technically incompetent.[1]

'Even we had no respect for Ramsbottom's knowledge and I commented at the time, if they had another one like him they could count me out.'

To the programmers, Ramsbottom symbolized the weakness of the O & M department – lack of computer expertise. At the time of the NTL 200 feasibility study, Neil Turner remarked, as noted earlier:

'We thought it was stupid of Mills to ask Ramsbottom; he knew nothing about computers.'

Another programmer commented:

'Relations between O & M and us were particularly bad, largely because of Ramsbottom. He had little respect from his own staff and we thought less of him.'

It would be inaccurate to take that comment at its face value and suggest that Ramsbottom 'caused' the conflict between the two groups. Ramsbottom merely occupied the stage on which the drama was played out. His role as successor may have exaggerated structural conflicts over the reality of interdependence and may have helped to provide a focus for such conflict, but he was not a causative agent. In fact, he became something of a scapegoat for both groups, providing a target that they could attack with a public show of unity whenever the strain of competition exhausted them.[2] Like Peele, Ramsbottom chose to fight back when threatened from all sides. This had the effect of adding to his troubles; people began to trust him even less. Ted Morgan observed:

[1] It is common for technical subordinates to over-dramatize their superior's weaknesses when things are not going well for them. See Kaplan (1959) and Glaser (1963).
[2] Both Coser (1956) and Gluckman (1956) deal with the theoretical issues of how unity can be achieved amid diversity and differentiation.

'Ramsbottom was the common enemy. Nobody trusted him. He was forever trying to get a knife in Jim's back.'

By the end of 1963, Ramsbottom's only tangible support lay with the company directors. During the decision process that resulted in the purchase of the Newton 350, a combination of Kenny's power strategy and Ramsbottom's already weakened position finally lost him that support.

The Decision to Buy the Newton 350: Drama No. 2

Throughout 1963 and early 1964 Ramsbottom pressed for further computerization of the business. When the issue of replacing the outdated SE 100 arose he argued that the new machine should be used to do both the work the SE 100 was doing and the work of one of the clothing administrative offices. It was his insistence on the latter point that finally lost him the support of the directors and allowed Jim Kenny to move back into formal control of the O & M department.

Ramsbottom's explanation of his lack of success, cited earlier (Chapter 3), was as follows:

'It was my intention to leave the NTL 200 on the furniture accounts and assign the new computer to do SE 100 work and one of the administrative offices. The directors weren't too keen on having computers in the administrative offices. This was the main side of the business where feelings were strongest and where the most entrenched systems were to be found. To me it was a prolific area for computerization, but in the minds of the entrenched this was the heart and soul of the business.'

Neil Turner offered the most complete description of what happened in the Newton 350 decision process: [1]

'Ramsbottom raised the issue of the administrative offices and got himself in trouble with the management. But then they asked him to look at one of the administrative offices and to replace the SE 100. They then changed their minds and told him to forget about the administrative office and see about replacing the 100. We didn't take any part in this. We just said something ought to be done about replacing the 100. Then Fred [Ramsbottom] came

[1] This version of what happened has been checked by cross-interviewing and with documentary sources.

round to us to find out why we had to do something about the 100. We told him that it was costing Michaels about £50,000 a year in maintenance. We could rent a new one cheaper than that.

Fred kept on fiddling about with the administrative office plus the SE 100, and eventually completed a report recommending BCD. The very next day he saw a Victor representative and proceeded to change the name on the report to recommend Victor while leaving the main body of the report untouched.'

At this point in the interview, I could no longer maintain my neutral, interested interviewing face. Turner continued:

'It's absolutely true. I've seen the stencil. Eventually he was told by the management to stop buggering about and get on with replacing the 100. He came to see us again, and when he left he was all in favour of BCD again. We told him, taking the available configurations, you must put BCD first, so he recommended BCD. Then somehow Jim got onto it. He asked me to go and see Newton, mainly because he had met some Newton people in the USA. I saw Newton and built up a configuration. We now had two, BCD and Newton.

We – Parkin,[1] Jim, and I – had a meeting to decide between BCD and Newton. Ramsbottom wasn't invited. He was left to make his own decision. Parkin thought Newton was the best, which, of course, Jim was all for then. I didn't care either way. BCD wanted to do the job by supplying first a 1700 and then a 250, which had just been announced. We knew Newton would do the job. BCD had better logic and design, but we didn't fancy the changeover to 250 as soon as we had got the job off the ground . . .

We stated right from the very beginning, we wouldn't have NTL under any circumstances. This caused some real rows with NTL and Mills, but this time we had plenty of experience to prove that their access device was too unreliable. We recommended Newton and left Fred [Ramsbottom] to keep mumbling about BCD, but nobody took any notice of him.'

Bill Reilly argued that Mills's identification with the furniture division of the company meant that he could have little influence on

[1] Parkin succeeded Gerald Lane as manager of the programming group in mid-1961.

a decision concerning the purchase of a computer for the clothing division:

'Mills did a bit of scurrying. He made a few noises in NTL's direction, but since he was a furniture director he couldn't really have much sway. In fact, this was a sort of anti-NTL factor.'

Ramsbottom suggested that the directors rejected NTL for technical reasons and because the company did not wish to become too dependent on one supplier. With the NTL 200 purchase the directors had been attracted to NTL because of the cross-ties of dependency between the two companies. Now they were seeking to manage the dependency, in a situation where NTL might have acquired an ascendant position, by preventing any new commitment to NTL:

'The directors felt that it would be unwise to have all your eggs in one basket. They considered we should go to yet another supplier.'[1]

The Michaels board had to sign the cheque, but the crucial intervention in the Newton 350 decision process was made by Kenny. The following is Kenny's version of what happened:

'Ramsbottom was putting up a BCD 1700 with a painless transfer to a BCD 250. I said "Not on your life". I mentioned this to one of the directors. He said he wouldn't go along with it either. Ramsbottom changed his mind for a Victor 300. I wasn't happy about this either. I knew their maintenance was poor. I rang up the managing director and told him I was worried. He said, "Sit back and wait".

It was in this worried state that I met Henry de Ville. (Kenny interjected that his story was beginning to sound like a Greek drama.) De Ville said, "I understand you're considering buying BCD. If you don't buy Newton you're mad. The BCD isn't off the production line yet." This was just sales talk. I hear it every day. I wanted to have a look at some of their installations. I called in Neil Turner and asked him what Newton were like. He said he knew nothing about them. I told de Ville, "You won't convince

---

[1] Becoming overdependent on one supplier is, of course, a familiar problem for retail men. Many large companies have tried to monopolize the productive capacity of small suppliers so that they can control price and quality (see Chandler, 1962, Chapter 5).

me with your sales talk. I want Turner to see some of your installations.''

De Ville made a wise move. He sent an experienced software man called Sanderson around with Turner. They were away a week. Turner was impressed when he came back. I saw de Ville again and all the top people in London. They convinced me I would get good backing. I finally came back convinced.'

Ramsbottom must have realized that any support he had was now gone. He later described how the decision was made while he was on holiday:

'If anything, I favoured BCD because they offered more systems support at that time. They had a local office and local servicing facilities. Newton were in their infancy in this country. They had no local support. We would have to go to London for that. To me these were the telling factors and I recommended BCD. After making this recommendation I went on three weeks' holiday. In the usual manner, Michaels always pressing, the managing director decided to make a decision on the fact that the Newton sales manager made an impassioned plea to Jim Kenny.'

Kenny's success in this decision process and the dismissal of Ramsbottom were a clear demonstration of his power. He was now in a much stronger position to carry out his earlier threat to control the programmers.

Summary of Programmer–O & M Officer Relations 1962-4

A comment by Bill Reilly, the systems manager, neatly describes the situation:

'Essentially the problem of systems analysts and programmers is who does what and why. This is a matter of us arguing with them. Always our area of knowledge is advancing year by year.'

The aim of this and the previous chapter has been to show how the task environment of specialist groups emerges over time through a process of negotiation. Such a process requires as a prerequisite a poorly 'institutionalized social system as a base'. According to Eisenstadt (1965: 40), 'the institutionalization of any social system means that certain norms, sanctions, and organizations which regulate the access to different positions and establish certain norms of exchange are set up'. In the absence of such clarity and consistency in role definition a process of role crystallization takes place (Eisenstadt, 1965, pp. 30-1). Strauss *et al.* (1964) have described the strategic aspects of this crystallization as the negotiation of order. Using the psychiatric hospital as a case, they define the problem of inter-specialist relationships as 'which specialist shall treat whom, how and under whose aegis'. As a result of this process of negotiation, the occupational identities of the various specialties emerge and change.

The relationship between the programmers and the O & M officers may be understood as a process of negotiating occupational identities. Conflicts developed in this process over the reality of interdependence. In a relatively fixed task environment, as one occupation expanded its jurisdiction the other group's spheres of activity were threatened with diminution. These struggles took on many of the features of win–lose interest-group conflicts. Apart from the generation of negative feelings and stereotyping, a cyclical pattern of aggressive–defensive behaviour developed.

The O & M officers, whose skills had not long been applied to computer systems, tended to be expansionist and aggressive since they had not yet been accepted in that sphere and were still trying to prove themselves.[1] The programmers, as we shall see, were the group declining in status, although not necessarily in power. Their generalized reaction was to go on the defensive and emphasize their technical skills. This defensive behaviour was seen as threatening by the O & M officers, who were lacking in technical expertise. Their response was to stress their forte and thus perpetuate the cycle of attack and defence.

The big difference between the periods 1957-61 and 1962-4 was in the degree of interdependence of the two groups (see *Table 3* above). As the level of interdependence increased, so did the level of perceived hostility. A content analysis of the history interviews showed a significant increase in the proportion of negative comments made by each group about the other from time period 1957-61 to time period 1962-6.[2] As far as O & M officers' perceptions of programmers are concerned, *Table 4* shows that the ratio of negative

1 See Thompson (1961) and Strauss (1964).
2 Since the summary data in *Tables 4* and *5* relate to time periods 1957-61 and 1962-6, the change in attitudes that they indicate will be affected to some extent by events that took place in Michaels in 1964-6. These are reported and discussed in Chapter 7.

to positive attitudes had risen from 1·8 : 1 at time period 1 to 23 : 1 at time period 2. For programmers' perceptions of O & M officers, shown in *Table 5*, the corresponding ratios are 2·1 : 1 at t_1 and 51 : 1 at t_2.

TABLE 4 *Attitudes of O & M officers*
to programmers:
1957–61 and 1962–6 compared

Period	Positive	Negative
1957–61	20	36
1962–6	2	46

Significant beyond ·002 level (McNemar test for related samples).

TABLE 5 *Attitudes of programmers to*
O & M officers:
1957–61 and 1962–6 compared

Period	Positive	Negative
1957–61	14	29
1962–6	1	51

Significant beyond ·001 level (McNemar test for related samples).

This strong relationship between increased interdependence and increased perceived hostility has been noted by others.[1] Studies of psychiatrist–psychologist–psychiatric social worker relationships (Zander, Cohen, and Statland, 1966; Strauss *et al.*, 1964) show that there is greater conflict in the psychiatrist–psychologist relationship than in the psychiatrist–psychiatric social worker relationship, where interdependence is not so critical. Both studies indicate that status is also an important factor. The psychiatrist feels less comfortable with the psychologist than with the social worker because he perceives the psychologist as having higher status and greater technical competence than the social worker.

[1] See Zald (1962) for a study in a prison setting.

Changes in the level of perceived conflict between the programmers and the O & M officers in Michaels from t_1 to t_2 can be
explained to some extent in terms of status. In the 1957-61 period
there was no question who controlled computer activities. Using
salary levels and educational qualifications as indices, we shall see
that the programmers undoubtedly had higher status than the
O & M officers. In time period t_1 the status discrepancy between the
two groups was clear and large. During 1962-6 it narrowed, and
status differences became blurred. As the level of interdependence
increased, so the status criteria became unclear and the level of
perceived conflict went up.

However, the increase in the negative feelings of each group
towards the other may not have been a result only of ambiguity over
interdependence and relative status; it may also have been a function
of a discrepancy between the expected and the realized. Apart from
their perceptions of each other in their particular locale, most
occupational groups, and especially those operating in a seller's
market for labour, have some awareness of what is happening in
their external occupational environment. If an occupational group
saw that, relative to its immediate competitor, the environment was
turning in its favour, but for some reason it was unable to translate
its consequent expectations into accomplishments in its home
situation, one might expect aggressive behaviour and conflict to be
its response. In the remainder of this chapter, data are presented on
the occupational environment of the Michaels groups with a view
to demonstrating a lag between the status position of the Michaels
analysts and that of analysts in the industry as a whole.

In the comparison of the Michaels and national data, a major
difficulty is the confusion between the titles and roles of programmers, O & M officers, and systems analysts. In the early period,
1957-61, the Michaels programmers did the systems work, although
they were not defined as systems programmers. Furthermore, as
noted earlier, the Michaels O & M officers were not called systems
analysts until 1966, and they continued to be trained as O & M
officers until 1968. Nevertheless, they were beginning to fulfil the
funtion of systems analysts from around 1962. On the national
scene, the newer occupational category of systems analysts had
already overtaken both programmers and O & M officers in terms
of salary level by 1961, and they kept ahead until 1967. Seen as
systems analysts, then, the Michaels O & M officers failed to keep

up with the way the environment was moving. The relative power of the programming and O & M/systems analysis groups in Michaels over the whole time period will be considered in order to explain how this status lag came about.

CHANGES IN THE RELATIVE STATUS OF THE MAJOR OCCUPATIONAL
GROUPS IN THE BRITISH COMPUTER INDUSTRY 1957-68

To examine relative status in the industry as a whole, two indices are used: rewards offered, and educational qualifications demanded for admission to the occupational role.[1]

In the absence of any national statistics broken down into the categories required for the purposes of this study, another way of gathering valid data had to be found (see Chapter 4). It was thought that a content analysis of newspaper advertisements for the various occupational groups in the computer industry would supply unambiguous statistics on three important areas:

1. Changes over time in the demand for the occupational groups.
2. Salary levels and how these might change over time by occupational group.
3. Changes over time in the educational qualifications requested for each group.

One national Sunday newspaper, the *Observer*, was used. All relevant advertisements in every edition between 1 January 1957 and 31 December 1968 were content-analysed from microfilm. In order to obtain a national norm with which to compare the data on relative salary levels, the Retail Price Index and the Index of Average Earnings were abstracted from statistics published by the Department of Employment and Productivity. The RPI was selected as the more appropriate measure, and the relevant salary levels and the index were reduced to standardized scores so that meaningful comparisons could be made.[2]

[1] The analysis of the relative status of the Michaels programming and O & M/systems analysis groups takes into account additional indicators of status – those that are usually referred to as the perks that go with the job.
[2] For further details concerning the choice of newspaper, the statistical treatment of the material, and the computation of standardized scores, and for a discussion of some of the problems posed by this kind of trend analysis, see Chapter 4.

Demand for the Occupational Groups

Table 6 constitutes one way of approximating the demand for the main occupational groups over the twelve-year period. The main problem with data collected from advertisements is that they cannot represent overall demand for the obvious reason that some of this demand never appears in newspaper advertisements. Some firms both advertise and train internally. Brian Michaels, for example, recruited its first four O & M officers internally, although they were trained outside by a firm of consultants. Presumably, the drop in the demand for programmers (80 per cent) and for analysts (72 per cent) between 1965 and 1968 can be attributed, in part at least, to a tendency for firms to recruit and train internally. The public behaviour of the industry is a little clearer with regard to the analyst than to the programmer on this point. Since about 1966 the industry has shown great interest in the training of analysts, as published material indicates.[1] This interest is also reflected in the opening of the National Computer Centre. Moreover, I have heard it said on many occasions that it is quicker to train a company man to be an analyst than to train an imported analyst in company business systems (Pettigrew and Gates, 1968). The availability of formal systems analysis courses from 1966 onwards had no doubt encouraged this practice. Apart from internal recruiting and the recent availability of training courses to encourage that recruiting, the drop in demand after 1965 may be due to a natural relapse after the surge effect of the previous nine years. The possibility of a relapse of this sort seems extremely questionable when one looks at projections of total computer installations. The National Computer Centre estimated (*c.* 1966) that 5000 computers would be in use in Britain in 1970, and 10,000 in 1975, compared with 1000 in 1965.[2]

Nevertheless, although *Table 6* does not represent overall demand it does give some indication of the large increase in the demand for programmers/senior programmers and analysts/senior analysts that occurred during the period studied. The number of advertisements for programmers rose from twelve in 1957 to a peak of 201 in 1965. The corresponding figures for analysts were one and 159 – here

[1] See, for example, an article in the *Computer Bulletin* (1967) on the education and training of systems analysts, and publications by the Department of Education and Science (1967) and the Department of Employment and Productivity (1969).
[2] Quoted in Mumford and Ward (1968a: 443).

again 1965 was the peak year. It is clear from *Table 6* that the demand for programmers was both earlier and greater than the demand for analysts: between 1957 and 1961, 281 advertisements appeared for programmers and only forty-nine for analysts. In this respect the national figures mirror the Michaels scene, where the programmers were the first group to become involved with computers. The national data are also consistent with the Michaels situation as far as the early position of the O & M officers is concerned.[1] Between 1957 and 1961 the demand for O & M officers was greater than the demand for systems analysts. Michaels, therefore, was one of many firms to recruit people under the title of O & M officer at that time. After 1961, however, systems analyst became the more accepted title nationally, and demand for analysts far exceeded that for O & M officers. In this respect Michaels was not typical.

Another point of interest in *Table 6* is the position of the group called computer engineers. This group presented a difficult coding

TABLE 6 *Overall number of advertisements for computer personnel by occupational group:*
1957–68

Year	Senior progr. and Progr.	Senior analyst and Analyst	Computer engineer	Senior O & M officer and O & M officer	Analyst progr.	Progr. analyst
1957	12	1	35	1	–	–
1958	28	2	87	9	–	–
1959	73	8	116	24	–	–
1960	77	14	95	17	1	–
1961	91	24	55	25	2	1
1962	96	35	27	19	3	1
1963	140	69	17	19	22	6
1964	177	92	16	37	30	9
1965	201	159	38	27	35	3
1966	173	139	15	23	52	10
1967	127	103	18	7	26	5
1968	40	44	28	3	11	5

[1] The only advertisements for O & M officers that were coded were those that stated that the successful applicant would be working with a computer system as distinct from other office systems.

problem. The title more exactly represents two occupational categories, computer maintenance engineers and computer research engineers. The demand for these groups reached its peak in 1959, then declined steadily until 1964; it rose again briefly in 1965. It is to be expected that there would be a greater impetus for research early on in the development of a new technology; and also that maintenance problems would ease with advances in the technology – as when the second-generation computer equipment came on the market in 1961-2. Again, the drop in the demand for computer engineers corresponds broadly with what happened in Michaels. The firm employed eleven engineers to service its first-generation machine; as the SE 100 was phased out these engineers lost their jobs. The maintenance engineers have been hit even harder than the programmers by changes in computer technology. Today most firms employ no maintenance engineers; servicing is carried out, usually on a 'fire-fighting' basis, by the computer manufacturers.

We have already noted, in the Michaels case, the problems created by the fluid and uncertain task boundaries between O & M officers and programmers. For a variety of reasons these issues were highlighted in the 1962-6 period. One generalized indicator of a problem over task boundaries would be the rise of hybrid occupational groups. *Table 6* shows that, in the same period in which Michaels computer people were having trouble over task interdependence, two hybrid occupational groups started to appear in the industry. The first advertisement for an analyst programmer appeared in 1960, and the first for a programmer analyst in 1961. Of the two titles, analyst programmer eventually became much the more popular: between 1960 and 1968 there were 182 advertisements for analyst programmers and only forty for programmer analysts. These figures may be some indication of the relative status of the two hybrid groups and of the relative demand for the two skills: firms wanted analysts who were competent programmers rather than programmers who could be trained to be competent analysts.

Trends in Rewards for Computer Specialists: National and Michaels Data

Table 7 sets out the salary levels for the various occupational groups, at two grades for analysts and programmers. Our main concern is to compare programmers with O & M officers and analysts, but first we may briefly note how the two hybrid groups fit into the overall picture.[1] Data are available on both groups only for the years 1964-8, and the indication is that in salary level they are closer to O & M officers or analysts than to programmers. There is just the slightest suggestion that analyst programmers tend to be paid more than programmer analysts.

TABLE 7 *Salary levels by occupational group:*
1957–68

Year	Senior analyst	Senior progr.	Analyst	O & M officer	Progr.	Analyst progr.	Progr. analyst
	£	£	£	£	£	£	£
1957	—[a]	—	—	1400	—	—	—
1958	1250	—	—	—	1180	—	—
1959	1350	1490	1000	1350	1280	—	—
1960	—	1750	1000	1500	1250	—	—
1961	2000	1720	1400	1370	1180	—	—
1962	1750	1780	1600	1100	1420	—	—
1963	—	1600	1570	1000	1250	1740	—
1964	1750	1680	1520	1580	1390	1610	1610
1965	2040	1820	1830	1560	1460	1610	1695
1966	2260	1980	1990	1620	1470	1900	1600
1967	2340	2180	2000	2000	1520	1840	2000
1968	2480	1915	1880	2000	1455	2000	1730

[a] For some years insufficient salary data were quoted to permit the calculation of an average.

The relative positions of the programmers, O & M officers, and systems analysts, in terms of salary level, changed over the period studied. Up to 1961, O & M officers had the highest salaries and analysts the lowest. After that, O & M officers lagged behind analysts (except for the year 1964), until eventually they caught up with them in 1967-8. With the exception of 1962-3, when O & M officers suffered a substantial drop, programmers' salaries were the lowest of the three groups over the period 1961-8.

As far as the comparison between the national and the Michaels data is concerned, the two groups that are relevant for time period

[1] Because of the gaps in the data, care must be taken in interpreting these findings. For all groups there were some years when only a small proportion of the advertisements quoted salaries. For example, in 1960 only one of the nine advertisements for senior analysts quoted a salary; by 1966, twenty-seven out of fifty-five did so. However, since the interest is in a trend analysis and not in variations between individual years, the data can be treated with some confidence.

1957-61 are senior programmers and O & M officers. Finding accurate information on salaries at Michaels during this period was difficult: no clear salary-grading system existed, and records were incomplete. All that could be done was to compare the salaries of the individuals in the Computer and O & M departments for whom data were available. In the period 1957-61 the average starting salary for a Michaels senior programmer was £1208 ($N = 5$), and that for an O & M officer was £975 ($N = 5$).[1] On this dimension, clearly the senior programmers were the higher-status group. This status differentiation is accentuated when the average age of the two groups on job entry is taken into account: the average age of a senior programmer was twenty-seven years; of an O & M officer, thirty-three.

The higher status of senior programmers as compared with O & M officers is found also in the national data in the early years. The difference between the average salary levels of the two groups rose from £140 in 1959 to £350 in 1961. On the national scene this status differential was maintained over the next five years, though the actual amount of the difference fluctuated considerably (from a peak of £680 in 1962 it dropped to £100 in 1964). Since data were available on only one senior programmer in Michaels for the 1962-6 period, no comparison can be made at that level.

When we look, however, at the relative rewards of O & M officers and programmers in Michaels in the period 1962-6, we find that the average salary for O & M officers over that period was £1332 ($N = 7$), and the average salary for programmers was £1200 ($N = 7$). The average age of the programmers was twenty-five years, and that of the O & M officers was thirty-seven years. Thus the average age differential was twelve years – a large differential for a salary gap of only £132. These figures give some indication of the relative power and importance of the two groups in Michaels computer activities because, by this time, Michaels O & M officers were fulfilling the functions of, and should have been equivalent in status to, systems analysts. That they failed to keep up with their counterparts in the wider environment says a great deal about the successful power-maintenance strategies of the Michaels programmers.

Figure 2 offers a comparison of the salary levels of systems analysts (two grades) and programmers (two grades) with a

[1] An N of 5 represents 70 per cent of the population of both groups at the end of 1959.

nationally computed index (the RPI) over the period 1957-68. The surprising finding is the extent to which the RPI has kept above both the analyst and programmer curves, Of the four occupational groups, only the senior systems analysts have, apart from a few months in 1958, maintained a salary level above the national index. This is especially noteworthy when one considers both the supposed high demand for these groups and the high salaries with which they have been credited.

FIGURE 2 *Relative salary levels compared with Retail Price Index: standardized scores allowing for vertical dimension: 1957-68*

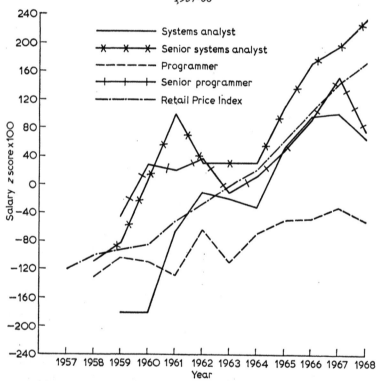

Figure 2 also makes clear the early higher salary levels of both programmers and senior programmers as against systems analysts and senior systems analysts. After 1961, as was predicted, both analyst grades kept above their programming counterparts, the analysts consistently more so than the senior analysts. This finding

is replicated in the Michaels case. In 1968, just as the computer decision was reaching its climax, the firm's salary scale for programmers was £950-1880 over a four-year time period, with a maximum of £2600 for senior programmers. The systems analysts were on a slightly higher scale of £1050-2200 over a five-year time period, with an upper maximum for the senior grade of £3000.

The only relationship implied in *Figure 2* between the RPI and the four salary curves is that of height. By calculating the standard deviation of each distribution independently instead of collectively, it is possible to see how each distribution relates to each of the others around the mean. The extent of the relationships can then be calculated by means of the product-moment correlation coefficient (see Chapter 4).

Figure 3 shows how the five curves relate to one another. With

FIGURE 3 *Relationships between salary levels and Retail Price Index: standardized scores: 1957-68*

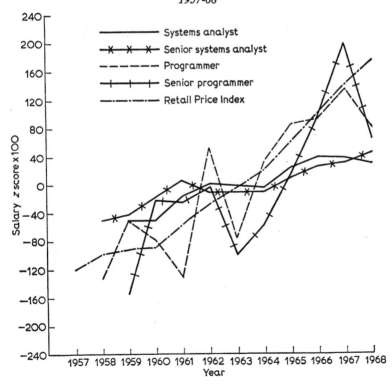

regard to relations between the four occupational groups and the RPI, the highest correlation, $r = \cdot74$, is between the RPI and the programmers; the lowest, $r = \cdot24$, is between the RPI and the senior systems analysts. The correlation between the RPI and the senior programmers is $\cdot68$, and that between the RPI and the analysts is $\cdot25$. These results indicate that the two systems analyst groups are, in terms of salary level, more out of keeping with the movement of the economy than are the two programming groups.

Correlations between the four occupational groups confirm the small relationship between the salary curves of systems analysts (both grades) and programmers (both grades), and also the high relationship between the salary curves of the two grades within each category. Thus $r = \cdot21$ for programmers and analysts, $\cdot22$ for programmers and senior analysts, $\cdot23$ for senior programmers and analysts, and $\cdot19$ for senior programmers and senior analysts. The within-category correlations are $r = \cdot60$ for programmer–senior programmer and $r = \cdot67$ for analyst–senior analyst.

The general conclusion on the reward dimension is the predicted one. In the industry as a whole, the programmers lost out to the analysts, and the senior programmers to the senior analysts, from around 1961.[1] In Michaels, however, the programmers were able to maintain their higher status relative to the O & M/systems analyst group for a longer period.

Trends in Educational Qualifications: National and Michaels Data

The main prediction on educational qualifications was that there would be a trend against asking for degree-level qualifications for programmers after 1960 or 1961. This prediction is very clearly borne out by the national data presented in *Figure 4*.

In 1957, 50 per cent of advertisements for programmers requested a degree only, of which 41·7 per cent specified a degree in mathematics. A further 41·7 per cent of advertisements wanted a degree (any subject) plus programming experience. Michaels was therefore following the national norm at this time in wanting people with a degree (preferably in mathematics) and experience for its first programmers.

---

[1] The same trend occurred in the USA and Canada (see Mann, 1968).

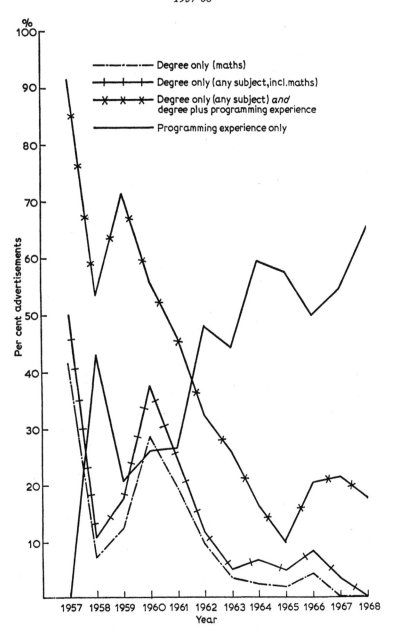

FIGURE 4 *Programmers: qualifications requested:*
1957-68

- ·—·—·— Degree only (maths)
- +——+——+ Degree only (any subject,incl.maths)
- x——x——x Degree only (any subject) *and*
  degree plus programming experience
- ———— Programming experience only

Per cent advertisements

%
100
90
80
70
60
50
40
30
20
10

1957 1958 1959 1960 1961 1962 1963 1964 1965 1966 1967 1968
Year

The national data show further that there were no advertisements in 1957 that requested programming experience only.[1] The following year, as many as 42·8 per cent of all advertisements were in that category, while the proportions requesting a degree only, in mathematics or in any subject, dropped substantially (from 41·7 to 7·1 per cent and from 50 to 10·7 per cent, respectively). Presumably the early rush for mathematicians absorbed a great part of the supply and, when the demand persisted, firms had to lower their educational requirements to find anyone at all. After 1958 the demand for graduates rose again at the same time as the total number of advertisements for programmers began to climb steeply (see *Table 6*). By 1961 the proportions of degree-only and degree-plus-experience advertisements had started a drop which persisted with minor exceptions until 1968.

Figure 5 illustrates clearly the overall drop in the demand for programmers with formal qualifications only (a degree) and the corresponding large increase in the demand for programmers with programming experience only. The proportion of advertisements requesting only formal qualifications dropped from 50 to 0 per cent between 1957 and 1968, whereas the proportion requesting only experience rose from 0 to 65 per cent in the same period. A test of statistical significance would seem superfluous with such data.

For comparison, *Table 8* shows the proportions of advertisements for systems analysts and O & M officers that requested similar types of qualification. The range of qualifications asked for in the advertisements for systems analysts was large: the data were coded into thirteen categories which included, at times, a fair-sized 'other' category (the 'other' category was at its largest in 1963 and 1967 when it constituted 20 per cent of all advertisements for analysts). Only seven coding categories were necessary for the O & M data. The large number of categories required to code the qualifications requested of systems analysts may reflect a generalized uncertainty about what their job involves and what kinds of skill are required for it.[2] This impression is strengthened by the fact that there was a small but appreciable number of advertisements for systems analysts

---

[1] There could have been few people with programming experience at the time.
[2] This task ambiguity has been noted by Mumford and Ward (1968b) and Robinson (1968). Reports on the training of analysts have attempted to deal with this problem (see *Computer Bulletin*, 1967, and Department of Employment and Productivity, 1969).

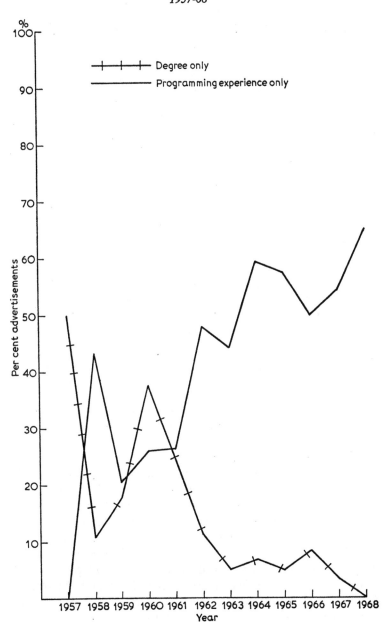

FIGURE 5 *Programmers: qualifications requested: formal only versus experience only: 1957-68*

in which the only qualification specified was 'relevant experience'. In 1963 the 'relevant experience' category represented 10 per cent of the total number of analyst advertisements; in 1967 it represented 15 per cent.

TABLE 8   *O & M officers and systems analysts:
percentages of advertisements requesting particular qualifications:
1957–68*

Year	Analysts: degree only	O & M officers: degree only	Analysts: degree only plus degree and experience[a]	O & M officers: degree only plus degree and experience[a]	Analysts: programming experience only
	%	%	%	%	%
1957	0	0	0	0	0
1958	0	0	0	44·4	0
1959	0	12·5	25·0	37·5	25·0
1960	0	41·2	7·1	41·2	14·3
1961	12·5	8·0	41·7	32·0	4·2
1962	0	0	22·9	21·0	14·3
1963	1·4	5·3	21·7	15·8	14·5
1964	2·2	2·7	7·6	24·3	31·5
1965	1·9	3·7	8·8	40·7	39·6
1966	6·5	6·2	21·6	47·8	33·1
1967	2·9	0	19·4	28·6	16·5
1968	0	0	31·9	0	6·8

[a] 'Experience' in these advertisements was not specified as programming experience.

Apart from 1960, the proportions of advertisements for O & M officers and systems analysts that requested only a degree are remarkably similar. For both groups they constitute under 15 per cent of the total number of advertisements. By 1968 such advertisements had disappeared altogether. The main difference between the qualifications requested for the two occupational groups is that programming experience is required of a fair percentage of systems analysts whereas it is hardly ever specified for O & M officers. Clearly, systems analysts are much more often seen as requiring programming skills than are O & M officers.

Table 9 compares programmers and systems analysts in terms of the frequency of requests for certain qualifications. Programmers have always been seen as requiring more degree-level qualifications than analysts, although the groups are alike in that requests for degrees without experience show a consistent decline. Similarly, subject to the important limitation that degrees have always been more frequently desired in programmers (particularly between 1957 and 1961), the degree-only plus degree-and-experience categories in the two groups are alike in overall shape. In both cases there is a decline until 1964-5 and then an overall rise during the next three years. This rise coincides with the marked drop in demand for both groups recorded in *Table 6*. If we assume that there was a continuous supply of applicants, then the possibility is that firms became more discriminating in their recruitment procedures as demand dropped.[1]

TABLE 9 *Programmers and systems analysts:*
percentages of advertisements requesting particular qualifications:
1957–68

Year	Program-mers: degree only	Analysts: degree only	Program-mers: degree only plus degree and experience	Analysts: degree only plus degree and experience[a]	Program-mers: program-ming experience only	Analysts: program-ming experience only
	%	%	%	%	%	%
1957	50·0	0	91·7	0	0	0
1958	10·7	0	53·6	0	42·8	0
1959	17·8	0	71·2	25·0	20·5	25·0
1960	37·7	0	55·8	7·1	26·0	14·3
1961	24·2	12·5	46·1	41·7	26·4	4·2
1962	11·4	0	32·3	22·9	47·9	14·3
1963	5·0	1·4	25·7	21·7	44·3	14·5
1964	6·8	2·2	16·4	7·6	59·3	31·5
1965	5·0	1·9	10·0	8·8	57·2	39·6
1966	8·1	6·5	20·2	21·6	49·7	33·1
1967	3·1	2·9	21·2	19·4	54·3	16·5
1968	0	0	17·5	31·9	65·0	6·8

[a] 'Experience' in these advertisements was not specified as programming experience.

[1] This argument should be qualified by the fact, emphasized earlier, that the data in *Table 6* cannot represent *overall* demand.

One of the most interesting findings in *Tables 8* and *9* concerns the frequency with which programming experience is requested in advertisements for systems analysts. From 1958 to 1965 the overall trend was upward. It is also worth noting that in the two periods in which demand for programming experience dropped, 1959-61 and 1965-8, there are peaks in the demand for degrees only or degrees with systems analysis experience. The frequency of these requests for programming experience suggests that many firms regard progression from programmer to system analyst as the natural line of promotion. Such a career progression would seem to be an open acknowledgement of the analyst's superior status. In Michaels, the programmers never allowed it to take place.

If, then, we take requests for degrees as the prime indicator of status, there is clear evidence that programmers have declined, in the industry as a whole, over the period studied. In 1957, 50 per cent of advertisements for programmers requested a degree only, usually in mathematics; by 1961, only 24·2 per cent did so. When requests for a degree plus experience are added to requests for a degree only, a similar drop is seen: from 91·7 per cent of advertisements in 1957 to 46·1 per cent in 1961. In terms of requests for degrees, the programmers continued to decline in status to the end of the period. Since systems analysts were never seen as requiring degrees to the same extent as programmers, they have declined much less on this criterion of status.

As with the reward dimension of status, the national pattern was not completely replicated in Michaels. *Table 10* presents data on the educational qualifications of Michaels computer staff at four different time periods.

The overall tendency, which is consistent with the national picture, is for programmers increasingly not to have a university degree. Of the fourteen programmers in Michaels in 1957-61, eight were graduates; by 1968, only four out of seventeen had a degree. There is some indication that the 1957-61 programmers achieved a better class of degree than did the most recent group, but the numbers are very small.

The main difference between the national data and the Michaels data is that, in Michaels, in both the programming and O & M/ systems analysis groups there were proportionately more graduates. In fact, the figures show that there was an overall rise in the proportion of graduate O & M officers/systems analysts in the firm over the period. If, however, the Michaels figures are looked at against the categories of *all* degrees (that is, degrees only plus degrees and experience) in *Table 9*, the difference is less marked. The appreciable increase in the proportion of graduates in the Michaels Systems department was due to a recruitment policy that began in 1965. The aim was not to recruit graduates with experience, but to attract the newly graduated.

TABLE 10 *Educational qualifications of Michaels computer staff at four different time periods*

Staff	Univ. degree	Withdrew from or failed univ.	Technical or commercial college	No full-time further educ.	No infor- mation
1957–61					
O & M officers	1	–	3	3	–
Programmers	8	1	–	–	5
1957–67					
O & M officers/					
systems analysts	1	–	5	5	–
Programmers	15	1	1	2	7
1967					
Systems analysts	2	–	1	12	–
Programmers	6	–	–	5	–
1968					
Systems analysts	4	1	1	12	–
Programmers	4	5	–	8	–

Thus the Michaels analyst people were not asked for program-ming experience as a prerequisite job skill. In this regard the firm's recruitment pattern followed the national recruitment pattern in respect of O & M officers, but differed from the national pattern in respect of systems analysts. More significantly, perhaps, the Michaels group were not trained in rudimentary programming once they had arrived. Not until mid-1968 did the systems analysts in Michaels even have the opportunity to go on courses to improve their technical computing skills. These are key factors in explaining the success of the programmers' power-maintenance strategies right up to 1966.

CONCLUSION: PHASE TWO

In Michaels and nationally, then, programmers have declined in status relative to systems analysts on the two dimensions of rewards and qualifications. There are two main reasons for this overall trend. First, changes in computer technology have downgraded the ordinary commercial programmer's job; second, a widely recognized need has emerged for another occupational group to deal specifically with the design and implementation stages of computer systems.

Bowden (1970: 43) has described, with a sense of personal involvement, the changes that have affected programmers:

> 'Twenty years ago, there were only a few dozen programmers in the world. They were all very competent professional mathematicians, and I think I knew most of them myself. Today there are hundreds of thousands of them, but most of them are not even graduates. A few inspired mathematicians have invented some astonishing techniques which make it possible for ordinary men to communicate with computers and explore them. Today a schoolboy can use a computer to solve problems that would have baffled experienced mathematicians only fifteen years ago.'

Ward (1968: 1) has also noted the speed of technological change in the industry:

> 'In commercial terms the computer has been around for only about twelve years. During this time the development of computer hardware and software facilities has been so great that any individual trained on the early (1950s) computers and isolated since that time would have no idea whatsoever about how to utilize the capabilities of the so-called third-generation machines.'

Bowden (1970: 46) holds that the computer revolution has depended on the simultaneous development of completely new electronics and mathematics. The machines have become faster, cheaper, more complex, smaller in size, and much more reliable. Programming has been simplified by the development of computer languages. The development of master programs has meant that the ordinary programmer has much less to do. Now, part of his job is being done for him by the machine, which computes the details of its own operations from the relatively brief outline instructions that the programmer writes.

Bowden stresses that two groups of programmers have developed over the years. The first and largest group, the one that concerns us in this study, he describes as ordinary programmers. It has been their job to write the 'simple' instruct programs. The others have developed languages like FORTRAN, PL1, and COBOL, the last of which can interpret English prose instructions such as 'perform tax calculation'.

It would seem all the more surprising, therefore, that the Michaels programmers managed, right up to 1966, to hold onto a significant, though always decreasing, part of the power they acquired between 1957 and 1961. How they were able to maintain control over the core of their expertise, their main power resource, in the face of deliberate encroachment by the systems analysts, is the next major research question to be pursued.

CHAPTER 7

Strategies of Power Acquisition and Maintenance 1957-66

> Political activity cannot be assumed to take place within predetermined boundaries. . . . Political activities occur in a space–time arena. . . . The field of action is continually being modified as different groups seek to further their interests.
>
> R. W. Nicholas (1966)

Earlier, it was emphasized that the importance of a power structure should not deflect attention from the details of the processes by which that power structure is sustained, threatened, and changed. Our consistent argument has been that time reveals the instability and imbalance in power relations.

The theoretical implications of such a time-based approach have not gone unnoticed. Crozier (1964) has discussed the evolution of expert power: 'As soon as a field is well covered, as soon as the first intuitions and innovations can be translated into rules and programs, the expert's power disappears' (p. 165). In spite of this awareness of the processual aspects of power, Crozier's analysis is essentially static. In this respect he follows the field. Quoting Crozier's work and an earlier study of his own, Perrow (1970: 67) argues: 'Neither of these analyses sufficiently takes into account the ability of those who once gain power to manipulate the source of uncertainty, at least over a span of, say, ten to fifteen years.' The present analysis is an attempt to deal with that deficiency in the literature. It will focus on the following questions:

1. What have been the specific sources, material or otherwise, of the emergence and decline of the contending groups?
2. What forms of social action, intended and unintended, have

contributed to the attainment, maintenance, and dissolution of power?

3. What implications have changes in power had for the distribution of status attributes between the contending parties?

POWER RESOURCES AND DEPENDENCY

Dahl (1957: 205) has suggested that the main difficulty, when one is studying power, is not to determine its existence but to make comparisons about its relative distribution. Such comparisons can be achieved by identifying the resources held by, in Dahl's case, the actors in a dyad. Unlike Dahl's, this analysis seeks to go beyond the dyadic case. As was noted earlier (Chapter 2), to understand the relative power of A and B one needs to know details of their relations with X, Y, Z, to n, since in this way the power structure is revealed. Our analysis, at this point, is of power at the group level. The relative power of the O & M/systems analyst group and the programmers in Michaels is assessed in the context of their relations with a third party, the Michaels directors.

Following Wrong (1968), Bannester (1969), and others, the task is to identify the system-relevant resources possessed and controlled by each group. Knowing what resources a group possesses does not tell us how it uses them. How a group uses its resources, and with what consequences, will be a major issue. Finally, in accord with the interest in social process, it is assumed that resources are detachable.[1] They may be gained and lost depending upon environmental change and/or upon a group's skill in using or misusing those it originally possessed.

A further major theoretical assumption of this approach is that social relations entail ties of mutual dependence. Individuals build up dependency relations with others by supplying needed services which go unreciprocated. Dependency is thus a result of an imbalance of exchange between individuals, together with the associated ability of one individual to control others through his possession of resources.

A group placed in a position of dependency need not accept subordination. Whether and to what extent it does so is likely to depend on the social alternatives, or lack of them, available to it.

[1] Both Thompson (1967) and Zald (1969) deal with theoretical issues around the fluidity of resources.

Thus if the weaker group has a resource base from which it can offer needed services to the strong group, it may be able to reduce the imbalance of exchange. Alternative strategies might include the weaker group's going elsewhere for a service, perhaps to a group where it had an appreciable balance in its favour, or doing without the service altogether. The weak group might also seek to reduce its dependence by stimulating competition between the suppliers of a service.

The resource of technical knowledge plays a significant part in the following analysis. Crozier (1964) has shown that the technical specialist's ability to control uncertainty, especially in an otherwise routinized set-up, is a major power resource. By using this resource assiduously the expert may be able to develop a dependency relationship with his titular superior. Using the control of uncertainty to create an exchange imbalance has also been noted in work on non-business organizations. McCleery (1960: 58), in a prison study, observed: 'Leadership in the inmate society involved the ability to explain, predict or control to some degree a situation in which others were uncertain and helpless.' Zald (1962) found that the degree of uncertainty in the relation of administrative means to organizational ends was a contributory factor to both the power balance and the level of conflict in five correctional institutions. As we shall see, the main problem for the programmers was to maintain their resource base in the face of the dual challenge of technological change and encroachment from another occupational group.

POWER RELATIONS IN MICHAELS 1957-61

The Programmers' Resources

In this period, role relationships were fairly stable and status and power differentials well defined. The senior programmers in the Computer department were unquestionably in control of computer activities. The reasons for this are equally clear. Installing a computer system at that time was a high-risk affair. There were no standardized solutions to any of the problems. Pete Taft recalled, as noted above:

> 'Scientific computers had been in use for a little while but the art of writing programs for commercial applications, using machine languages, was more or less in its infancy ... It wasn't

just programming either – the whole concept of EDP was pioneered in Michaels. Data preparation and transmission all had to be done from square one.'

Quite specific mathematical and technical skills were required to deal with these problems; the programmers alone possessed those skills. Reilly was the only non-programmer to attempt to acquire programming expertise. Later he acknowledged his lack of success:

'We spent a lot of time looking at programming manuals. I hardly understood a thing that was going on.'

By 1959, Gerald Lane had recognized that Reilly would not make it as a programmer and arranged for his transfer (1960) to the O & M department.

At this period, then, the programmers' power was based on the resource of technical knowledge. They alone possessed it and they used it to deal with a relevant source of organizational uncertainty. As a result of this power, the programmers controlled the task environment they shared with the O & M officers:

'The systems analysts at that time were not a breed by themselves. The programmers did the systems work. They were systems programmers, though they weren't defined as such.'

'There were no real technical arguments because we were involved in the actual systems design. They [O & M] weren't in a position to argue over technical points anyway.'

The Directors' Dependence on the Programmers

Not all services can be used to create an exchange imbalance. The essential requirement is that the service offered should be in great demand by the potential recipient. The Michaels board needed computers in 1957. The current chief stock controller recalled the state of the business at that time:

'In 1957 we were in real lumber trying to operate. With the rapid growth of the company, which, as you know, was around the corner, it was obvious that we had to have help, either that, or five new buildings, and another say 150 to 200 staff. Even then our output of information from the warehouse – that is, sales, stocks, calls, etc. – was taking us anything from five to ten days to complete; whereas, once we got onto the computer, we were receiving output, of a limited form, on the Monday morning following the close-down of the balance. This was something unheard of before.'

Harry Bell conveyed a similar impression:

'The firm was going through a difficult period. There had to be a better use of clerical labour. The business was growing fast, yet its techniques were obsolete. If something hadn't been done it would have been necessary to have an enormous increase in staff.'

Given the demand for the service they offered, then, the programmers were clearly in a strong position relative to the company management. Their power would remain as long as there was uncertainty about the success of the task they were performing, and as long as the management remained dependent upon them for special skills and access to certain kinds of information.

The suggestion has been made that the degree to which one group has power over another depends on what alternatives are open to the subjected group. One course that the Michaels board might have taken in order to reduce its dependence on the programmers would have been to go elsewhere for the expertise they had. Likely sources of outside help might have been consultants, or programming assistance from a computer manufacturer. Neither was possible at the time. Even the programmers complained that they had 'virtually no help from the manufacturers'. If Brian Michael had bought the computer his business associate Miller was manufacturing, he might have had an outside check on his own specialists; but, as we have seen, the SE 100 was chosen essentially on technical grounds by the technicians. The Michaels board did try to make internal checks on the early computer people. Reilly acknowledged that he and Philby, both recruits from the Work Study department, had spied on the Computer department at a director's request. The Computer department was aware of these activities and managed to remove both offenders on the ground that they were technically incompetent.

A further indication of the programmers' power was the intervention of the board to silence user department resistance against the computer. Ted Morgan supplied a good example:

'Just out of the blue, Gerald and I were called to a directors' meeting in which Taylor [a clothing director] had just finished reading out a report critical of our work. Gerald and I were told to sit down there and then and read and comment on the report. Fortunately for us we were in a position to refute the error rates quoted by Taylor and to show that they were lower than those under the previous manual system. The result was that Brewster [the managing director] publicly gave Taylor a hammering and told him it was his responsibility from now on to make the computer work.'[1]

Status: A Visible Attribute of Power

Mitchell (1956: 76), in a study of power relations in a Yao village, observed: 'The struggle of the headmen for power and prestige, both among themselves and against the chief . . . is expressed mainly in the competiton for various symbols of prestige.' Ultimately, the power struggle between the analysts and the programmers in Michaels centred on the pattern of interdependence of the two groups. Initially, however, while their power was relatively unchallengeable, the programmers gathered various items of prestige which increased their status and made their power visible to all. Unlike the Yao headmen, the programmers' power was not symbolized in the wearing of a red band or an extra large knife; rather, it was made visible through their salary and educational levels and their apparent ability to flout the bureaucratic rules in Michaels:

'People worked overtime at weekends without being rewarded and without asking for it. Eventually one of the directors said that this was ridiculous. The programmers must be rewarded for all the extra work.'

'At that time, the rules of the company stipulated that, over a certain salary, if you worked overtime you had to take time off in lieu. But first the operators and then the programmers were paid Sunday overtime.'

There was also the issue of time off for overtime during the week:

'If we stayed after work late we put it down as time off in lieu of overtime. This applied to everybody at Wolverhampton, but they needed to ask somebody pretty high up for permission to stay late – we could stay on when we liked.

---

[1] Gerald Lane related the same events without any interviewer solicitation. One of Taylor's deputies also acknowledged that they were suddenly told to 'get on with it'.

L

People used to notice we were walking in and out when we liked. We used to make an effort to be in by 9.40 in time for break. It was very unusual for anyone to be in at 8.30.'[1]

In spite of a vigorous attack by the Personnel department, the programmers remained intransigent. Eventually the Personnel department gave in and formally acknowledged the overtime payment and time-off-in-lieu privileges.

Mechanisms for Maintaining Functional Autonomy

A major problem for a group generating power in interaction with others in its environment is to establish the legitimacy of its power. The stability of a power base depends on its legitimacy. From the beginning, the programmers failed to stabilize their power. In fact, they engendered collective disapproval and opposition[2] from many groups in Michaels.

Predictably, those who had exceptionally strong negative feelings about the programmers tended to be those whose power and status in the organization were threatened by them. The earlier discussion of programmer–stock controller relationships, and, in particular, of Kahn's behaviour, demonstrates this point.

The programmers did not endear themselves to the Personnel department. One programmer recalled that on one of the many occasions he had to see the chief personnel officer for being late, the latter said to him: 'You computer people make me sick.' The programmer explained: 'He thought we were bolshie.'

The criticism most frequently made of the programmers was that they were arrogant – that they openly displayed their disdain for company rules; then they were criticized because some of the rules were modified and became their privileges. The programmers were aware of the ill feeling, yet they persisted. This was not an effective use of their resources:

'Mind you, the other staff at Wolverhampton felt as if they had plenty to moan about. The programmers didn't just consider

[1] My own experience working in the Systems and Programming departments in 1967 and 1968 suggested that the above laxity in time-keeping had not changed. Whereas rules were rigidly enforced in the Systems department, the programmers' work environment was much more easygoing.

[2] The theoretical issues associated with power and discontent are dealt with by Gamson (1968) in a book entitled *Power and Discontent*, and also by Blau (1964, Chapter 9).

themselves to be different. They thought they were better than everybody else. People became aware of this attitude. They saw the programmers taking what they considered to be liberties: coming in late, having afternoons off to play golf, going out drinking in the evening when they should have been operating the computer.'

In addition to these groups, the programmers had the directors to deal with. It has been suggested that the programmers were able to create a dependency relationship with the directors because of their singular possession of computer expertise. There is the possibility that the directors attempted to control the programmers by generating their own brand of uncertainty. Discussing the problems of purchasing agents, Strauss (1964: 144) noted: 'The sporadic nature of top management intervention makes many PAs insecure; they do not know where they stand.'

It might be crediting the members of the Michaels board with more political acumen than they possessed to state that they used a strategy of control through ambiguity. After all, their dithering and inconsistent behaviour towards the Computer department might have been a product, as Bell said, of their inability 'to understand what was going on'. Nevertheless, however unintentional their actions may have been, they were real in their consequences.[1] By keeping distant from the scene of conflict, by giving the programmers some freedom from the system of bureaucratic rules, and by keeping job assignments uncertain, subject to change at any moment, they prevented the programmers from consolidating a stable power base, and still managed to extract from them the knowledge and work necessary for the company's continued prosperity.

There is plenty of evidence that the programmers were disturbed by the directors' sporadic intervention:

'Brewster and Mills picked up the rudiments extraordinarily quickly. They took it in turns to be responsible for us so as to learn quickly, even though, as you can imagine, this was very unsettling to us.'

'We had progress meetings on key dates, then we would be left for a couple of months on our own.'

---

[1] We are following the famous dictum of W. I. Thomas that 'if men define situations as real they are real in their consequences'.

I asked a programmer if the Computer department had had any clear idea of what the directors were thinking:

> 'No. This was a real problem while I was there. The situation kept changing; rethinks would be undertaken. This considerably affected those in continual contact with the directors. On three or four occasions I can remember great bust-ups, with people screaming out, "What the hell are the bastards up to now!" The system would work, of course, but feelings were always high at the time.'

Another programmer said:

> 'There's one thing that sticks in my mind. At one time we were all dissatisfied. They were messing us about. They would let us start a job and then stop us. Mills came and talked to us. He said, "Bear with us". Of course, it didn't do any good.'

Faced with this sort of harassment, the programmers used two strategies. The first was to retreat behind any available barrier in order to protect their functional autonomy. As Gouldner (1965b: 422) has noted: 'Mechanisms for the maintenance of functional autonomy may entail the use of various "material props" as devices which both symbolize and constrain a degree of social distance between role players.' He goes on to quote Lombard's (1955: 185) example of a department-store sales girl's use of the sales counter as a barrier between herself and the customer. Another example is Whyte's analysis of the use of the 'spindle' to limit interaction between waitresses and pantry help in restaurants (1948: 75).

The programmers had no material props they could utilize as insulators, but they were able to use ecological mechanisms[1] and other individuals as barriers. The programmers were, of course, in the early years, situated twenty miles away from direct everyday contact with the company directors and the O & M department. The main barrier they possessed, however, was the aggressive leadership style of their manager, Harry Bell:

> 'Harry regarded any contact he had with the directors as taking place on a battle-ground. . . . He kept the wolves from the door and

[1] Both Mack (1954) and Long (1958) deal with ecological mechanisms for maintaining functional autonomy, the first in an industrial shop, the second in the community sphere.

allowed the boys to get on with the job. This was absolutely the right approach in that situation and with these people.'

'Harry was reasonably technically capable but he had plenty of drive. He stuck his chin out and got it hit, but he went boldly forward – he didn't bother – on he went.'

'Harry was one of the best businessmen I've ever met. He was a great boss. He would say black was white to people outside the department if he thought it would further the Computer department's interests. He's the only man I've met in this company who could handle our board of directors.'

Later, when Harry Bell had left, Gerald Lane, then senior programmer, and the person most likely to have to deal with the directors' inconsistencies, thought that the new O & M manager, Kenny, would provide a good barrier:

'There was a continual fear that management would change their minds about objectives and the time period you had to attain them in. It was felt that Jim [Kenny] would be a good buffer between us and them.'

If the first strategy that the programmers talked about appeared defensive, the second one most certainly was not. Sayles (1958) has found that the greater the group solidarity and self-esteem stemming from social status and/or professional homogeneity, the more likely a collective identity is to be found. Assuming certain historical constants, Williams (1947) and Coser (1956) find that an outside threat generally produces internal group solidarity. It has been demonstrated that the programmers perceived their environment to be threatening. There is plenty of evidence to suggest that they had high self-esteem, high group solidarity, and a good sense of collective identity:

'Nobody else in the business was obviously backing computers. We were the only group interested in proving they were worthwhile. We were bound to be a close-knit group.'

'The main thing that struck you was the number of very good people around – a fantastic number – maybe because it was the early days. You wouldn't assemble that sort of calibre team today. Today you can expect only a few graduates. If anybody applied at that time without an honours degree in maths, you more or less asked them why they were applying. You needed A levels just to be an operator.'

Like the printers in the study by Lipset, Trow, and Coleman (1956), the programmers were driven together partly by out-of-the-ordinary work hours. There was also the challenging work, and the hostility and suspicion they had to live with. They were a group by themselves – outsiders.

In this sort of situation, they behaved very similarly to the maintenance men cited by Crozier (1964). The power of both groups was contested. It was not legitimate power. Both groups felt insecure. Their reactive strategy was to cultivate a cohesive, aggressive group spirit to keep opposing power-seekers on the defensive and to shield their own power resources from unfriendly eyes.

An unintended consequence of this strategy of the programmers was to generate still further discontent and opposition, and to strengthen certain people's resolve to control them. It was, above all, the programmers' aggressive *esprit de corps* that was sensed and despised by most of the Michaels organization. Many of the comments that have been quoted describe the programmers as aloof and arrogant. As the person most immediately threatened by the programmers' power, Jim Kenny was most garrulous on the subject:

'Trying to get to grips with them was extremely difficult.... I suppose a lot of their behaviour was partly defensive. They were an odd group. They had to protect themselves.... I thought, I must get control of them.'

POWER RELATIONS IN MICHAELS 1962-6

In this period the power of the programmers was further threatened by technological change and by management-inspired O & M encroachment on their task environment. In fact, by the end of the first period, the programming group had already suffered a severe blow, with the departure of virtually all the senior programmers who had designed the system for the SE 100.

TABLE 11 *Programmers: labour turnover:*
1957–67

1957	1958	1959	1960	1961	1962	1963	1964	1965	1966	1967
0	1	1	4	5	1	1	6	2	5	2

Table 11 shows the pattern of programmer labour turnover over the years 1957-67. There are clearly two peaks, at 1960-1 and 1964-6. Four of the nine programmers who left in 1960-1 were traced. Two principal reasons were given for leaving at that time. First, as far as they were concerned, by 1960 the SE 100 job was well 'bedded in'; they had to move on in order to keep learning. Second, they were unhappy with both the Michaels and the Wolverhampton environments; they wanted to move back to London. The biggest blow for the programmers was the loss, late in 1961, of Gerald Lane, their senior man. He was replaced as joint computer manager by a non-programmer, Phil Parkin.

Power-maintenance Strategies under Technological Change

The technological changes that so influenced the computer industry have been discussed. Likewise, it has been noted how technological changes can break up configurations of expected status characteristics by altering the occupations from which those status characteristics develop. An important related area that has not yet been dealt with, however, concerns the power-maintenance strategies that are likely to be used by an occupational group when it is faced with technological change that is eating into the core of its expertise, its major power resource. How an acquisitive group might react to such strategies must also be considered.

Literature dealing with active and reactive strategies under conditions of technological change is practically non-existent. Thompson (1963) examines the impact of technical change on nineteenth-century craftsmen. He argues that, in the first half of the nineteenth century, the skilled trades were like islands threatened on every side by technical innovation and by the inrush of unskilled or juvenile labour. Invention simultaneously devalued old skills and elevated new ones. In this situation 'the artisan was as much concerned with maintaining his status as against the unskilled man as he was in bringing pressure upon the employer'. According to Thompson, the artisans used two protective strategies. First, they looked to their trade unions to protect the knowledge base of their skills through the apprenticeship system. Second, they became politically involved. Thompson holds that the political radicals of that period came from the ranks of the 'debased trades' and not from the unskilled or semi-skilled workers who flocked into the cities from rural England.

Cottrell (1962) discusses the 'big four' occupational groups in the

American railroad industry. He was interested in what happened to these big four when diesel and electric locomotives were introduced. The pattern of dilution and elevation that occurred with the nineteenth-century artisans was repeated here. The boiler-makers declined and the auto-mechanics and electricians increased in power and status. The engine-drivers were no longer required to have a 'strong back and weak mind'. A knowledge of auto-machinery was now a more critical job skill. The engine-drivers used protective strategies similar to those of the artisans: through trade-union activity they kept control of the recruitment and learning processes for their trade.[1]

The Michaels programmers did not have an interest group like a trade union or a professional association to bargain for them. Nevertheless, in the 1962-6 period, a number of factors helped them to protect their power base and their occupational identity, although the strategic implications of these factors as perceived by others induced reactive strategies which further weakened the programmers' position. The programmers used four main strategies:[2]

(i)   norms that denied outsiders' competence
(ii) protective myths
(iii) norms of secrecy
(iv) protection of their knowledge base through control over training and recruitment policies.

Turner, the chief programmer in the 1962-6 period, was the most outspoken on the first protective strategy:

'We knew it wouldn't work. People trying to tell programmers what to do – they knew nothing about computers. . . . We objected to suggestions from people who didn't know what they were talking about. This was particularly so with Ramsbottom, who tried to dictate what we did.'

In a programmer group interview, the following comment received wide acceptance:

'We hardly saw them [O & M] until we moved into the new head

[1] This strategy is also a familiar one in the building trade industry (see Myers, 1946).
[2] It might be thought that the concept of strategy has been imposed on the actors. The interview data show, however, that the participants were aware of, and generally willing to discuss, their strategies.

office and there hasn't been much contact since then and you could hardly say that's been much use. If you asked any of the O & M in the early days they knew nothing about the specifications. They used to write their reports after jobs had been put on.... They kept on changing their ideas.... The trouble was they didn't know what they wanted in the first place.'

The second mechanism, the generation of myths, is less easily characterized as a strategy in the Michaels case. Myers (1952: 273) has suggested that myths are likely to appear when an occupational group is faced with change and is seeking to protect its power and identity. H. L. Smith (1962) prefers the term 'fiction' to myth: 'Every profession operates in terms of a basic set of fictions about itself. These provide the profession with a comforting self-image and some stereotypes to help meet and adapt to the varied and often drastic contingencies of everyday operation' (p. 223). This point has also been made in the anthropological literature on myth: 'If we view social relations through a longish period of time, we see how various parties and supporters operate and manipulate[1] mystical beliefs of varied kinds to serve their interests' (Gluckman, 1965: 235).

It is possible that the widespread *belief* in the Management Services department that the early programmers were especially well qualified was such a protective myth. Clearly it was in the programmers' interests to stress both that special skills were required to perform their task and that they possessed those skills in abundance, especially when that was no longer true.[2] In fact, there was never a time when all the programmers had first-class honours degrees in mathematics. Taking 1957-61, the most likely period, of the nine programmers for whom records are available, one had a first-class honours degree, four had seconds, two had thirds, one had a pass degree, and the other had not completed his degree course.

Another myth that Neil Turner liked to use was that programmers could not operate under time constraints:

'People are always pressing for things to be put on the machine, but it's difficult to forecast the time periods for doing anything.

---

[1] Kapferer (1969a) provides some fascinating data on manipulative behaviour in a Zambian copper mine.
[2] See Chapter 6 for a comparison of the programmers' educational qualifications in the two periods 1957-61 and 1962-6.

The computer either works or it doesn't. There are no 75 per cent correct answers.'

This is emphatically denied by one of Turner's deputies, Malcolm Burlington:

'Neil's always argued we cannot work under time constraints. This isn't true. It's just his way of giving himself plenty of room for manoeuvre.'

Gerald Lane, talking of an earlier period, showed that the programmers could operate under harsh time limitations. I had asked him what his relations with the directors were like:

'If they wanted something done, they wanted it in a hurry. When they finally made up their mind to do the furniture stock control, they asked me how long it would take to implement the first phase. I said five weeks. They said three. I was eventually "conned" into saying I could do it in three. We all sat down, split the work up, and did the programming bit by bit. We were rather proud we did it in three weeks. The department spirit was high. We were a group apart from the rest of the company.'

The third strategy used by the programmers, withholding information that might have reduced the uncertainty and/or mystique of their task, is one that has been noted by several authors. Crozier (1964: 153) discusses the maintenance workers' strategy: 'Their strategy is a very simple and rigorous one. It aims, first, to keep the area under their control, free from outside interference.... Maintenance and repair problems must be kept secret. No explanation is ever given. Production workers must not understand.' The industrial relations officers in Goldner's (1961) study augmented their power by keeping union–management agreements 'secret', or failing this, making them vague: 'They continually stressed that a contract was not what it seemed and agreed to make it specific only under pressure.' Similarly, Scheff (1961: 96) found, in his study of a state mental hospital, that if physicians broke the trading agreements they had set up with the ward attendants the latter could sanction them by withholding information and cooperation.

The programmers who mentioned the withholding strategy were prepared to admit that it was a deliberate device but not that it was a protective one:

'From their point of view, they [the O & M group] thought of us as being bolshie. We were the fellows who wouldn't tell them why they couldn't do things. But what was the point? They couldn't understand our language.'

'There was a feeling that those fellows [O & M] didn't know what they were doing, that they knew nothing about computers. I never withheld information but some of the programmers couldn't be bothered to explain what was going on. They would say: "It would take too long; just take my word for it." I know that some of the systems analysts felt that the programmers were deliberately keeping them in the dark. We had to spend a lot of time telling them that things couldn't be done. It was either that or spending a lot of time training them about the NTL 200.'[1]

Evidence concerning the programmers' fourth strategy – controlling the training and recruitment policies that protected their power base – is presented and discussed in a later section of this chapter (see pp. 161-5).

The Directors' Strategy towards the O & M Department

By 1962 the directors had firmly placed the O & M group between themselves and the programmers. I asked Ramsbottom what his functional relation was to the Computer department:

'It was my job to specify the systems that were required by management and our systems investigation. You could say then that the Computer department worked to my instructions[2] except in personnel matters and program developments.'

A consequence of this strategy was that it relieved the directors of some of their dependency on the programmers and placed the burden of dependency on the O & M group. It now became the O & M department's responsibility to get the work out of the programmers. The department's ability to do this was not made any easier by the directors' somewhat ambivalent behaviour towards it. From the directors' point of view, of course, they had created an O & M department to deal with the user departments and counter the threat of the programmers, and this new department had to be

---

1 Clearly, from the programmers' point of view, the second alternative would have done them more long-term harm.
2 This, of course, was hotly contested by the programmers.

controlled too. There is some evidence that they used the strategy of divide and rule.

President Franklin D. Roosevelt is said to have been one of the noblest practitioners of this strategy. To quote Schlesinger (1959: 522-3): 'Roosevelt's persistent effort was to check and balance information acquired through official channels by information acquired through a myriad of private informal and unorthodox channels and espionage networks.' Roosevelt also attempted to generate information by recruiting strong personalities and structuring their work so that clashes would be certain: 'His favourite technique was to keep grants of authority incomplete, jurisdictions uncertain, charters overlapping' (Schlesinger, 1959: 528).

Whether the directors' behaviour was strategically contrived or not, it has been shown that their sporadic and inconsistent interventions unsettled the programmers. Moreover, in the 1962-6 period, their behaviour had the further effect of stimulating conflicts between the O & M and programming groups.[1] I asked a programmer if there was any formal difference in status between his departmental head, Parkin, and Ramsbottom:

'No, though Ramsbottom thought he was superior to Parkin. This was a big fault with the system then. Nobody knew who was in overall charge. The whole thing was uncertain.'

Another programmer commented:

'We had a bit of trouble with Ramsbottom. He got violent at times, especially with Parkin. Parkin was responsible to Mills, while Ramsbottom was under Brewster. This caused trouble. Mills would ask us what was the matter. Parkin often could only reply, "We can't do anything, Ramsbottom is holding us up." '

Ramsbottom seemed equally uncertain:

'I did not control the computer operations side although I was certainly involved with them in systems implementation. Really, the operating side was split in two. The programmers and operations versus data preparation. This appeared to be responsible to

---

[1] Anthropologists interested in factionalism in tribal societies hold that it is often a product of a 'dominant external society selectively influencing a group in a manner which is covert and which tends to accentuate existing cleavages within the group' (Siegel and Beals, 1960: 112).

Mills, although everything was a bit airy fairy – nobody was really in overall charge of the whole lot.'

A consequence of Brian Michael's asking Kenny to withdraw his resignation after Ramsbottom had been recruited was that competition between Kenny and Ramsbottom was encouraged. Ted Morgan echoed many a sentiment when he remarked of the 1962-6 period:

'I suppose everything was dominated by his [Kenny's] fights with Ramsbottom – it used to be hell going into the new head office.'

A likely reason for Kenny's being kept on was that he could act as another source of information and advice for the directors.[1] Kenny was given a management development assignment but still retained his office in the O & M department. Ramsbottom described Kenny's role like this:

'Well, Kenny was not in the computer field at this time. . . . He was not directly involved with the Computer department – well, not at least until he became assistant to the directors and they involved him.'

In the previous chapter we described the confusion that resulted among the O & M staff. Kenny and Ramsbottom would go to meetings with the directors, often at the same time, and come back with different versions of what had occurred. Both Lane and Ramsbottom made unsolicited references[2] to the divide-and-rule strategy. They indicated that they were not the only people to be affected by it:

'The company philosophy was to set people in pairs – two people for every job.'

'They operated with a philosophy of divide and rule. They liked to operate a system where two blokes did every job, e.g. they appointed two head stock controllers at £10,000 and played one off against the other. This also happened to Jim and I. They would rather employ another buyer at £5000 a year than have a proper division of responsibility. That was the trouble with the whole place. There was no defined area of responsibility; everything was left to evolve.'

[1] The directors had, of course, used Reilly and Philby for this purpose in 1957-8.
[2] The responses quoted were given to the question: 'What was Michaels like as a place to work in?'

The insecurity that Ramsbottom felt was shared by his staff. For strategic and other reasons[1] the directors had supported the O & M department in its encroachment on the programmers but the O & M group did not yet feel accepted. Ray Ashton, an O & M officer, summed up his feelings about his department's relations with the directors:

> 'It's a strange relationship, more like being kept than married. If you take the Stock Control department, the directors, they need you, it's a permanent sort of relationship. Our relationship changes day by day depending on the success of our last report. Our relations are dependent on our ability to attract ourselves to them.'

Table 12 shows that, in spite of the role that the directors had given them in the NTL 200 and Newton 350 installations, the O & M people felt no better about Michaels, its management, and user departments at time period 1962-6 compared with time period 1957-61. In fact, proportionately more negative comments were made in respect of the later period. The ratio of negative to positive comments increased from 1·8 : 1 in 1957-6 to 3·2 : 1 in 1962-6. The difference was not, however, significant.

TABLE 12 *O & M officers' perceptions of Michaels, its management, and user departments: 1957–61 and 1962–6 compared*

Period	Positive	Negative
1957–61	38	71
1962–6	15	48

No significant difference from time period 1957-6 to time period 1962-6 (McNemar test for related samples).

Ramsbottom was on his own, then, in thinking that the O & M people were 'the darling boys of the directors'. The ambivalent relationship they had with the directors, together with their internal squabblings, did not put the O & M department in a very strong position to deal with the power-maintenance strategies of the

[1] The hope was that the O & M department would get on better with the user departments than the programmers did.

programmers. In effect it was not until Kenny had built up his power sufficiently to challenge Ramsbottom on the Newton 350 decision that he was in a position to act on his threat to control the programmers.

Kenny's Power Strategies against the Programmers

The O & M officers were quite aware of the programmers' withholding strategy and understood why it was in the programmers' interests to be secretive. Ray Ashton said:

> 'The explanations they gave were clipped. If you knew what they were talking about, the explanation was satisfactory, but if you didn't catch on first time, well, that would be too bad. ... As far as I'm concerned it wasn't till 1964 or 1965 that the split between the two departments was reduced. All the time it was in the Computer department's interests to be obscure in order to give themselves freedom of action.'

What really infuriated Kenny and Reilly was the realization that the programmers' norms of secrecy were making them completely dependent on the programmers. Kenny, because of his 'assistant-to-the-directors' role, was in a very good position to exploit the questionable legitimacy of the programmers' power through obviously legitimate channels. Reilly offered this description of the programmers' behaviour and his own department's predicament:

> 'This worked out all right while we had a static team (the brainstorming sessions on the SE 100), but the moment changes occurred in the team we found there was no record of what had been happening. We found we were becoming terribly reliant on the persons who did the system or programming. Therefore we got to the stage where we were specifying what the job was and Turner would state how it should be done.
>
> Then two further problems arose. First, what level of detail and in what form should we specify the job? Second, what record will or should the programmers keep of what they do, so that if one of them happened to walk under a bus, somebody would be able to take up from where they left off?
>
> In its worst light it seemed that programmers were trying to openly manipulate the situation. It looked like their attitude was

"I know what's going on, therefore I'm indispensable". That situation was clearly not tolerable.'

As a project leader in the O & M department, Reilly was not in a position to challenge the programmers. Kenny was. In order to provide 'impartial' evidence of the programmers' behaviour and at the same time protect himself, Kenny persuaded the directors to hire a consultant to look at the Computer department. The directors let Kenny choose the consultant. Kenny takes up the story:

'I raised the issue of the programmers. The situation was chaotic.... Mills or anybody could check on the operating efficiency of the system, but it was the programmers. I got in Palmer to do a piece of consultancy to find out the actual state of affairs among the programmers. His basic conclusion was that the only reason the computer system worked at all was because the programmers were at hand to deal with troubles with the programs as they arose. Nothing was written down; few programs were written out properly.[1] We were dependent on individual programmers to get us out of trouble. I knew it was going to be a long hard job. There were a lot of anarchists about.'

I suggested to Kenny: 'Really, you were taking away some of the programmers' autonomy.' He continued:

'Yes. I felt I must have more control over them.... In those days there wasn't a single program written up in standard speci- fication form. When a programmer called Maynes left, I was nearly faced with the problem of keeping off the 350 installation for six months.'[2]

In 1964 the Newton 350 was purchased under Kenny's supervision and over Ramsbottom's dead body. Kenny described this purchase as a 'high-risk decision'. Now that he was formally in control of the O & M department again, his dependence on the programmers became even more starkly real:

---

[1] The maintenance men described by Crozier (1964) used similar rule-of- thumb procedures to protect their knowledge base.
[2] Given the pressure of work (the NTL 200 came in 1962 and the Newton 350 in 1964), the marked scarcity of programmers was a major power resource for them. In a group interview, the programmers talked of holding the company to ransom. They described pretyped letters of resignation with gaps for names and dates. This may have been one reason why Kenny referred to them as anarchists.

'I was responsible for its success, but had little control over the programmers.'

In the actual decision process, Kenny felt compelled to consult the chief programmer, Turner. The latter offered the following reasons why:

'He wanted somebody to back him up. He knew if he didn't ask us we would be deliberately destructive.[1] Therefore, he had to ask us even though we weren't in his department. This way he was covering back two ways.'

In this situation of dependency, Kenny chose to cut into the programmers' power base by bringing in an alternative source of programming expertise. In this respect Newton was a very willing accomplice:

'I had four Newton programmers plus our own lot. The Newton boys were on my side because I got the contract for them. Gradually I got control over the programmers in this way.'

Using the Newton men to undercut his own programmers' power base could be only a temporary relief for Kenny. Assured that the Newton 350 was successfully installed, and with his reputation intact, he persuaded the directors to accept a major structural change in the organization of computer activities. At the time, Kenny argued that bringing programmers into his head-office team would reduce the level of conflict between the O & M officers and the programmers, and would also enable the latter to get on with research and development work unimpeded by day-to-day production problems. Later he admitted that there were additional strategic reasons for bringing the cream of the programmers into his newly created Management Services department:

'What used to happen was, they wrote the programs, the specification for which they kept in their heads; consequently, the operation system was dependent on them. I wanted to get them away from the machines to hand over the running of the programs to the operators. Therefore, I thought I must bring them in here. . . . Really, I transferred by stealth eight or ten programmers into this department. I convinced management that I had

---

[1] Compare the attendants' withdrawal of cooperation as a sanction in Scheff's (1961) hospital study.

M

to train batches of programmers by new methods, attempting to select them by more scientific means. We now trained three batches of programmers. Most of these were trained in the Management Services department environment, not in the Computer department at all.'

I asked Kenny if the programmers offered any resistance to these moves:

'Yes, they used to stay in Wolverhampton and wouldn't come down here at all.'

One might have predicted that a group with a strong sense of collective identity would come together when faced with an external threat. Kenny, however, dealt with the programmers' group solidarity by redirecting it. He chose the programmers' primary group leader as the transmission mechanism for the change:

'I had to work through Turner. I had to drag him into a managerial role, to make him responsible, although he's still one of the chaps as far as the programmers are concerned.'

Splitting the programmers into the site operations and development groups also had the consequence, perhaps unintended, of further weakening their solidarity. Kenny's decision to pay the development group more than the site programmers had an immediate divisive impact:

'A bit of competition arose. They were supposed to be the development section but development work was also being done at the production centres.'

A programmer recalled:

'There was a time when the development people got more money – they were considered the elite, with us just keeping the jobs running on site.'

Gareth Jones, one of the two new computer managers, commented:

'I kept the site programmers for program maintenance and Turner had the development bods. This caused trouble. Kenny was under the impression that they were races apart. The development bods were the elite doing the exciting things. It started to reflect in salary scales until I changed it.'

Having isolated the senior programmers from the main source of their power, the computer, Kenny then placed them formally under his control. His further activities had the effect, inadvertently or not, of creating divisions in their ranks, thus weakening them still more. The status attributes the programmers had collected as a visible sign of their power in an earlier day were the next items to go. Kenny changed their Sunday overtime and time-off-in-lieu privileges and adjusted the salary scales of the O & M/systems analyst group to bring them first up to and then above those of the programmers.[1] The latter now had only one tangible way of expressing their discontent – to leave. *Table 11* (p. 148) shows that six programmers left in 1964, the year Kenny announced his structural change, and five left in 1966, the year he altered the reward system for the Michaels computer people. Kenny was now in a position to say:

'I've now written off a whole generation of programmers. Some of them wanted to come back, but I've always refused until very recently, when I let one guy in.'

There was no question that, by 1966, Kenny had greatly reduced the programmers' power. He was still dependent on them, however, for the programming and computer skills that they alone possessed. Since many of the other senior people had now left, much of this dependence was expressed in his relationship with Neil Turner, the person he had recently appointed manager of the programming development section.

The Relative Power of the Programming and Systems Analysis Groups in 1966

While Kenny was improving his own power position in the organization relative to that of the programmers, he either directly or indirectly helped the analysts to improve their status by increasing their rewards and encouraging graduate recruitment. He did not, however, help the analysts to reduce their dependency on the programmers. One way he could have done that would have been to provide the analysts with unquestionable computer expertise. In fact, up until 1968, the analysts were still being trained as O & M officers and not as systems analysts. This placed them at a grave disadvantage in interaction with the programmers.

---

[1] The figures were given in the preceding chapter.

TABLE 13 *EDP experience of Michaels computer staff before joining Michaels*

	Last job was in EDP; all previous jobs were in EDP	*Last job was not in EDP; no previous jobs in EDP*	*No reply; no previous jobs*	*Total*
Programmers	2	5	10	17
Systems analysts	—	11	6	17
Total	2	16	16	34

Tables 13 and *14* indicate the amount of electronic data-processing (EDP) experience that each group had.[1] *Table 13* shows that only two of the seventeen programmers and none of the seventeen systems analysts had held EDP jobs in other companies before joining Michaels. However, as *Table 14* makes clear, once they had joined Michaels the programmers had had more computer experience than had the analysts: seven of the programmers had held previous EDP jobs in the firm compared with only one of the analysts.

TABLE 14 *EDP experience of Michaels computer staff within Michaels*

	Last job was in EDP; all previous jobs were in EDP	*Last job was in EDP; but not all others*	*Last job was not in EDP; no previous jobs in EDP*	*No reply; no previous jobs*	*Total*
Programmers	7	3	3	4	17
Systems analysts	1	1	8	7	17
Total	8	4	11	11	34

The problems the analysts had with the programmers as a result of their initial lack of computer experience were not made any

[1] The data on computer experience, training, and career aspirations, presented in *Tables 13-19*, were gathered by questionnaire from all the programmers and systems analysts employed in Michaels in 1968. Interview data would suggest that there were few changes in these factors between 1966 and 1968.

easier by the inadequate training they received once they arrived in Michaels. *Table 15* suggests that, whereas the programmers tended to take an internal course as well as to have on-the-job experience, the analysts had on-the-job experience only. Neither group had access to external courses.

TABLE 15 *Initial training offered by Michaels to programmers and systems analysts*

	External course plus on-the-job experience	Internal course plus on-the-job experience	On-the-job experience only	O & M training plus experience	Total
Programmers	—	13	4	—	17
Systems analysts	1	1	13	2	17
Total	1	14	17	2	34

The majority of both groups were, moreover, critical of their training (see *Table 16*). *Tables 17* and *18* report how they thought

TABLE 16 *Overall attitude of programmers and systems analysts to their initial training*

	Critical	Non-critical	Total
Programmers	14	3	17
Systems analysts	14	3	17
Total	28	6	34

TABLE 17 *Improvements in training desired by programmers and systems analysts*

	Better teachers	More practical approach	Better planned courses	More specialized courses	More formal courses	No reply	Total
Programmers	1	1	2	—	4	9	17
Systems analysts	1	—	—	1	12	3	17
Total	2	1	2	1	16	12	34

TABLE 18 *Types of course desired by programmers and systems analysts*

	Program-ming	Systems analysis	Manage-ment	Several different kinds	No reply or not intending to take further courses	Total
Programmers	2	7	1	2	5	17
Systems analysts	1	9	2	1	4	17
Total	3	16	3	3	9	34

their training could be improved. Twelve of the seventeen analysts as against four of the seventeen programmers wanted more formal courses. However, in answer to another question asking what kinds of course they would like to take, nine of the analysts and as many as seven of the programmers specified a course in systems analysis.

This desire on the part of the programmers for systems analysis training probably reflects their perception of the higher external status of analysts and their own weakening position. *Table 19* gives some indication of the career aspirations of the two groups. A note-worthy finding is that more than half of the programmers were looking for promotion outside programming: six wanted to become systems analysts and five EDP managers. The analysts, on the other hand, hoped to stay in systems analysis or to become O & M or systems managers.

TABLE 19 *Career aspirations of programmers and systems analysts: position anticipated in five years' time*

	Systems analyst or senior systems analyst	Progr. or chief progr.	Mgmt Services or EDP manager	O & M or systems manager	Non-EDP manager	No reply	Total
Programmers	6	4	5	—	1	1	17
Systems analysts	10	—	—	5	2	—	17
Total	16	4	5	5	3	1	34

The differential amount of computer experience and training possessed by two groups is of the utmost importance in accounting for their relative power.[1] Like the threatened railroad workers in Cottrell's (1962) study, the programmers could maintain their power over the analysts as long as they had control over the recruitment and learning processes that supported their power base. This Neil Turner has been able to achieve. No programmer has ever been recruited from outside into the Michaels analyst section. No Michaels analyst has ever been transferred into the programming section. No Michaels senior programmer has ever been promoted into the systems analysis group. Several of Turner's senior men have reluctantly left the company to become senior analysts elsewhere because in Michaels, as senior programmers, no further career progression was open to them. Apparently this is a cost that Turner has been prepared to accept in order to maintain his power. As one senior programmer rather dispiritedly put it:

'The whole question is a matter of whether Bill [Reilly] or Neil is top dog.'

Apart from the analysts' inability to challenge the programmers' power with unquestionable computer expertise, the reorganized O & M/Systems department got off to an unfortunate start with Kenny. Reilly had expected to be offered the O & M manager's job, but, as Turner said:

'Jim and Bill got off to a bad start because Jim didn't recommend Bill for the O & M manager job. Jim obviously didn't approve of Bill completely, though there was no absolute friction.'

Reilly was greatly disturbed by this rebuff. It had a lasting impact on his relationship with Kenny:

'Jim Kenny started to put Brown in for Ramsbottom's job. I was furious. I went to see Brewster [the managing director] over Jim's head and eventually got the job after being grilled by some consultants who were called in. He [Kenny] couldn't have welcomed me as head of the department. He claims that all anti-feeling has broken down. He thought that within twelve months all acrimony would have gone. I'm not sure that this is true.'

---

[1] Control over recruitment and training as a power resource has been discussed by Gouldner (1965b: 415).

Turner was not really concerned which of the two Michaels candidates got the job. He felt that technically he was more than a match for either of them. I asked Turner how he felt about Reilly's computer experience:

> 'It was mainly on the installation of the SE 100 job. He's never had any programming experience; in fact he was taken off the computer team and put in Kenny's department. This happened at a point in time when we were developing the system. It wasn't until two years later that things were really working properly, and of course in that crucial period Reilly had nothing to do with computers. He was out of touch with the 200 job apart from input and output documents and the like, and of course the systems people weren't involved with the Newton 350 because it was just a machine change.'

CONCLUSION

The aim of this and the two previous chapters has been to use historical data to reveal the social structure of Brian Michaels. The analysis has not been a static one. The consistent aim has been to show the elaboration of social structure. In particular, the focus of the analysis has been the changing patterns of conflict, status, and power among those groups concerned with computer activities in Brian Michaels.

The main theoretical assumption has been that an individual's behaviour is governed not only by the structure of the situation in which he participates but also by his ability to shape and mould that structure to suit his own interests. The individual in question may be a free agent or he may be representing his group's interests. In any case, his ability to change the social structure will depend on whether he possesses sufficient power to impose his will on others despite their opposition. The weapons of such contests are the resources that individuals possess, control, and can manipulate, and the ties of dependency they can form with relevant others.

The purpose of the following chapters is to show how the network of power relations, the likes, dislikes, and organizational attachments just discussed, were played out in the particular social drama of the Michaels 1966-8 computer decision. Following Swartz,

Turner, and Tuden (1966: 26), the assumption will be that: 'Every terminus is a new beginning, though each beginning represents the results of an earlier phase of action or a set of linked and cumulative phases.'

CHAPTER 8

The Disparity of Demands in an Innovative Decision Process

Only in the limited and extraordinary case where one member
of a system could raise matters for consideration, consider
them by himself in isolation, arrive at a decision and act on
it, could we say that demands played no part.

David A. Easton (1965: 50)

A theory of decision-making as a political process was presented in
Chapter 2. The basic components of this theory are as follows. The
division of labour in an organization creates sub-units which develop
interests based on specialized tasks and responsibilities. Such sub-
units are often interdependent. This interdependence may be played
out within a joint decision process.

Within decision-making processes power strategies are employed
by the various interested parties through their demands. Strategies
'are the links between the intentions and perceptions of officials and
the political system that imposes restraints and created opportunities
for them' (Wildavsky, 1964: 63). A demand 'is an expression of
opinion that an authoritative allocation with regard to a particular
subject matter should or should not be made by those responsible
for doing so' (Easton, 1965: 38). A distinction is made between an
interest and a demand: 'The expression of an interest in a matter
is not identical with the input of a demand. To become a demand
there needs to be voiced a proposal that authoritative action be
taken with regard to it ' (Easton, 1965: 42).

The more complex, heterogeneous, and differentiated a political
structure is, the more likely are disparate demands to be made. Such
disparities are a product of the uncertainty and complexity of the
task at hand; of organizational position, professional training, and
adherence to subgroup values and reference groups; of pressures

168

from external forces contributing to internal uncertainty and conflict; and of the history of relationships and attitudes between those in the demand-generating process. Not all demands can be met. In the absence of a clearly set system of priorities between those demands, conflict is likely to ensue. The processing of demands and the generation of support are the principal components of the general political structure through which power may be wielded. The success any claimant has in furthering his interests will be a consequence of his ability to generate support for his demand. The final decisional outcome will evolve out of the processes of power mobilization attempted by each party in support of its demand.

The involvement of sub-units in such demand- and support-generating processes within the decision-making processes of the organization constitutes the political dimension. Political behaviour is defined as behaviour by individuals, or, in collective terms, by sub-units, within an organization that makes a claim against the resource-sharing system of the organization. Those resources may be salaries, capital expenditure, new equipment, or control over people, information, or new areas of a business.

Political behaviour is likely to be a special feature of large-scale innovative decisions. These decisions are likely to threaten existing patterns of resource-sharing: 'Political conflicts appear out of situations in which changing circumstances constitute a threat to existing parts of the working community' (Burns and Stalker, 1961: 199). New resources may be created and appear to fall within the jurisdiction of a department or individual who has not previously been a claimant in a particular area. Those who see their interests threatened by the change may invoke resistance in the joint decision process.

In an innovative decision process involving executives and change agents, the issues that are likely to arise will have to do with the relative contribution that either side can claim for its knowledge or skill contributed as resources, and the right thereby to the greater or lesser share of command over total resources. The generalized demand by the innovators is likely to be for increased recognition of the importance of technical information as a business resource (cf. Burns and Stalker, 1961: 191), and therefore for increased standing as the controllers of such information. This may be seen by executives as a demand for quasi-elite status. It often is. In these ways new political action is released and ultimately the existing distribution of power is endangered.

This analysis does not assume such a finite distribution of organizational resources as that a gain for Peter must mean a loss to Paul. It does not rest on a zero-sum conception of power. The power of all can be increased. Allocation, however, is still a critical problem. The distribution of power at any point in time is a major factor in determining who will gain a disproportionate share of new resources as these become available. Consideration is given, therefore, both to the pattern of distribution of power and to the dynamics of redistribution in the context of an innovative decision process.

The preceding chapter explored the issues surrounding the distribution of power in the social arena of the Michaels Management Services department, and the following chapter will examine how the various parties used their power in the 1966-8 computer decision process. Here our concern is to recognize and explain the disparity in the demands that were made by the different parties.

A general description of the decision process was given in Chapter 3. In addition to providing an overview of the main events in the decision process, it indicated the preferred alternatives of the various interested parties, and also those alternatives that were actually translated into demands on the authority system of the organization. It should be noted that the locus of authority is likely to vary according to the position an actor occupies in the organizational structure. Thus, for Kenny, the locus of authority is the company directors, and he addresses his demands to them. His subordinates, Reilly and Turner, are expected, at least formally, to put their demands to Kenny, who in turn may pass these upward to the board of directors.

Before we discuss the factors producing disparity in the demand-generating process of an innovative decision, however, the reader has to be convinced that the behaviour reported in Chapter 3 did in fact take place. The initial aim of this chapter is therefore to set out, on the basis of data obtained from interviews, observation, and documents, the conflicting preferences of Kenny, Reilly, and Turner.

THE CONFLICTING PREFERENCES OF KENNY, REILLY, AND TURNER

The 1966-8 decision process can be split into three phases:

1. *August 1966 – January 1967:* In this period brochures were sent

to seven manufacturers asking them to submit proposals for the computerization of the accounting procedures of the administrative office of the Michaels clothing division. Six of the seven sent in proposals. Of these six, Reilly and Turner shortlisted Wilson Electric and BCD. As head of the Management Services department, Kenny insisted that Newton also be shortlisted. At two board meetings, on 5 and 9 January, it was decided to shortlist Wilson Electric and Newton. The board also expressed a preference for a document-reading form of input.

2. *February – August 1967:* In this period there was a lack of contact between the Management Services department and the Michaels board. Turner began to have serious doubts about Wilson Electric and switched his interest to manufacturers with other input and software solutions. Reilly and his assistant Ashton made consistent and unflinching demands for Wilson Electric hardware equipment and document readers for input. At the end of the period, however, in a report to the board they came out in favour of Newton. Kenny continued to push for Newton hardware, though he was uncertain about input equipment, while his subordinates changed their minds and fresh initiatives came in from BCD.

3. *September 1967 – April 1968:* On the initiative of Brewster, the managing director, the parameters of the job were widened in this period. At two meetings, in September and October, it was decided that the job should include all the procedures in the administrative office, and subsequently Kenny was asked to look at CRT (cathode ray tube) equipment for input and to consider the computerization of all the company's offices. After his defeat over the Wilson Electric issue, Reilly kept in the background for a time. Now that the job had expanded in scope, Turner finally came out into the open with a demand that BCD should be reconsidered. Reilly gave Turner some support, but Turner's main support came from the active marketing strategies of the BCD salesmen. Kenny maintained his belief in Newton right up to the time the decision was made, in April 1968.

Phase 1: August 1966 – January 1967

For much of this period the conflict and mistrust between Reilly and Kenny were dormant. They finally came out during an informal meeting of the systems analysts on 16 December. This meeting had been called to discuss which companies should be shortlisted.

The discussion was framed almost entirely in terms of the Systems department's interests. Because the analysts' knowledge of computer hardware was almost exclusively limited to input equipment, this was the main criterion they used to evaluate the manufacturers. Reilly started the meeting off by saying:

'As this is essentially an input problem, the most useful way we can compare the proposals is in terms of their input capabilities.'

Later he confided:

'Which machine we take from a programming point of view I kept out of it; that's not my area. It's up to Neil [Turner] to advance his own arguments and put forward his own interests.'

After coming down firmly in favour of Wilson Electric and document readers, Reilly and Ashton rounded the meeting off with a discussion about what they called some of the 'political' considerations likely to influence the decision. They began with the directors. Reilly commented:

'Of course, there's Mills [a director] and his tie-up with NTL. This might influence irrationally the sort of consideration NTL gets. . . . And Newton's – they're likely to get pushed because the last machine we bought was from them. As far as the prejudices of Kenny are concerned, he's likely to make a go for a system that can be adapted for CRT input and output facilities.'

This was almost a classic 'speak of the devil' situation. No sooner had Reilly mentioned Kenny's name than the latter walked into the office. It was now 6.30 p.m. on Friday, well after finishing time. Reilly and his team of analysts were really surprised by Kenny's sudden appearance. They became alarmed when they saw that Kenny noticed that the meeting was being taped. As soon as Kenny left Reilly said to Ashton:

'He saw the tape. We'd better get rid of it now. He'll be in here tomorrow morning to play it back. We don't want him to get any pre-warning of our arguments for Wilson Electric. There's a big meeting with him and Neil next week.'

That episode gives a clear idea of the suspicion, mistrust, and competitiveness that Reilly felt towards Kenny even at this early stage in the decision process. The meeting that followed the next Thursday confirmed my impressions.

Reilly called Ashton and me into his office to discuss strategy before the meeting began. Reilly was suspicious of both Kenny and Turner. Ashton said that a major problem for them was that they 'didn't know what Turner was thinking'. Unfortunately, I was in the same position. I had not, at that time, widened my net of close informants to include Neil Turner. The main reason for this was that I had noticed very little work-related or social contact between the programmers and the analysts, and I did not want to endanger my brittle relationship with Reilly and Ashton by being seen talking to the manager of the programming group.

As it turned out, we were little wiser about Turner's position at the end of the meeting than we had been before it. Reilly went into the meeting 'determined to put our [the analysts'] case forward as forcibly as I can'. He conducted a monologue on input equipment for the first half-hour. Turner and his two assistants sat back and did not say a word. Kenny, realizing this, tried to steer the discussion towards the software capabilities of the various manufacturers. Turner's only comment in the first hour was that 'Alpha would be a brute to program'. After two hours of argument, largely between Reilly and Kenny, the meeting broke up with everybody agreeing to rule out NTL and American Electronics. There was no agreement on whether only manufacturers with document readers should be shortlisted – a suggestion made by Reilly – or whether Newton and Alpha should be considered further. Turner remarked:

> 'A shortlist of two would be quite enough in terms of the work-load it would give the department, but if another one had to be included [in addition to Wilson Electric and BCD] it should be Newton.'

Reilly and Ashton insisted that Wilson Electric and BCD were the only proposals worth putting on the shortlist, while Kenny was determined to include Newton. The meeting ended with this air of disagreement.

After Christmas 1966, Kenny took the initiative and insisted that Newton be shortlisted along with Wilson Electric and BCD. He stated:

> 'I think that there are two things you need to bear in mind as the

things that influence us here. First of all, as far as the systems people are concerned, there is a great deal of attraction about document-reading input, of which there were two possibilities – BCD and Wilson Electric. The systems chaps would have preferred, I think, to have gone along with just these two. However, I feel very strongly that we've had a great deal of investment in Newton in terms of know-how, association, and programming – we could start programming on that machine this afternoon if we wanted to – and therefore we shouldn't ignore their contribution even though it doesn't quite meet the specification we had in mind. And we had a great fight and argument about this, but I'm afraid I insisted.'

Reilly's version of Kenny's insisting on Newton was as follows:

'Obviously he's got the right to do this. What I'm concerned about is that from the outset he should make it clear why Newton are being included. I don't want them included for some mystical reasons which might be difficult to refute in the long term.'

In the interim report Kenny sent to Brewster, Taylor, and Hall on 2 January 1967 he justified the inclusion of Newton partly on the ground that:

'A certain amount of inflexibility is implied in both these systems [because BCD and Wilson Electric recommended document-reader input] and it is proposed that consideration be given to including one conventional input form (Newton) in the further discussions we are proposing to have with the manufacturers.'

In an interview two weeks later Kenny was arguing:

'First of all, the Newton input proposals are not acceptable to us. They have proposed Class 83 teletype input machines which we wouldn't want to go along with as machines anyway, and we don't want on-line input, or any kind of punch operator controlled input.'

This is a good example of the kind of vacillation that can take place in a decision process where uncertainty is great and the criteria for making choices are multiple and flexible. It will be an issue we shall return to in explaining the conflicts in the demand-generating process.

In the interview just mentioned, Kenny went on to say:

'We are, I think, linked to accepting document-reading input, and therefore we have said, "Newton, you have got to find another input solution." '

The linking of the administrative office computerization to a document-reading form of input had been made by the managing director, Brewster, at a meeting with Kenny on 5 January.

On 9 January, Kenny, Reilly, and Turner met the directors, Taylor and Hall. This was to be the only directors' meeting that Reilly was allowed to attend throughout the decision process. The outcome of the meeting was very satisfactory for him. Both his demands – for Wilson Electric and document reading – were accepted. But he was far from satisfied about the shortlisting of Newton:

'Neil and I had separately listed possible computers in order of preference. We both put Newton low down the list at around fourth or fifth place. [In fact, Turner had listed Newton in third place.] Wilson Electric submitted the cheapest estimate, around £100,000 less than the others. However, Newton is now one of the two top choices. This is entirely because Jim Kenny is emotionally involved with Newton.'

Kenny seemed equally sure that the analysts were not acting like rational economic decision-makers:

'It's a fact that, if some of our systems people had their way, Newton wouldn't even be in the final selection. Now they have at least a 50–50 chance of getting the job, and they wouldn't even have gone forward if some people had had their way. Now this is very largely a matter of prejudice. There's no doubt whatsoever of that.'

BCD was rejected even though it was one of the only two firms – the other was Wilson Electric – that recommended the form of input the directors preferred. Just after the board meeting, Kenny confided that displays of emotion had not been confined to his technical advisers:

'There were a number of factors which influenced the directors. They too were impressed with the document-reading type of approach to the problem, but weren't prepared to go along with

N

BCD's proposal. Some of this represents a bit of anti-BCD feeling which exists in this company. . . . You see, there's not a great will to get around any difficulties, so any objection that can be raised gets a sort of murmuring assent immediately.'

Phase 2: February – August 1967

If the problems of identifying criteria in terms of which a choice could be made were difficult enough in Phase 1, they were more difficult now. At least when the choice was being made between the original six manufacturers, all six had been asked to quote for the same job. Kenny describes well the new situation:

'Now what you've got to note here is that these are two quite different proposals. On the one hand you are saying to one firm, Wilson Electric, please put proposals forward to cater for one and a half administrative offices on your installation, and therefore achieve a higher utilization of the hardware; or you are asking the Newton people to upgrade their configuration so that they can do the administrative office job while at the same time doing the merchandising for the total business, as they now do. And so, although these things are competing with each other, they are obviously competing on quite different terms. They are aiming to do quite different jobs.'

In fact, Wilson Electric did not have a chance. The company and its spokesmen in Michaels were outmanoeuvred at every turn by Kenny, Turner, Allison (the Newton salesman), and by the marketing strategies of BCD. By the beginning of February, Kenny was having serious doubts about Wilson Electric as one of the first two choices. He had received a visit from one of the Alpha people who had expressed great astonishment at the selection of Wilson Electric, pointing out that it had no software. Kenny mentioned this criticism to Neil Turner and, much to his surprise, Turner agreed, although previously he had not shown any signs of uncertainty about Wilson Electric. As far as Newton was concerned, Kenny's attitude from then on was to be, 'We're not just buying a machine, we're buying a relationship'.

Meanwhile, his two technical advisers tried to use various technical criteria to evaluate the proposals of the two remaining manufacturers. Since the main technical uncertainty continued to be input equipment, this was the issue around which much of the action took place.

Newton's initial problem was to find a document reader to compete with Wilson Electric. In February, Kenny remarked:

'The problem is still with Newton's input. This could be solved if Wilson Electric would sell Newton one of their readers. They can't refuse to sell Newton one, but you can be sure they'll put a five-year delivery date on it. You can't blame Wilson Electric for this, Obviously they don't want Newton to get the contract.'

Turner and his chief technical assistant, a Scotsman called Angus Bull, provided Newton with what seemed to be a viable reader:

'Angus and I saw the Larco reader in operation in another division of Michaels. To all intents and purposes the Larco reader was designed in Michaels. Brown, the computer head up there, knows more about optical scanning than anybody in the country. All this experience in the business meant that we would be fairly well covered, and dealing with such a small concern as Larco would mean that they would find it easy to adapt to our requirements. I said, "If we've got to have a reader, why not better Wilson Electric and go for Larco?" '

Kenny seemed pleased by Turner's discovery, although he hinted that Reilly was not:

'The three of us discussed it over lunch one day. Bill obviously wasn't in favour of it. He said very little. He may have felt that people were doing things behind his back.'

When I asked Reilly about the Larco reader he pointed out its main technical strength and its main weakness. Its strength was that it was faster than the Wilson Electric reader because it used magnetic, not paper, tape output. Its main disadvantage was that, because of the technical way in which it read the data, it could not operate with a turn-around document. The turn-around advantage of the Wilson Electric reader was raised time and again by the analysts over the next few months. Furthermore, no sooner had the Larco people announced their reader with its magnetic-tape advantage than Wilson Electric informally proclaimed that its Mark 2 reader, which was just about to appear, would also have this facility. This was just one of many information leaks that allowed a competing manufacturer to make a fortuitous appearance to rebalance its waning position.

By March, Turner was starting to think that BCD should not have been eliminated. He said:

> 'All other things being equal, I'd go for BCD. Their software is more fully developed than anyone else's. The knowledge within BCD of computer applications and techniques is streets ahead of anyone else. They will be in the front of any future developments in computer science.'

Kenny regarded Turner's attachment to BCD as emotional. His own to Newton, however, was justifiable:

> 'Neil's highly identified with BCD. He's a great friend of their local salespeople. He's still putting forward proposals suggesting that their equipment should be considered. Neil's a pretty rational, logical person but his choice here is influenced by personal considerations, in particular his close relationship with BCD management.'

Meanwhile, the analysts were identifying more and more with Wilson Electric. Ray Ashton, the senior analyst in charge of the project, talked of resigning if his choice was not awarded the contract:

> 'If Newton get the order for the computer system and the reasons given by Jim Kenny are in any sense wilfully irrational – and they can only be irrational since Wilson Electric have the best system – then I'm definitely leaving the company. Somebody else can get on with implementing the system. I'll have had enough of Michaels by then.'

Again Ray mentioned that he and Reilly were unsure of what Turner was planning:

> 'One of the big question marks for us is Neil's position. Bill and I are never exactly sure where he stands. We suspect he's heavily oriented to Newton because of his experience with their software. Wilson Electric software would mean a lot of change and trouble for him.'

For the first time Ray came out in the open and criticized Reilly. It is argued later that this was because Reilly was beginning to waver in his support for Wilson Electric. Ashton certainly implied this when I asked him if Reilly's authoritarian behaviour at this time was due to his realization that Wilson Electric's chances of getting the contract were poor:

'This might be an important factor to Bill, but it's much more important to me. Bill's essentially concerned with what is best for Michaels and he's quite willing to accept any decision that Michaels make. I'm more concerned with making an objective decision rather than one which fits in with the preconceptions and prejudices of a number of people at the top of Michaels.'

The argument that the systems group had consistently put forward in favour of Wilson Electric was that it had an excellent reading device. Now the basis of their case was removed, at least in part, by an alliance in May 1967 between Allison, Turner, and Kenny in favour of teletype input. The chain of events was as follows. Allison's boss at Newton persuaded him that reading machines would be bad for Michaels. This may have been because Newton did not have a reader and was unhappy at having to rely on the small Larco company. The public reason given by Newton was that teletype would offer better development prospects. 'Development' was to become the catchword for teletype in the next few months. Turner takes up the story:

'Michaels had really forced readers on Newton. A number of people in Newtons had never been satisfied with this right from the start. In fact, when McGregor came up to be sales manager for this area, he was very much against it. . . . Recently, Allison has been thinking in this direction as well. He went to tell Kenny that teletype would be a better form of input.

Meanwhile Angus and I quietly re-did the volume figures for input and decided that teletype would be better. We kept quiet about this for a time. Yesterday I went to see Jim Kenny about it. Jim's gone off to see the Newton people now. I suspect they'll put a supplement in their report recommending teletype.'

At the time, neither Reilly and his analysts nor myself had any idea that this was going on. Reilly later told me that he had first heard about it the day before he went on his summer vacation. Separately, first Allison, then Turner, and then Kenny came up and said to me that really, as far as Newton was concerned, teletype would be better for the job. For the remainder of the decision process Reilly was always very nervous just before and during his vacations. We shall see that, eventually, he took to telephoning in while on vacation, to check up on what was going on.

While Reilly was on holiday, Allison, Bull, and Turner made a number of visits to talk to the analysts. In my field-work notes for that period I noted:

'This morning [17 May 1967] a rather unusual event happened in the Management Services department. One of the members of the programming section came into the analysts' room to talk about the administrative office job. This is especially unusual since the visitor was Angus Bull, who rarely ventures from Neil Turner's side.'

At the end of the week I noted:

'This is the third time this week that Sam Allison has been in to see Neil and Angus. It's especially interesting since Reilly has been on holiday all week and it's very unusal for Allison to come into Michaels more than once a week.'

The purpose of Angus Bull's visit was to inform the analysts of Newton's change of mind on reading machines. Ray Ashton offered this explanation to his fellow analysts of Newton's change of mind:

'Newton are now beginning to realize that the Larco reader isn't as good as the Wilson Electric one. Either Jim or Neil has told Allison that Wilson Electric can produce a usable turn-around document. With this piece of information Allison probably thinks he's losing out. Anyway, a couple of weeks ago (Kenny has just told me this) Allison went to see Kenny and more or less told him that readers were out as far as Newton was concerned. In this, Allison appears to have found allies in Neil and Angus. Have you noticed how often Allison is seeing Neil these days? He may now be thinking that Neil has more influence over Jim than Bill has.'

The analysts were thoroughly dejected after this statement. It looked as if all their work on reading machines would be wasted 'because of some political manoeuvring between Allison, Neil, and Jim Kenny'. A few days later their spirits rose as results started to come in from transcription tests of the two readers. It appeared that the Wilson Electric reader could transcribe documents faster and with less error. In a state of near euphoria, Ray Ashton announced to the other analysts:

'At last we have some rational objective evidence to show that Wilson Electric are the most suitable company as far as input is concerned.'

Reilly was not so convinced. On his return from holiday he told me that he was resigned to the fact that both Neil and Jim were now so heavily in favour of Newton that there was very little he could do about it. Kenny told me that he had said to Reilly:

'You're wasting your time with Wilson Electric. Any further tests with input devices are irrelevant; we have enough information to make a decision now.'

To Reilly's reply, 'I agree, if you're making a political decision', Kenny had retorted:

'It's not a political decision at all. Unless Wilson Electric can demonstrate that in some way they are very much superior to Newton, the choice is obvious.'

Bill then tried to get Neil's support. He asked Neil which manufacturer he supported. Neil replied: 'Newton, and teletype input.'

With the open support of Turner, Kenny now arranged a meeting with three directors and told them, 'We now have enough information on which to make a decision'. The directors reacted with instructions that he should go cautiously. Kenny said to me:

'However, I argue that unless Wilson Electric can show substantial advantages in its performance specifications, the question is "Why not Newton?" This argument was accepted by the directors and written into the minutes. [Kenny added at this point, "No one except you knows this".] This means we shouldn't waste time with Wilson Electric.'

While this was going on, Kenny was trying to persuade the Newton people to state categorically which input device they were recommending. Newton's attitude now was 'either will do'. Kenny therefore decided to let the tests on the Larco reader go ahead, despite his present preference for teletype. Unfortunately, these tests were proving difficult to arrange. The Larco company had already postponed them four times. In this situation of indecision and uncertainty, BCD made a telling intervention. Bill Reilly takes up the story:

> 'At the end of last week the sales manager of BCD invited Jim Kenny out for a game of golf. The next day the local salesman invited me out riding. The position is that they feel they can still interest Michaels in the BCD reader to solve our input problems. We would still use Newton hardware. Even though Jim has always been prejudiced in favour of Newton and against BCD he may see in this situation a way out of one of his dilemmas. At the moment, Wilson Electric, the company he doesn't appear to be considering at all, have to all intents and purposes solved the input problem and worked out a good system with a turn-around document, whereas Newton have not solved this problem at all. With BCD supplying their advanced reader with Newton hardware, this might solve the problem and still maintain the influence of Newton in the Michaels organization.'

Kenny said he could now see 'a clear solution' to the computer job problem. He then went on to describe the BCD recommendation that its new reader would act as the common input for all the Michaels machines. This would probably take two years to set up. 'In the meantime,' said Kenny, 'it doesn't really matter whether we use the Wilson Electric reader with Newton hardware or the Larco reader.'

At this juncture the Wilson Electric people arranged one of their rare meetings with Kenny. Reilly described, with characteristic emotion, what happened at that meeting:

> 'Ostensibly, the meeting had been arranged to improve the contact between Jim Kenny and Wilson Electric higher management. Up until now 99 per cent of the contact between Wilson Electric and Michaels had been through my systems lads or me. . . . In fact, what happened was that Kenny gave one of his speeches, one of his tirades, in which he more or less told Wilson Electric his life-story. He ended his speech in a burst of nervous energy half-way through a sentence, told them that was all, and threw them out. There was no chance for the Wilson Electric people to participate in the meeting at all.'

Kenny's version of what happened was less dramatic:

'I told the Wilson Electric people what the position was and pointed out that they were starting from way back. They must not kid themselves that they were starting on equal terms with Newton.'

Kenny was then asked if Wilson Electric did not resent all the money and effort they had wasted. 'No,' he replied, 'they knew this was real life! '

The effect of this meeting on Reilly and his team of analysts was instant and remarkable. They did a complete about-turn and started putting forward complex accounting-type arguments in favour of Newton and the Larco reader. Ray Ashton even found a journal article using the discounted cash-flow technique to assess the long-term savings of a computer installation. He wanted to use this 'to prove that Newton are the best proposition for the administrative office job'. He was dissuaded only after a visit from the chief accountant who told him and Reilly that the board would not want to know about discounted cash flow. The *pièce de résistance* was yet to come. On 3 August I was sitting in the analysts' room when I heard a quite amazing conversation between Ray Ashton and Liam Ryle, a systems analyst. Ray was talking to Liam about the report the systems group was preparing for the board. Ray said to Liam:

'It's imperative Newton are seen to be the best manufacturer for this job. We'll have to be real careful how we present the material, Nothing is to be put in the report which is in any way ambiguous, otherwise, knowing the directors, they might latch onto something and come out in favour of Wilson Electric.'

The reader will recall that, only a few months previously, Ashton had said that he would resign if Newton won the contract. The systems group's report went in (2 September) recommending Newton and the Larco reader. Reilly did, however, manage to write into the report the following dig at Newton and at Kenny's consistent argument about the company's special relationship with Michaels:

'In recommending Newton equipment we have been influenced by the existence of Newton equipment at Wolverhampton which is available for use on weekdays. The existence of this equipment has enabled Newton to provide for better standby facilities than Wilson Electric could offer at comparable cost. However, it can-

not be assumed from this that Newton equipment is of itself
better value than that supplied by all other companies. There is
therefore no guarantee that in considering the extension of a
successful first installation to the remaining companies we would
necessarily recommend Newton.'

Phase 3: September 1967 – April 1968

The analysts had lost the first round of the battle. They seemed now
to be saying publicly, 'But we are prepared to fight another day'.
They soon had a chance because, at two board meetings in September and October, respectively, the directors asked their technical
advisers to look at CRT input in relation to the computerization of
all the procedures in the Wolverhampton office, and also to consider an integrated system covering the company inventory procedures and all the procedures in all the administrative offices. This
became known as 'the all singing, all dancing job'. It introduced
further complexity and uncertainty into the decision process and
gave fresh impetus to a new round of demands and political debate.

The period September to November 1967 can be characterized
as the 'warm-up before the big fight'. A certain amount of sparring
with ideas and alternatives went on between Kenny, Reilly, and
Turner.

Faced with what seemed to be, for the first time, a coalition
among his subordinates, Kenny called a meeting on 15 November
'to clarify policy'. This meeting is reported here in detail, first, to
reveal through their arguments the positions the three men were
taking at the time, and, more particularly, to give the reader some
idea of the intensity of debate that perennially occurred in meetings
between Kenny and his two subordinates.

Reilly went into the meeting expecting a fight. When I asked him
if I could attend the meeting, he said:

'Why not go and ask Jim Kenny? I doubt if he'll want you to go
to the meeting as he must know there's going to be a hell of a row
and he may try to prevent you from seeing it.'

Bill then went on to discuss Turner's recent behaviour:

'One of the most remarkable things that's happened over the last
few weeks is that Neil has suddenly started to come out and argue
with Jim. You know what Neil's like. He just sits there and

grunts; he never really says anything in meetings; he doesn't argue with Jim. Well, this is starting to change. The other night, when we were in the pub, Neil suddenly turned on Jim and said, "The trouble with you is that you'll twist anything to suit your own arguments. You won't listen to reason; you won't listen to logic. You just want to push forward your own prejudiced ideas on this whole project." '

On this happy note we left Bill's office and walked across to Jim Kenny's office to begin the meeting.

Kenny started the meeting off:

'The aim of this meeting is to thrash out our ideas on a number of fronts so that I can go to the directors as soon as possible and get some concrete decisions out of them.

There are two things we've got to look at first. How should we tackle the Wolverhampton job if we are going to tackle that on its own? Secondly, if we're going to consider the total integrated data-processing job, how do we tackle that and in what way does this affect our existing thoughts on handling just the Wolverhampton job? Finally, if we are to look at the integrated data-processing job for the whole company, does this mean we have to look at other computer manufacturers?'

Agreement was reached on the first issue. They all decided that, if the Wolverhampton job was to be tackled on its own, Newton were probably the best people to do it.

Jim then said:

'Now what about the input for this job? Can we reach any sort of agreement about this? There are three possibilities: teletype, mark-sensing, and CRT. Which would you choose, Bill?'

Reilly replied:

'From the tests we've done, Larco is the best at the moment. I have reservations about Larco, however, because Newton, and therefore Michaels, have no control over the Larco organization. They could hold us to ransom.'

Kenny leapt in and said:

'Nonsense – that's a completely stupid attitude to take. Nobody is going to hold anybody to ransom. Manufacturers like Newton can't afford a bad implementation. It's not a matter of setting down legal constraints about what people can or cannot do.'

Bill hummed and hawed, saying, 'That wasn't the point', but really he was not willing to argue the matter. Jim then asked Neil what he thought would be the best form of input. Before Neil could answer Bill jumped in and said:

'Neil's always been in favour of teletype input as a start for this job.'

Neil sat back and to some extent agreed:

'If you want to develop this job forward, *and* if you want it to be a success immediately, it's best to start off with teletype. But there are a lot of considerations.'

Jim Kenny then started off an argument which raged for half an hour. Jim said:

'What about CRT equipment? I'm not interested in the economics of the matter. Clearly, using economic criteria, CRTs are too expensive. What I want you two to tell me is whether or not CRT equipment is technically capable of handling this job.'

Without listening to the end-point of Jim's question, Reilly aggressively said:

'It's worthless to try to establish whether CRTs are technically feasible. The real point is whether they're justified organizationally for this particular job in this particular company.'

The argument continued for what seemed an interminable time with the two men shouting at each other and continually repeating their views. Reilly's approach was particularistic, Kenny's universalistic. Reilly would insist that, in terms of this particular job in this company, with these contraints, the answer was no. Kenny would proclaim that this organization and that organization were successfully using CRTs. Kenny's continual reference to outside situations infuriated Reilly even more. Bill said:

'I'm not bloody interested in what you heard some character on one of your trips saying. I'm thinking of Michaels.'

Neil, Ray, and I sat back and listened as the dispute became more emotional and more and more personal. Eventually Neil concluded the issue by saying:

> 'As far as I'm concerned, CRT equipment does exist and it's technically possible to implement it in Michaels at this moment if the company is willing to spend the money on it.'

Jim got the final dig in at Bill:

> 'The trouble with you, Bill, is that you're too damned conservative. You won't look at ideas and consider them properly. You're too cautious.'

Bill went red in the face, looked at me, but said nothing.
Jim continued:

> 'What about the total integrated processing job? What do you all think about that?'

Bill's reply was:

> 'This is an entirely different level of project altogether. It involves a completely different level of expenditure from anything we've experienced in the computer field. We should stop and think again which way we are going to move with regard to manufacturers. The first thing we'll have to do on the total job is put the central processor in the head office [in Birmingham], and if you're going to do Wolverhampton first, put two small computers in there. [Neil agreed with him at this point.] This means that the present Newton machine at Wolverhampton cannot be considered as part of the hardware for the total job. Therefore there's no intrinsic reason why Newton should start off with an advantage over anyone else.'

There then followed another bitter altercation, this time involving Kenny, Reilly, and Turner. I have the following comment in my notes for that day:

> 'I was very surprised to see how open Neil Turner was. This is the first time I've seen him get really annoyed and start arguing with Jim Kenny. He obviously thinks this is the point to get up and say something.'

Kenny's position was:

> 'Until somebody proves they're better than Newton, as far as I'm concerned Newton will get the contract for the total job.'

Neil and Bill continually repeated that this was a grossly biased view. Kenny was taking the wrong approach altogether:

'You shouldn't be trying to defend Newton. You should be asking yourself the question: What are the alternatives for this job and which is the best one?'

Neil and Bill were agreed that if one did ask what the alternatives were, one would have to consider BCD. Neil said:

'With the level of expenditure BCD are making on research, it's inevitable they'll continue to lead the field, particularly in software, which is probably the most difficult part of any computer installation.'

Bill observed:

'There is also the point that if existing trends in machine development continue, Newton will soon have to bring out a new range of machines to compete with BCD. If we start buying their old range and then they spring the new machines on us and they're not compatible, we'll be in all kinds of mess.'

Kenny vehemently disagreed with these comments:

'They're too vague. They don't prove anything. It's no good making vague statements about the amount of money BCD spend on this or that or the next thing; or saying that Newton can't handle a job of this size when they have done so. The existing Newton machine in this company has been very successful. If I went to the board with a statement about BCD like the one you've just given me, the first thing they'd say is, "But what about Newton? What about all the experience we've had with them? Why have you suddenly changed your mind about Newton after saying that they had such good equipment in all these reports?"

I need more evidence than this before I change my mind. I'm going to see the deputy chairman tomorrow. I'm going to tell him that Newton are the people for the total job. If you want to say anything to the contrary it's up to you to stick your necks out and go and see him and tell him that BCD is better for the job. But you'll have to supply him with a lot more convincing evidence than you've put before me.'

Bill then made a variety of comments to the effect that Kenny was biased. He would not even allow them to consider BCD for a job that would cost in excess of £3 million. Kenny replied:

'I've had enough. I'm not arguing any more. I'm sick to death of it. I've got to be somewhere else. That's the end of the meeting. I'm going to tell the deputy chairman[1] that Newton is the best manufacturer for the job.'

Exactly a week after this meeting, Kenny and Turner met the deputy chairman. Kenny also wrote a report recommending the directors to go ahead only with the accounting job for the present; he advocated using document readers for this job, but having tele-type input available so that the firm would be able to move on to CRT later. In his memo covering this report to the board Kenny said:

'I am mindful of the responsibilities of this department in recom-mending that the directors give consideration to a future computer policy for the company, rather than a decision on a particular configuration.'

There was no question that future policy was to involve Newton. Kenny came out of this meeting with the deputy chairman sure that the latter 'is now very much on my side and prepared to support my views on further computerization in Michaels'. The deputy chairman did, however, ask Turner to put down on paper his arguments in favour of BCD.

Meanwhile, Reilly had been left out in the cold again. He said to me:

'I suppose you know that while I was away on another job Jim and Neil had a meeting with the deputy chairman.'

I asked Bill if Neil was still committed to BCD. He replied:

'He's fairly committed, but the real question is whether he'll stand out on a limb and fight for his ideas when the head of the depart-ment is supporting another manufacturer. I doubt whether he will do this. Neil's always one who likes a quiet life.'

Neil later remarked:

'Bill never had a chance with Wilson Electric. When he realized

[1] At the end of May 1967, Kenny had been made responsible to the deputy chairman instead of the managing director, Brewster.

this he pestered me to make a challenge for BCD. My attitude was, if you're doing a job of the size the directors were considering, then you had to look at BCD,'

When I asked Reilly where he stood on the BCD–Newton issue his reply indicated that his days of aggressive challenging were over – at least for the present:

'All I'm worried about is that Jim Kenny shouldn't reduce the autonomy of his advisers to such an extent that he doesn't even allow us to get some facts together. Just recently Kenny's attitude has been, "Whatever you say I'm recommending Newton, and you can run along and do what the hell you like". I'm not as openly committed to BCD as Neil is. I just want them to be given the opportunity to say what they can do.'

BCD was eventually given such an opportunity at a seminar it arranged for the Michaels directors. The manufacturer brought technical experts from all over Europe for this seminar. However, only one Michaels director, Hall, turned up, and the BCD people were left talking to Kenny, Reilly, and Turner.

On 7 December the board met to make a final decision. In the event they did not do this, but asked the Management Services department to provide more information on the suggested alternatives. Brewster, the managing director, favoured CRT equipment, but Brian Michael himself was questioning the economics of this form of input. On 30 January, Brewster, Taylor, and Hall met with Kenny and told him to go ahead with the total integrated system. No decision was taken on input or on the computer supplier for the job.

Prior to this meeting, information had accidentally been leaked to the press indicating that Newton had been given the contract. This caused sheer panic among the analysts. Reilly said:

'We'll all get minced if the directors read this. [All copies of the offending journal in Michaels were quietly destroyed.] And another thing, between you and me, do you know what happened last week? One of Neil's lads went up for some reason to Durham, and while he was there he asked if he could look around the Newton factory. Do you know what he saw? A bloody computer with Michael's name plastered all over it. And the directors haven't even decided yet to go ahead with the project, never mind say yes to a particular manufacturer! This has never been a problem-solving exercise. It's been an exercise illuminating Kenny's prejudices.'

On 2 February the directors met again to consider input. Turner had by this time procured a quotation from BCD for 'the all singing, all dancing job'. This quotation was discussed in the Management Services department, but it is not clear whether Kenny took it to the board meeting with him. The outcome of the meeting was again ambiguous. Brewster and Kenny favoured the use of CRT equipment, but the chairman was still worried about the cost. The directors therefore decided to ask the Newton sales director to visit the company and answer some questions about CRT. This was the first time a top-level computer man had been formally received by the Michaels board.

With regard to what to computerize first, now that the project had become so much larger, the directors opted for starting the new system by computerizing the Wolverhampton administrative office (clothing division). After this had been completed, the system would be extended to the administrative offices of the furniture division. The directors asked the Management Services department to look into the costs of this approach.

Relationships among the computer people were still tense. Allison thought Reilly was verging on a mental breakdown:

'Bill was in a real mental turmoil on Friday. He hung around Michaels until well after 6 o'clock waiting for Jim Kenny to come back from the board meeting. He's like the over-taut strings of a harp or a guitar; he's liable to snap at any moment. His room was littered with half-drunk cups of coffee – he couldn't keep still – his hands were quite literally shaking.'

Reilly said to Allison:

'If the management doesn't buy document readers it will be a vote of no confidence in myself and my department.'

My impression of Reilly was similar. He talked like a defeated man:

'I've decided to withdraw completely from the situation. I've advised the directors that a limited job with document readers would be the best approach. They've decided not to take my advice, which is their prerogative of course. I don't want the

o

responsibility from now on. It's up to Jim Kenny to do all the talking and proposing for the "all singing, all dancing job".'

I asked Bill Reilly about Neil's current attitude to BCD:

'I'm still not sure if Neil has the courage to stand up and fight. This time I'm going to sit back and watch. I'm afraid to get drawn into it again. Both Jim and Neil are looking for allies.'

On 1 March the directors took a final decision to go ahead with the proposed system. They accepted Kenny's recommendation that CRT input should be used for the integrated system job on the administrative offices. They did not specify which manufacturer should be given the contract.

In the face of a concerted selling drive by BCD aimed at all levels of Michaels management, Kenny finally persuaded Brewster to give the contract to Newton. Kenny was overjoyed. Reilly said of Kenny: 'You can't show a blind man anything.'

FACTORS PROMOTING DISPARITY IN THE DEMAND-GENERATING
PROCESS

The demands made by Kenny throughout the 1966-8 computer decision were, for the most part, both consistent and clear. He wanted Newton to supply the computers and he preferred teletype leading to CRTs, or CRTs immediately, for input. Reilly backed Wilson Electric computers and the document reader form of input. Later he gave some support to Turner when Turner eventually came out in the open and demanded that BCD should be considered for the integrated computer project. Turner was also fairly consistent in his attachment to teletype and CRT forms of input.

In addition to making his own positive demands, each of the parties attacked the preferences of the others. Kenny would have nothing to do with Wilson Electric or BCD computers, although when he was having difficulty in finding an alternative input solution to the Wilson Electric reader favoured by Reilly, he did consider a BCD reader. Reilly repeatedly came out against Newton computers. His views were often expressed in the form of a personal attack on Kenny and were directed, in particular, against what he saw as a special relationship between Kenny and Newton. There is no question that Kenny objected to these personal attacks, and his attitudes towards the demands made by Reilly were probably as much influenced by his personal feelings as by his irrepressible belief in the value of Newton hardware. Turner came out against both the early demands made by Reilly and his systems team – for Wilson Electric computers and Wilson Electric input equipment.

The Michaels computer decision was characterized, above all, by the disparity of the demands made. The first and obvious research question to ask of these data is: Why the conflict? Why were particular individuals attached to particular computer suppliers? I hope to answer these general questions by reference to the political element in the context of this innovative decision process. In Chapter 2 it was argued that, if the present analysis is to add to existing work, an attempt must be made to explain processually the relationship between the strategies pursued by the various interested parties and the final decisional outcome. Such an analysis involves tracing out the generation of demands and the mobilization of power for those demands. The former will be dealt with here; the latter in the following chapter.

An earlier theoretical discussion highlighted four factors likely to be sources of conflict in a demand-generating process involving an inclusive leadership system, its innovative subsystem, and subsystems within the innovative system:

1. Structural differentiation and the concomitant development of particularistic subgroup attitudes and values.
2. The history of relationships between, and the attitudes and predispositions of, those involved in the demand-generating process.
3. A complex and uncertain task.
4. External pressures contributing to internal uncertainty and conflict.

These factors are separated here for analytical clarity; they are, in fact, closely interrelated. The notion of structural differentiation permeates them all. How past actions affect present ones may be a consequence of the way in which a differentiated structure has persisted or changed. How individuals cope with a complex and uncertain task may be a function of the habits, values, and expertise they have acquired in a particular role or an organizational subsystem. How those individuals respond to external pressures may be a product of their past attachments or of their present identification with the reference groups that support their values.

Earlier it was suggested that structural differentiation and

consequent task differentiation in a condition of interdependence
are likely to lead to the development of particularistic subgroup
attitudes and values and intergroup conflict. Such processes have
already been described and analysed in the context of computer
activities in Michaels. In particular, the focus of our historical study
was the power conflicts between the Michaels directors, the programmers, and the O & M officers/systems analysts. Detailed
attention was also given to the conflicts between the two innovating
groups. The importance of structural differentiation as a variable
for explaining conflict is a continuing theme in the discussion of the
Michaels computer decision. It acts as a linking pin in the following
analysis which attempts to show its explanatory significance through,
first, the historical relationships, then, the uncertainty, and, finally,
the external pressures operating on the actors concerned.

THE HISTORICAL FACTORS

The importance of precedent, of past experience, in influencing
present decisions has been noted by several authors. For example,
Devons (1950: 17), describing the formulation of aircraft pro-
grammes in the Ministry of Aircraft production in World War II,
observes: 'No programme was ever drawn up on a completely
rational basis. Each aircraft programme was a development from
the amendment of the previous programme, the original first
programme being hidden in history.' Similarly, Wildavsky (1964:
13) has said of the United States Bureau of Budget: 'The largest
determining factor of the size and content of this year's budget is
last year's budget.' Most of the budget is a product of previous
decisions. Wilensky (1967: 17), referring to foreign policy decision-
making, remarks that 'stereotyped solutions – captured in felicitous
slogans – can for years remain impervious to evidence'. He then goes
on to quote as an example the strategic bombing of Germany by the
Allies during World War II. Lindblom (1959) suggests that
'incrementalism', considering only small changes in the alternative
raised, is an adaptive device for dealing with uncertainty in a
decision process.[1]

The importance of precedent is seen also in the way in which
individuals become identified with particular solutions to problems.

[1] Cyert and March (1963) also make this point when they talk about standard
operating procedures.

In the study referred to above, Devons (1950: 51) reports: 'There was a tendency for individual production officers to identify themselves with the firms for which they were responsible, and to regard as their main function the defence rather than the criticism of their actions.' He explains the production officers' identification as a product of their lack of knowledge of production problems. The Ministry of Aircraft production men thus became dependent on the technical skills of their outside suppliers. Allen (1965: 19), discussing problem-solving in an engineering context, makes the point that, when a technical approach to a problem becomes preferred over any other, it is not easily rejected; and the longer it is in a dominant position the more difficult it becomes to reject. He suggests that old ideas have a decay time, and he finds an average time of six or seven weeks.

Unlike Devons, Allen puts forward an essentially psychological explanation of the tendency of individuals to become committed to solutions and to resist disconfirming information. He quotes the work of Bruner and Postman (1949) on perceptual identification, and argues that the key explanatory variable, in the case he cites, is the cognitive system of the individual engineer. A process of closure takes place whereby 'openness to additional cues is drastically reduced, and either normalized or "gated one".' This view has certain similarities with that of Herbert Simon. Dearborn and Simon (1958) conclude a paper on the departmental identification of executives with the following comment: 'Presented with a complex stimulus, the subject perceives in it what he is "ready" to perceive; the more complex or ambiguous the stimulus, the more the perception is determined by what is already "in" the subject and the less by what is in the stimulus.'

The critic might argue – but why? Dearborn and Simon, and Allen, have described only the process of perceptual identification. The Dearborn and Simon conclusion begs the question why the subject perceives in the complex stimulus only what he is ready to perceive. If he does retreat to what he already knows, why does he do this?

Exploring the cognitive limits on the rationality of the individual decision-maker is undoubtedly an interesting and useful approach. However, I question the value of imposing a model of individual decision-making on the firm and calling it a model of organizational decision-making. This point was made in the earlier discussion of

March and Simon's book *Organizations*. It was suggested that March and Simon show too much concern with the individual as an information-processing system and not enough with the organization in these terms. In *Organizations* there is an overemphasis on attempting to reconstruct the world from the perspective of the decision-maker, and not enough attention is given to how the world impinges on the decision-maker's perspective.

The view adopted in the present work is that an adequate theory of organizational decision-making must assume that decisions are made not by individuals or by role occupants, but via processes that are affected by properties of the unit or units in which the decision is to be made. Decision-making in organizations is not merely a thought process that balances goals and means, or a choice process in which the environment is discriminated as a limit to choice only through the mind of the decision-maker. Rather, it may be understood as a political process that balances various power vectors.

It has been argued that this is especially so of large-scale innovative decisions. Such decisions are likely to threaten existing patterns of resource-sharing. They will be perceived at least as affecting current organizational resources in some way. The implication, for a theory of organizational decision-making, is that those participating in the decision process may attempt to control the decisional outcome in the hope of establishing claims on the resources newly entering the organization. As was noted earlier, the assumption need not be made here of a finite distribution of resources. The fact that the total resource cake is continually increasing in size should not deflect attention from the important matter of its allocation, and particularly from the influential role of the existing distribution of power in determining that allocation. In fact it might be argued that the more rapidly resources become available the more likely are people to be aware of the issue of allocation.

Questions concerning the allocation of resources have been critical to the development of computer activities in Michaels. With each computer, the Management Services department, or its earlier equivalent, attempted to impose its own particular brand of technical rationality on a retailing organization that had developed very successfully by 'the logic of the market place'. In making a generalized demand for increased recognition of technical information as a business resource, the computer specialist, if successful, is effecting a major change in the distribution of organizational resources. Mumford and Banks (1967), for example, give detailed examples of how computers can alter expected career paths to the advantage of some occupational groups and the disadvantage of others, Goldstein and Farlee (1970: 5) show how the introduction of a computer system upset previously established bargains between different interest groups in a hospital.

In Chapter 6, evidence was presented of the extent to which the early stock controllers in Michaels were afraid that the SE 100 installation would reduce their power and status. The fact that it did exactly the opposite was beyond their or anybody else's comprehension at the time. The Michaels directors were also aware of the increasing role of computers in the business and of how they might act as constraints on their freedom of action. Brewster is said to have remarked to Neil Turner, just before he agreed to purchase the company's third computer: 'I suppose it's too late to turn back, we can't do without them [computers] now.' Another director, Hall, has said: 'Intellectually I'm in favour of them; emotionally I'm all against them.' Kenny has remarked of that last observation:

'From his point of view, why should he change? His empire is so neat, so tight. He knows every area of the business – how every last clerk works. Once we get in there with computers he won't know where he is.'

In a critical vein Kenny has also pointed out the dilemma of the directors:

'The thing they never seem to realize is the irreversibility of the data-processing revolution. Their machine-thinking is hopeless. They've got to learn to live with it. They can't take it out once it's in.'

As the number of computers has increased, so the opportunities for the specialists to intrude into fresh areas of the business have widened. In this sense their share of the resource cake has grown Allocation problems have not been confined to the specialist–user department interface. There have also been recurrent difficulties arising from the nature of the interdependence of the specialists themselves. We have seen how the arrival of a new computer – the NTL 200 – had significant implications for the state of interdependence of the programmers and the O & M officers (see *Table 3*, p. 106 above). Evidence has been presented also to show how the power positions of the two groups at different times affected their ability to claim the resources that were made available with the arrival of each computer. For each group, of course, the critical resources lay in the task environment surrounding the new installation.

Again, the 1964 decision to purchase the Newton 350 computer was seen by the participants as a political process in the sense that the resources it made available were mainly distributed to Kenny, the person who backed Newton in the decision process. Reilly described Kenny's part like this:

> 'It was a different sort of decision from the other two. There was no innovation involved. We were merely replacing the SE 100 because it was just a machine changeover. The analysts weren't involved. Programming changes had to be made so Neil was in on it, but the decision was largely Jim's. This was the first opportunity that Jim had to buy a machine, and knowing Jim it had to be a change.'

The above comment is interesting in that it reveals Reilly's perception of his and Neil's part. The implication is that the division of labour between the analysts and the programmers largely determined each group's participation in the decision. Reilly is as careful to point out why he was not involved as he is to play down Neil's part. He was clearly describing what to him appeared as a competitive situation. Jim won.

Turner, too, was aware of how Kenny used that decision to get rid of Ramsbottom and re-establish his own power position:

> 'Jim realized that unless he got in on computers he was a dead duck.'

One of the computer manufacturers intimately involved in the Newton 350 decision had this to say about Kenny's role:

> 'Newton got the recommendation because Jim saw this as a way of reversing Ramsbottom's recommendation. The board were led to think that Ramsbottom hadn't done a thorough job and he was asked to resign. The decision was used by Jim to oust Ramsbottom.'

There is evidence, then, that the first three computer-purchase decisions taken by Michaels released new resources into the specialists' environment, that there was conflict over the distribution of those resources, and that the decisional outcomes were seen by the participants to have an impact both on the state of the task interdependence of the two specialist groups and on the departmental power structure.

These findings can be considered in the light of the earlier discussion of the research literature on how past decisions can influence present ones and how the attachment of individuals to particular solutions can lead to programmed outcomes. It was felt that none of the authors mentioned described the process of incrementalism well or could adequately explain it. In particular, it was suggested that the cognitive approach of Dearborn and Simon (1958) and Allen (1965) offered only a partial explanation of incrementalism in the organizational sphere.

The present aim is to try to explain the impact of the Newton 350 decision on the 1966-8 decision, and, by implication, Kenny's commitment to Newton and the corresponding commitments of Reilly and Turner to Wilson Electric and BCD, in terms of a competitive struggle for power between the three men and their respective interests. The assumption is that 'social groups do not begin and end with the genesis and fruition of any single political process. The individual participant's acts in one process may affect the results that accrue to him in other processes' (Cahill and Goldstein, 1964: 376). It is also suggested that individuals in a competitive situation are likely to attempt to anticipate the future behaviour of their adversaries by reference to their past experiences with them. Finally, individuals come into the demand-generating phase of a decision process not only with various expectations concerning the demands that others are likely to make, but also with certain expectations of the weight that should be accorded to their own point of view. Therefore, hostility is as likely to arise because an individual does not receive the weight he expects for his point of view as it is because a decisional outcome runs counter to his view (Horwitz, 1964: 79).

Kenny's Relationship with Newton

Throughout the 1966-8 decision process the major argument Kenny used to support his demand for Newton and to undermine the claims of Wilson Electric and BCD was:

'Michaels have a successful relationship with Newton. They've never let us down. Why should I change?'

It was precisely this argument that led Reilly eventually to say: 'You can't show a blind man anything.'

The aim of this section is to show how Kenny built up his special relationship with Newton prior to the 1966-8 decision process, and how their perceptions of his behaviour influenced the demands of Reilly, Ashton, and Turner in the period leading up to the decision process and during the process itself.

We saw, in Chapter 6, that the intervention of Henry de Ville, a Newton sales director, played a crucial part in Kenny's support of Newton in the 1964 computer decision. At the time, Kenny was accused by his subordinates and others of recommending Newton on emotional grounds. Ray Ashton was one of the few people in Michaels to meet de Ville. He was impressed:

'Newton more or less sold the machine to Jim. They had a lovely sales director called Henry de Ville. What a smooth character! I've never met anyone like him since. He came up here for a meeting with Jim, and I had to take him down to the "Cat and Fiddle" for lunch with Jim and the chief accountant. Jim turned up one and three-quarter hours late. In this time de Ville didn't show the slightest sign of annoyance. His self-control was un-believable.

He sold Newton to Jim. He told Jim, we'll fly a 350 over. Here is a blank contract, have it on the conditions you want. Relations between Jim and Newton were cemented over the next twelve months before de Ville cleared off back to France. Jim's really susceptible to the good salesman.'

Reilly said of the 350 decision:

'It all boiled down to Jim's relationship with the people at the top of Newton. He was on personal-name contact with them.'

This is certainly the impression given by an analysis of Kenny's correspondence. In a letter (16 December 1964) to the European head of Newton, after the 350 had been installed, Kenny remarked:

'We are today taking over officially the Newton 350 from your installation people and I am very happy to tell you that every-thing has gone better than our expectations. . . . I hope that this is a forerunner of a long and fruitful association between our companies in the data-processing field.'

By January 1965 Kenny was negotiating with the deputy chairman of Michaels the opening of a new Newton office in Birmingham. Kenny took the liberty of writing a draft of a speech that the deputy chairman might make on that occasion. He said, in effect, of himself:

'We have every reason to believe our people have chosen well in deciding on the Newton 350. All the signs to date suggest to us that Newton are living up to their promises, which is not very common practice among suppliers today.'

If a researcher is trying to argue that an individual's special relationship with a supplier had a crucial impact at a later date on the demand-generating process of a decision, he must be in a position to compare that special relationship with the individual's relations with other suppliers. Relationships can be special only in a relative sense. In order to test the hypothesis that Kenny had a special relationship with Newton, four different but overlapping unobtrusive measures were developed from an analysis of his correspondence.

Kenny gave me access to all his correspondence to and from the six computer manufacturers prior to the 1966-8 decision period. For all the manufacturers except Newton, this correspondence covers the period January 1964 to August 1966. However, since Kenny did not really become involved with Newton until late in 1964, the Newton correspondence effectively starts in 1965.

The crudest way to compare the relationships between Kenny and the different manufacturers, on the basis of their correspondence with him, is simply to add the number of items of correspondence across all the manufacturers and then calculate the percentage of the total accounted for by each manufacturer. *Table 20* shows that, even though the correspondence with Newton relates to a considerably shorter period than that with the other manufacturers, it accounts for the largest percentage of the total. Since the two computers operating in Michaels in the period 1964-6 had been purchased from NTL and Newton, respectively, it is to be expected that the files of the companies would be the largest. It is noteworthy that Wilson Electric and BCD, the two manufacturers pushed by Kenny's subordinates and rejected by Kenny during the 1966-8 computer decision, occupied the fourth and fifth positions, respectively.

TABLE 20 *Amount of correspondence be-tween Kenny and manufacturers: before decision process*

Manufacturer	No. of items	% of total
Newton	55	28·3
NTL	54	27·8
American Electronics	34	17·5
Wilson Electric	21	10·8
BCD	20	10·3
Alpha	10	5·2

A further way of looking at the correspondence between Kenny and the manufacturers, for evidence of a special relationship, is in terms of its reciprocity. With Kenny as the maiden and the computer manufacturers as his suitors, a measure of the reciprocity of each relationship can be obtained by calculating the ratio of correspondence in to correspondence out. *Table 21* sets out the passion ratios.

TABLE 21 *Passion ratios: Kenny and manufacturers: before decision process*

Manufacturer	Correspondence 1964–6		Passion ratio in : out
Wilson Electric	In	11	1·1:1
	Out	10	
NTL	In	31	1·3:1
	Out	23	
Newton	In	35	1·7:1
	Out	20	
American Electronics	In	23	2·1:1
	Out	11	
Alpha	In	7	2·3:1
	Out	3	
BCD	In	14	2·3:1
	Out	6	

One might assume that the higher the ratio of correspondence out to in, the more balanced the strength of desire between maiden and suitor; conversely, the higher the ratio of correspondence in to out, the greater the strength of the suitor's desire as compared with the maiden's response. The table shows that BCD was a strong suitor: it made a considerable number of advances but received few responses in return.

The two unobtrusive measures considered so far offer rather crude indications of a special relationship. Few maidens are so undiscriminating as to receive all classes of men. For the present analysis it would be of value to know not only the relative frequency and reciprocity of the communications between Kenny and the six manufacturers, but also who were his correspondents. Kenny's correspondence with each manufacturer was therefore split into three groups, according to whether it was to or from salesmen, area managers, or directors, and the percentage of correspondence in each group was calculated. The results, shown in *Table 22*, are

TABLE 22 *Correspondence between Kenny and manufacturers*
at three levels:
before decision process

Manufacturer	Salesman	Manager	Director
	%	%	%
Newton	20·0	47·3	32·7
American Electronics	58·8	41·2	0
Wilson Electric	66·7	28·6	4·7
Alpha	70·0	30·0	0
NTL	77·8	18·5	3·7
BCD	100·0	0	0

extremely revealing. Newton is clearly the odd manufacturer. In the salesman column BCD is prominent: 100 per cent of that company's correspondence is at this level, compared with only 20 per cent of Newton's. The other four manufacturers all have much more correspondence than Newton at salesman level, the percentages ranging from 58·8 for American Electronics to 77·8 for NTL. In the area manager column the positions are reversed: 47·3 per cent of Newton communications are at this level whereas there is nothing to or from BCD managers. The percentages for the other manufacturers range from 41·2 for American Electronics to 18·5 for NTL. The most significant finding recorded in *Table 22* concerns the correspondence with directors. Of all the correspondence that Kenny had with Newton from late 1964 to August 1966, 32·7 per cent was at director level. In the case of three of the other manufacturers there were no board-level contacts with Kenny. With the remaining two companies, only a small amount of correspondence was at the highest level, 4·7 per cent in the case of Wilson Electric and 3·7 per cent in the case of NTL.

The final unobtrusive measure of a special relationship was based on the number of invitations Kenny received and accepted from each manufacturer. People in Kenny's position who, as part of their job, are expected to keep in touch with the outside world are, as we have seen, pursued by that world. Kenny was repeatedly invited to golfing and social occasions, as well as to equipment demonstrations as one manufacturer after another released its latest piece of electronic gadgetry. For each manufacturer, a count was made of the items of correspondence that concerned golfing, social, and equipment-demonstration occasions, and the percentage of invitational correspondence to total correspondence was calculated.

TABLE 23 *Manufacturers' invitations accepted by Kenny: before decision process*

Manufacturer	Invitational correspondence as percentage of total correspondence	No. of actual invitations	No. of invitations accepted
Newton	36·4	8	7
Wilson Electric	19·0	1	1
BCD	20·0	4	1
NTL	29·6	5	1
American Electronics	35·3	5	0
Alpha	50·0	4	data unclear

Then counts were made of the number of actual invitations each manufacturer issued, and of the number that Kenny accepted. These data are given in *Table 23*. It will be seen that Newton had the second highest proportion of invitational correspondence, issued the highest number of actual invitations, and had the highest number accepted.

In sum, Kenny's special relationship with Newton was confirmed by the following evidence:

1. The Newton file in Kenny's office contained more correspondence than did the file of any other single manufacturer.

2. Kenny had little contact with Newton salespeople, whereas most of his correspondence with the other five manufacturers was at salesman level. In consequence, Kenny had more correspondence at area-manager level with Newton than with any other supplier. Most significantly, over 30 per cent of Kenny's contacts with Newton were at director level; he had practically no written contact with the directors of the other companies.

3. Kenny received and accepted more invitations from Newton than from any other manufacturer.

The Impact of Kenny's Commitment to Newton on the 1966-8 Computer Decision

Unlike previous authors who have discussed the importance of pre-dispositions and commitments on decision-making (Devons, 1950; Wildavsky, 1964; Allen, 1965), I feel that I have, to some extent at least, been able to describe and measure that prior commitment. The research questions to ask at this point are:

1. What impact did Kenny's prior commitment to Newton have on his behaviour during the decision process? Were the positive demands he made based on this commitment? Were the negative demands he made against Wilson Electric and BCD influenced by his identification with Newton?

2. Did the other participants form expectations about Kenny's likely behaviour in the decision process? Did these expectations have an impact on their own demand-generating behaviour?

A quick look at some of the comments made by Kenny in interviews and in memos to directors illustrates how his predisposition towards Newton influenced the positive and negative demands he made:

'The present Newton machine is my baby. I was responsible for choosing it, even though I did this on the basis of a hunch.'

Interview, 18 January 1967

'In buying Newton we're not just buying a machine, we're buying a relationship. Newton have always looked after Michaels well. They have a close association with the company. This is my main reason for wanting to go to Newton.'

Interview, 23 May 1967

'Unless Wilson Electric can demonstrate that in some way they are very much superior to Newton, the choice is obvious.'

Interview, 9 June 1967

'I told the Wilson Electric people . . . that they were starting from way back. They must not kid themselves that they were starting on equal terms with Newton.'

Interview, 7 July 1967

'As far as I'm concerned I do have a special relationship with Newton, but it's not an irrational one as far as the company is concerned.'

Interview, 18 October 1967

'The company's aim must be to have completely compatible equipment. . . . The advantages of BCD equipment are at best marginal while the economic considerations will always be against them. In addition, the company would incur considerable cost in changing over to new equipment. . . . It is therefore our [my] recommendation that the company's best interests are served by continuing to work with Newton.'

Report to board, 28 November 1967

'Our basic problem is why should we change to another manufacturer unless considerable technical or economic advantages accrue to the company, and no such advantage has been demonstrated to my satisfaction. I wish to reaffirm my previously expressed conviction that the company is correct in asking Newton EDP Ltd to provide the computer equipment for the administrative office computer project.'

Final memo to managing director, 26 March 1968

It would seem, then, that there is clear evidence that the positive and negative demands Kenny made during the decision process were influenced by his prior commitment to Newton.

The second question concerning Newton's commitment was how Turner, Reilly, and Ashton perceived Kenny's pre- and post-decision behaviour and what impact their perceptions had on their own demands. To answer this question it is necessary to jump back into the past again.

The Relationship between Reilly's and Ashton's Early Demands and their Expectations of Kenny's Decision-making Conduct

It was argued earlier (Chapter 5) that existing cleavages are of extreme importance in predisposing a group to action. The question was raised: What are the bases from which people respond in a conflict situation? A possible answer was that these bases may have less to do with the particular issue in focus at the time than with existing antagonisms between individuals and groups. This theory was operationalized in the context of the Michaels decision process in the suggestion that Kenny, Reilly, and Turner, individually, said 'I'm against it because he's for it'. The interest here is in looking at the feelings Reilly had for Kenny prior to the decision.

Much of the personal animosity between the two men can be traced to Kenny's preference for someone other than Reilly to fill the vacant post of O & M manager in 1965. Reilly was appointed only after going above Kenny's head to the managing director. Ashton had this to say about the relationship between his two superiors:

'[In 1965] relations between Jim and Bill were acid, mainly because Bill got the job in spite of Jim. There's a natural conflict implicit in their characters. The question is how much do they care to express it.'

Turner's comment was:

'Jim and Bill got off to a bad start because Jim didn't recommend Bill for the O & M manager job. Jim obviously didn't approve of Bill completely . . .'

Reilly's description confirms other interview data:

'When I first joined the department [1960] he was glad to have me as an establishment representative. I believe Jim is a very selfish person; even his altruism is self-motivated. . . . He couldn't have welcomed me as head of the department. He claims that all anti-feeling has broken down. He thought that within twelve months all acrimony would have gone. I'm not sure that this is true.

P

I don't believe Jim has ever forgiven me for getting the job. We mouth the right things. I had to go to the managing director. This announced to everybody that Jim's choice hadn't got the job.'

Thus there is strong evidence of bad feeling between Reilly and Kenny prior to the 1966-8 decision process.

The data also seem to suggest that, at an early stage in the process, Reilly and Ashton expected Kenny to push for Newton and CRT input equipment, and that this had an impact on the demands they made. Ashton said:

'We all knew that Jim would go for Newton. The only doubt was how strong it would be. In fact, Newton weren't shortlisted. He insisted on them.'

Reilly commented:

'Jim had a host of reasons for going for Newton. It's back to the problem of him not having done a data-processing job. He had no reason, apart from political, for going for Newton.'

Both Ashton and Reilly were willing to admit that Kenny's likely support of Newton influenced their own choice behaviour. I asked Ashton why he favoured Wilson Electric:

'They were cheaper. They had a better system. Bill was afraid that Newton would get in for non-technical reasons. I became influenced by the feeling that our standards were declining. I wanted to see fair play . . . You know there was a lot of conflict. Jim spent a lot of his time trying to stop discussions largely because Wilson Electric had support because of price and BCD because of technical capability.'

Reilly said:

'From the moment the job was first mooted there is no doubt that Jim was all for Newton. . . . There's no question we were all biased; you've got to make up your mind on something and look for information to support it.'

Aside from the issue of Newton in 1965-6, Reilly was very suspicious of Kenny's liking for CRT input. There had been some argument before September 1966 about whether the specialists should push for an initial accounting-only job without CRTs, or for a total job with CRTs. Kenny was in favour of the latter and Reilly was against it. Their feelings were expressed in memos to the managing director. In a memo to Brewster on 18 July 1966, Kenny noted:

'We have been investigating the CRT form of input and this seems to have great potentiality indeed for our future developments.'

In an interim report to the board, also in July 1966, Reilly dealt extensively with CRTs. When discussing the pros and cons of CRT he began his advantages section with: 'The advantages *claimed* for this type of equipment are...' There then followed nine lines of advantages. The disadvantages section started: 'The disadvantages *are*...' He seemed much surer of the disadvantages; the list he gave occupied twenty-one lines.

As part of his attempt to control the decisional outcome, Reilly favoured bringing in consultants to recommend which computer manufacturers should be asked to submit quotations for the Wolverhampton office job. On 23 August 1966 a meeting was held of the consultants and Kenny, Reilly, and Turner. The extent of Reilly's interest in the procedural aspects of the decision can be gauged from the detailed work schedule he sent to Kenny the day after this meeting. After making the point that the consultants selected which manufacturers were to be approached, Reilly was careful to mention that the job was not to involve the use of CRT equipment.

Perhaps the most revealing piece of evidence suggesting Reilly's suspicions of Kenny's attachment to Newton and CRT input is a memo Reilly sent to his boss on 30 September 1966, as follows:

'To: Mr Kenny
From: Mr Reilly
         Administrative Office Computer Application

Yesterday we issued the specification for this job to the seven selected suppliers.

This morning Mr Alf Swoop of Newton rang you, and in your absence spoke to me. The purpose of the call was "to clear up some policy issues" which he said needed clarification before they could continue work on their proposals.

As a result of previous discussions with yourself, Mr Turner, and Mr Bull, he had reason to believe that the job described yesterday would develop into "a more sophisticated application" involving the use of CRT equipment, whereas the job specified yesterday would not necessarily involve this equipment and may instead require some form of add-listing equipment. In the light of this he wanted to ask two questions. I reminded him that all questions should be addressed, in writing, to you. He replied that if necessary he would do this, but in case a quick answer was possible, would I listen to the questions and then decide.

Question 1.   Should the quote for this job include the equipment considered likely for the "more sophisticated application"?
Answer   Quote for the job specified yesterday.

Question 2.   If it was necessary to quote for the job described yesterday and a more sophisticated application was envisaged, the question arose as to whether this particular quote was "an exercise".
Answer   Quote for the job specified yesterday.

He suggested that he might confirm this conversation to you in writing. I asked him to do so.

This conversation speaks for itself. You will recall that I spoke to you about this problem on a number of occasions.

If any further suppliers ask the same questions they also will receive the same reply from me.

B. Reilly'

In this memo Reilly points out Kenny's special relationship with Newton and his attachment to CRT. After accusing Kenny, Turner, and Bull of plotting, he suggests, in the last sentence, that he is impartial. We shall return shortly to the Reilly–Turner issue, and, by implication, the analyst–programmer issue, and their impact on the decision.

The evidence presented so far indicates that Reilly played a very assertive role in the build-up to the decision. Much of his assertiveness was directed towards Kenny and the demands he felt Kenny would make. We have shown that Reilly persisted with this pattern of behaviour throughout the decision process. He and Ashton came out quickly with positive demands for Wilson Electric and document readers; furthermore, they made incessant attacks, first, on Newton hardware and, later, on CRT input. The question that arises is, then, why was Reilly so unrelentingly aggressive? For an answer, we have to examine again the status and power position of the analysts at the beginning of the decision process, the general problem of the analyst–programmer interface, and the impact that the decision was likely to have on the future status and power of the two groups.

The Programmer–Analyst Issue in the 1966-8 Computer Decision

In a sense it is not necessary to focus on particular encounters between Reilly and Turner before and during the 1966-8 computer decision in order to understand Reilly's behaviour. If Reilly's assertive behaviour towards Kenny had been successful it would have strengthened his position not only with Kenny but also with Turner, and, in consequence, over the programming function. That Reilly was interested in improving his own and his department's status cannot be doubted. Throughout the summer of 1967 and on into early 1968 when his demands for Wilson Electric and document readers had been repulsed, he repeatedly asked Kenny to make him his deputy. That was his way of formally asking for the power and status that his assertive behaviour had failed to win.

The reader will recall that the structure of the Management Services department was as shown in the diagram below. Formally, Kenny's three technical subordinates were of equal status. If the job of deputy had been created and given to Reilly it would have upset the status system in the department. Kenny's reason for refusing Reilly's suggestion indicates his awareness both of the competitiveness between the analysts and programmers and of the analysts' inferior technical position:

Head of Management Services department		
J. Kenny		
O & M/Systems manager	Programming manager	O R manager
B. Reilly	N. Turner	T. Carr

'Bill and I have argued this out on a number of occasions. Part of the issue is Bill's desire to acquire Neil's expertise as a technical slave. My attitude is that this doesn't just involve Bill. You've got to consider that you're not just telling one chap that he's got the job, but two others that they haven't. I refused outright and I'll continue to do so.'

Kenny's first refusal on the deputy issue was in July 1967, just after Reilly had given up all hope for Wilson Electric. In 1966 Reilly must have felt that he was in with a chance of using the decision as a springboard for the raising of his own and his department's status. He was certainly aware of the importance of the decision to the whole department:

'I'll spend 30 per cent of my time on the administrative office job. To me this is completely justified; any future developments in the department depend almost entirely on what happens on this particular job.'

Later, when there were doubts about the directors' willingness to go ahead with the project, Reilly commented:

'If the directors refuse this computerization they are refusing the most obvious and biggest area of the business which is as yet untouched, and in doing so they are effectively shutting the door to further computer developments in Michaels.'

It was comments like these that led me to disregard any variant of the zero-sum conception of power. As was pointed out earlier, the Management Services department 'resource cake' increased in size with every computer. In this decision Reilly was aware of how the interface between the analysts and the programmers could impinge on the allocation of those resources. Reilly's approach to the programmers was very similar to that taken by Ramsbottom in 1962. He thought that by arguing at the beginning of the decision that the analysts were in charge of the administrative office job he could control the project. He was wrong. Nevertheless, he tried to insist:

'The current situation is that responsibility for any project lies with the systems analysts. There is no doubt about this; it's the stated policy of the department. The conception of the system and its implementation is the analysts' responsibility.'

On another occasion he said:

> 'The responsibility for the project lies with the analysts. The first question they've got to ask is, "Is it a computer job or a non-computer job?" Then to specify the system. It's difficult to think what the programmers could do.'

These assertive statements made by Reilly about the interface between his group and the programmers probably stemmed from a feeling of the inadequacy of his own and his department's power in 1966. This was his first opportunity to participate in a computer decision. Turner had played a major role in the previous two decisions. The discussion in Chapter 7 of power relations between the two groups concluded that, in spite of major setbacks, the programmers had been able to maintain their power over the analysts. They were able to do this mainly because of their control over the recruitment and learning processes that supported their power base. If Reilly and the systems team were to increase their power, they had to do it through the 1966-8 decision. They knew the outcome of this decision would have repercussions in the Management Services department for many years. Reilly said himself that the administrative office job was 'the most obvious and biggest area of the business .., as yet untouched'.

Along with their demand that the analysts should control the administrative office job, Reilly and Ashton began the decision process highly distrustful of the programming manager. Ashton felt that Turner might try to take decisions on hardware which would limit the analysts' systems. I had asked him why he and Reilly were suspicious of the programmers in the decision:

> 'We felt if we weren't careful, decisions would be made on the hardware side which would affect our systems.'

After some experience of Turner's behaviour in the decision process, Ashton remarked:

> 'One of the big question marks for us is Neil's position. Bill and I are never exactly sure where he stands.'

Reilly said of the programming manager:

> 'Neil likes to manoeuvre in the background. He doesn't like overt issues.'

This tendency of Turner to withhold information and to operate quietly in the background was, of course, a major and a highly successful power-maintenance strategy used by the programmers between 1962 and 1966. Turner used it to good effect during the computer decision. He accepted this at the general level:

'There was and still is a funny relationship between us. Bill's convinced I only tell him half-truths. I argue it's a waste of time explaining things because he can't understand them.'

He then went on to quote a specific example which explained how the issue of CRT equipment came into the decision:

'I saw them [CRTs] in London at the time the administrative office job was first in the offing. They looked incredibly good. I arranged a demonstration for Jim, The big problem was cost. Scientific Electronics approached Angus and me at Datafair. They gave us a quote. The cost seemed astronomical at the time, but both Jim and I were very pleased about the idea of CRTs. Bill wasn't involved in any respect. He didn't go down to Datafair.'

Turner and Kenny came out in favour of CRT input during the decision process. Reilly was consistently against it. Reilly did not find out about the Scientific Electronics quote for CRT until January 1967, and only then because he inadvertently came across it in Kenny's office. This was not the only occasion on which Kenny and Turner formed a coalition during the decision. Turner at various times supported Kenny against Wilson Electric hardware and the Wilson Electric reader and in favour of teletypes, CRTs, and Newton. This is a classic case of the formation in a triad of a conservative coalition to preserve the existing power structure. It is an issue we shall return to in more detail in Chapter 9 when we consider how the power of the various parties influenced the decisional outcome.

Angus Bull, Turner's assistant, was also prepared to admit that the programming section kept information back from the analysts during the decision:

'Neil and I tend to work rather separately and keep things away from the analysts until the last minute.'

Angus went on to support a remark that Kenny made about the systems group being short of technical expertise and needing recruits to bolster their position against the programmers. He quoted himself as a case in point:

> 'I went to see Jim one day to clear up my future in the company. As you know, I'm neither programmer nor analyst. [He was an engineer.] Bill must have got to hear about this from Jim, for he recommended I move into the systems group. Neil resisted this. He knew Bill would try to use my technical know-how against him.'

A final quote from Ashton demonstrates that the analysts were aware both of the programming group's likely interference in their systems and of the mechanism they would use to do this. I had asked Ashton if Neil and Jim ever combined on issues:

> 'Yes, this happens. Sometimes they'll get together and make decisions on their own in systems areas. For example, in the early stages of the CRT issue, before we had even sent out the specifications, they had organized a quote from Scientific Electronics. Neil likes to make hardware decisions before the systems are known.'

Conclusion on the Historical Factors Encouraging Disparity in the Demand-generating Process

Evidence was presented in Chapter 7 indicating that, by 1965, the combination of their own lack of technical skills and the successful power-maintenance strategies of the programmers meant that the analysts were still some way from controlling the task interdependence of the two groups. The analysts had the aspirations but not yet the accomplishments. A major argument of the preceding section has been that the analysts' assertive behaviour before and during the decision was an attempt to attain those accomplishments.

However, our analysis has also shown that the social structure of the Michaels computer groups changed between 1965 and 1966. By the time the computer decision was under way, Kenny had created a new department. The development programmers and the analysts were brought together for the first time under one roof and Kenny controlled the destinies of both. The intra-specialist conflict which has been documented over the history of computer activities in Michaels was now to be enriched through the sociological significance of the third party.[1]

[1] For a detailed look at the triad, see Simmel (1950) and Caplow (1968).

This move from the dyadic to the triadic form greatly complicated the generation of demands in the decision process. The aspiring analysts now had to think not only of the programmers but also of their boss Kenny. In this case, the person at the apex of the triad was especially threatening to the analysts because of his seemingly intransigent belief in the virtues of Newton EDP.

Much of the disparity in the demand-generating process of the Michaels decision was a consequence of the analysts' attempts to increase their power and status. Kenny has said of the analysts', and in particular of their manager's, behaviour:

'Their choice of manufacturer in the decision process wasn't just a matter of their technical orientation. Bill was actively concerned with putting forward a different installation, one that was his alone.'

Turner was most voluble both about Reilly's singular pursuit of his own demands and about his implicit attack on Turner's and Kenny's demands. I had asked Turner why he thought Reilly supported Wilson Electric:

'Because he hadn't been connected with Newton in any way; he wouldn't like to admit they were any good because he had nothing to do with it. Any praise going wasn't reflected on him. It was also because Jim was sold on his association with Newton. He objected to this and therefore went in the exact opposite direction. He quite liked the Wilson Electric people, he seemed to get on well with them. . . . He seemed to take the attitude, "If I'm not involved with it it's no good". If we had Wilson Electric he could have said, "I decided alone". If Newton got the order this would have involved somebody else.

This was also seen in his attitude to CRT and document readers. Angus and I introduced the idea of CRT a while ago. Bill had nothing to do with it. When I came up there was a tendency for Bill to react against something which wasn't his suggestion. He has to find an alternative solution.'

If the cause of much of the conflict in the Michaels decision was the active power strategies of the analysts and the attempts by Kenny and Turner to preserve the existing task and power structure, further impetus was given to the disagreements by the complexity and uncertainty of the decision and by the marketing strategies of the computer manufacturers. Uncertainty is the issue we pursue next.

COMPLEXITY AND UNCERTAINTY IN INNOVATIVE DECISIONS

Complexity and uncertainty are features of organizational decision-making with which most organizations must live. Many writers have mentioned their significance. Devons (1950: 41) has referred to the 'inevitable uncertainties' of planning in conditions of rapid technical development. March and Simon (1958: 139) and Downs (1967: 75) consider various cognitive limits to rational decision-making. According to Downs (1967: 75): 'Important aspects of many problems involve information that cannot be procured at all, especially concerning future events; hence many decisions must be made in the face of some ineradicable uncertainty.' Cyert and March (1963) are less concerned with the causes of uncertainty than with its management. They hypothesize that organizations seek to avoid uncertainty by 'emphasizing short-run reaction to short-run environment' (p. 119).

The literature dealing with the impact of complex and uncertain environments on decision-making behaviour has had its critics. Duncan (1970) raises three issues. He notes that, while Lawrence and Lorsch (1967) found that different configurations of organizational structure are required to cope with different environmental conditions, they did not discuss the *processes* whereby organizations adapt to environmental uncertainty. The other points Duncan raises involve the way in which uncertainty and environment have been defined. March and Simon's (1958: 113) definition is at the micro-level: 'In the case of uncertainty the individual does not know the probability distribution connecting behavior choices and environmental outcomes.' At the macro-level of analysis, Lawrence and Lorsch (1967: 29) have defined uncertainty as consisting of three components:

– a lack of clarity of information
– a long time-span of definitive feedback.
– a general uncertainty of causal relationship.

In the present work, uncertainty is defined empirically. The following analysis relies on the participants' own *perception* of the determinants and impact of uncertainty on the computer decision.

Following Dill (1958), Thompson (1967), and Duncan (1970), the environment surrounding a decision may be comprised of two dimensions: the simple–complex dimension and the static–dynamic dimension.

Complexity relates to the number and variety of factors in a decision unit's environment that impinge on that unit's decision-making behaviour. The expectation is that a low-level production department is likely to be closer to the simple end of the dichotomy than is a boundary-spanning department such as a Management Services department, faced as it is with a wide set of, often conflicting, interdependencies and obligations.

The static-dynamic dimension refers to the degree to which factors in the decision unit's environment are stable or are in a continual process of change over time.

The matrix below combines the two dimensions. When the dimensions are related,[1] the expectation is that Cell 1 conditions would offer the lowest, and Cell 4 the highest, perceived uncertainty. While this matrix has a predictive feature which may be tested by empirically filling out all four cells, its role here is merely to suggest that Cell 4 offers a more elaborate way of conceptualizing the conditions under which the Michaels 1966-8 computer decision was made than do existing distinctions between programmed and non-programmed decisions.

	SIMPLE	COMPLEX
STATIC	*Cell 1* Low perceived uncertainty	Moderately low perceived uncertainty
DYNAMIC	Moderately high perceived uncertainty	*Cell 4* High perceived uncertainty

There are several justifications for the argument that Cell 4 conditions were evident in the Michaels case. With regard to the simple–complex dimension, there is the issue of structural

[1] See Duncan (1970) for a detailed discussion of the theoretical implications of this matrix.

differentiation. It has already been implied that the Management Services department was a social system with high boundary relevance,[1] that is, it was a department whose role incumbents had plenty of contacts with other departments, and those contacts were important to the department's effective performance. These contacts ranged throughout Michaels, but in this context the most significant ones were with the board, a number of would-be user departments, and manufacturers and consultants outside the company. Most importantly, perhaps, the innovating groups were themselves differentiated by structure and therefore by task. Our historical analysis has already shown that this differentiation within the innovating groups and across other groups led to problems that were often expressed in differences of attitudes and values. Part of the complexity in this decision process arose, therefore, from the number of disparate groups involved in the process. Thompson (1967: 139) provides theoretical credence for this suggestion when he observes that the potential for conflict in a decision process increases with the interdependence and variety of the groups incorporated.

The actual task on which these disparate groups were engaged was highly complex at the technical level. The Wilson Electric salesman admitted this, but suggested that the difficulties would have been reduced if the Michaels analysts had been better equipped:

'It was an advanced and difficult installation by normal electronic data-processing standards. The quality of the Michaels systems staff wasn't particularly high. In the context of the EDP world it was an ambitious and dangerous project, but if they had had the right staff it would have been OK.'

Kenny acknowledged his department's inexperience when he wrote his final memo to the managing director:

'The project we are about to undertake is of a different order of magnitude from our existing computer installations. We are moving into fields (on-line input, real-time and multi-programming) of which we have little experience.'

Reilly was unhappy about the technical difficulties he could foresee:

'I would have preferred a limited approach to the job: doing the

[1] See Kahn *et al.* (1964: 120) for a discussion of boundary relevance.

accounting side of one of the administrative offices and using document readers for input. In this way we'd be able to handle the job easily and then move on with more confidence to the technically more difficult problems.'

The dynamic nature of the computer task environment has been documented in earlier chapters. Between 1957 and 1968 three different generations of machines came onto the market. In that period programming was 'converted from a mystery to a discipline' (Bowden, 1970: 47). Changes in the backing and fast stores of computers since 1952 are tabulated below:[1]

Computer	Date	Backing stores	Fast stores price per bit	Access time
Mark 1	1952	600,000 bits at 1 penny	50 shillings	240 microseconds (10,000 bits filled a room)
Mercury	1955		2 shillings	10
Atlas	1960		4 shillings	2
1900	1968	100,000,000 bits at 1/100 penny	6 pennies	6·6 (1 million bits take about half a filing cabinet

The momentum of these technical changes continued throughout the period of the Michaels computer decision. Michaels was particularly affected by changes in input equipment. In a provisional report to the board in November 1965, the analysts stated that 'the principal remaining problem is one of input'. At that time the only viable form of input was paper tape. Reilly could, however, foresee the superiority of document readers:

'Clearly, if such machines can be developed they will solve our input problem. The key question envisaged in relation to time-scale is whether such machines will be developed by 1968-70.'

In fact, by the end of 1966, Wilson Electric was marketing the Mark 1 version of its mark-sensing reader. By 1967 an improved Mark 2 was on the market and was competing with a BCD hand-writing

[1] Taken from Bowden (1970: 47).

reader and the Larco mark-sensing reader. All these brands featured in the Michaels decision.

Faced with Cell 4 conditions, a complex and dynamic environment, the Michaels computer people certainly perceived the uncertainty. With regard to the factor of structural interdependence, there is evidence that the analysts were continually uncertain about their relationship with the programmers, Kenny, and the board. Ray Ashton said of the programmers:

'There's still a tendency for the programmers to keep things to themselves. . . . It's difficult to know what they think.'

Likewise he commented to Kenny:

'We're always complaining to Jim about being left in the dark. We never know what the directors think and I'm sure they only have a rough idea of what goes on in here.'

As we shall see when we discuss Kenny's assessed stature, he also had his periods of uncertainty with the board. These were associated with his low assessed stature at a particular point in time, and also with his periodic doubts about the directors' willingness to carry through the project. One day, in June 1967, the deputy chairman said to a researcher:

'Of course we may decide not to go ahead with the administrative office job despite the money we have spent on it.'

The researcher asked Kenny if this remark was to be taken seriously:

'Yes, it is. There's still a possibility that the firm will change its mind about the new system. If they do, several people are likely to resign.'

On another occasion Kenny commented:

'Some of the board are continually looking for excuses to draw back. I'm afraid they might use the resignation of another senior programmer to reinforce their fears.'

The directors' apprehension was partly a reflection of their mistrust of computers and their impact on the administrative office system. Kenny certainly thought so:

'Brewster was worried about moving into a field where we were going to affect customers. The business was growing fairly rapidly. They weren't prepared to take any risks. . . . In the administrative offices at the moment they can control things pretty well. There are a lot of highly determined jobs. Why upset this? The computer might go wrong. Therefore they demanded more and more evidence. They wanted all the i's dotted and t's crossed. It was a great delaying tactic. It was an extreme example of management avoiding contact with the computer.'

The major source of uncertainty mentioned by the computer specialists was the complex and dynamic technical environment surrounding the decision. Frischmuth and Allen (1968: 1) have pin-pointed some of the special difficulties of technical problem-solving. They mention that technical problems frequently have no terminal state; the solutions themselves are often dynamic. Kenny was aware of this:

'The great problem with this sort of decision is the uncertainty. Things are moving so fast you cannot be sure of anything. This means you've got to stop at some point and cut into the informa-tion you've got and say, "We want that. This is the best possible decision we can make at this point" – and then go ahead and implement it. If you're not careful there can be too many horizons in this field.'

Frischmuth and Allen (1968: 1) also note that the goals that act as constraints on the decision process may change over time. It has been shown that on three occasions[1] the Michaels board changed the goals of the administrative office project.

A further and critical source of uncertainty was that the criteria by which the solution was to be evaluated were dimly perceived and a matter of individual judgement. Kenny has spoken of the Michaels 1966-8 decision:

'The configurations proposed by the manufacturers may bear little resemblance to each other, and it is virtually impossible to com-pare them.'

He went on to quote specific examples:

'1. *Financial factors*
The resulting quotations, delivered to an agreed and specified

[1] January 1967, September 1967, and January 1968.

date, ranged from considerably less than £200,000 to significantly more than £450,000 for a tightly specified job. With hardware costs varying by a factor as great as this, how is one to justify the preference for a given proposal?

2. *Input equipment*

The types of input proposed were fundamentally different from each other and some methods required highly skilled operators, while others needed only low-grade clerks.

3. *Programming load and maintenance costs*

The estimates of programming load involved ranged from 19·5 to 41·2 man-months effort. . . . The maintenance costs of the proposed systems also varied between £5000 and £15,000 per annum.'

Kenny concluded:

'If one system had all the good features and another all the bad, at least it would be simple to compare the hardware, but examination of the various proposals suggested that the desirable and undesirable features (once they are defined) appear to be randomly distributed. What criterion is the client to employ in finding an optimum solution?'

Given this uncertainty, there is plenty of room for individuals, as we have shown, to reduce the uncertainty by appealing to criteria that suit their own interests. I asked Reilly if a decision to purchase a computer could be rational:

'Not at all. Certain things can be evaluated quite rationally but there are also areas where no precise knowledge is possible. In these areas politics and emotion are bound to play a large part.'

After discussing his distaste for Reilly's and Turner's belief that he was anti-BCD, Kenny said:

'You get involved with these kinds of value judgements when you're dealing with this amount of uncertainty. It's this which makes it a managerial problem. Their choice of manufacturer in the decision process wasn't just a matter of their technical orientation. Bill was actively concerned with putting forward a different installation, one that was his alone.'

Kenny repeated these feelings in his final memo to the managing director:

'Because of the size of the order envisaged and the prestige attached to the installation, the Management Services department has been put under considerable pressure by rival claimants extolling the virtue of their particular expertise. The particular difficulty of the situation is that few of these claims are subject to any scientific validation so that, paradoxically, one is left, in the selection of essentially scientific equipment, with large areas of belief. In this situation it is perhaps not surprising that agreement on selection of equipment does not even exist among informed opinion in the Management Services department.'

In the above comment not only does Kenny reiterate one of the general arguments of this study – namely that uncertainty tends to be a source of conflict – he also points to an additional factor promoting conflict in the decision studied – the behaviour of the computer manufacturers. The following section looks further at the manufacturers' marketing strategies.

EXTERNAL PRESSURES CONTRIBUTING TO INTERNAL UNCERTAINTY AND CONFLICT

A consistent theoretical assumption of the preceding section has been a link between uncertainty and conflict in social systems. This is a familiar point in the organizational literature. Hickson (1966: 224) has been somewhat critical of a convergence in organization theory around the lack of specificity in role expectations. To back up his argument he quotes the work of Gross, Mason, and McEachern (1958), Burns and Stalker (1961), Kahn *et al.* (1964), and others.

The approach of anthropological literature on factionalism is not to suggest a linear relationship between ambiguity and conflict: 'It is clearly not being asserted that ambiguity itself is a determinant of factional conflict in any significant sense' (French, 1962: 239). Rather, the emphasis is on linking ambiguity – for example, over the worth of remaining affiliated to a loosely structured Indian Reservation community as against formal disengagement – to various complexities in the social structure, like the history of cleavages in that community. Siegel and Beals (1960) and also French (1962) hold that factionalism is a result of external stresses affecting a group according to potential lines of cleavage within it. Specifically, Siegel and Beals (1960: 112) contend that it is a product of a 'dominant external society selectively influencing a group in a manner which is covert and which tends to accentuate existing cleavages within the group'. This section hopes to add to earlier ones on the role of historical factors and a complex and uncertain task environment in promoting conflict in the 1966-8 decision. The particular aim is to show how external pressures might have been fed into the existing conflicts during the demand-generating process of the decision.

Our analysis so far has suggested a relationship between a complex and dynamic environment and decision-making under uncertainty. There is reason to believe that the marketing strategies of the manufacturers contributed to this uncertainty. First, their interventions were sporadic and therefore unsettling to the Michaels staff. Second, part of the aim of each of the manufacturers was to generate uncertainty about the proposals of their rivals.

In an interview on 25 January 1967 Kenny remarked that he and his staff were now having some doubts about having Wilson Electric as one of their first two choices:

'I had a visit from Alpha to find out why we had eliminated them from the tendering process. They expressed great amazement at the choice of Wilson Electric and pointed out that it had no software and that BCD or some other manufacturer would have to be used. I mentioned this to Neil, and much to my amazement he agreed, yet previously he had not raised any objection to the selection. It looks like we have a machine as second choice which can't do the job. There are in fact few machines in operation in the country.'

Bill Reilly, about the same time, was using rumours he had picked up from BCD in order to question Newton's intentions. He was worried that Newton would soon bring out a new and incompatible range of computers. Allison, the Newton salesman, vehemently denied these allegations:

'The computer business is dirty. This sort of thing, this scandal-mongering, happens all the time, especially after companies have been put out of the running by a selection process like the one we've just had here.'

Even in April 1968 Turner was still worried about the compatibility of Newton's future models with its existing range. Aware of Neil's and Bill's doubts, Kenny arranged a meeting at the Newton head office. Kenny described one incident:

> 'The Newton representatives had said that new equipment would be completely compatible with old, as they could not let down previous customers. Neil queried this statement. The Newton representative said that he was sorry that Neil didn't believe him. All he could do was to state what he knew to be the case. If Neil didn't accept it, that was up to him.'

In fact, Neil was sufficiently experienced in his dealings with computer manufacturers not to take their statements at face value.

A further tactic used by the manufacturers was to write to the Management Services department pointing out the enormity of the task Michaels was setting itself and claiming that they alone were equipped to deal with the problems entailed. Such letters invariably ended with the announcement of a new piece of equipment. One manufacturer wrote:

> 'As we have discussed many times, this next stage of development is not merely an extension in size of the computers you have already installed. It involves techniques and computer expertise with complexities of a different magnitude. The facts that I have brought to your notice have really been concerned with these complexities and fall into three principal categories . . .'

The Michaels computer decision featured a mating search process (see Cyert and March, 1963: 80). Not only were the computer technologists searching for alternatives; alternatives were also looking for them. As we shall see in more detail in the next chapter, this was a selective process. Because Kenny made it clear that he was in favour of Newton, the other computer manufacturers concentrated their selling behaviour on Reilly and Turner. This added fresh impetus to the conflict in the Management Services department and thereby contributed to the disparities in the demand-generating process of the decision.

SUMMARY AND CONCLUSION

This chapter has tried to place the Michaels computer decision in a historical, social, and technological framework. The overall theoretical approach has emphasized social process. The concern has been to relate past actions and attitudes to present behaviour and future designs; to describe and explain the decision-making behaviour in the context of a social structure and a technological environment that were elaborating over time.

The essential research question asked of the data has been: Why the conflict? Why did Kenny, Reilly, and Turner make disparate demands on the Michaels authority system? The answer to that question has rested on a process of reciprocal causation between a number of factors.

The initial theoretical assumption was that existing cleavages play a primary part in predisposing a group to action; in other words, that 'the degree of group consensus prior to the outbreak of conflict seems to be the most important factor affecting cohesion' (Coser, 1956: 92). The analysis of relationships prior to the decision illustrated clearly the extent of the conflict between the various groups and individuals in the Management Services department. That analysis also showed the changing pattern of status and power relationships between the specialists and the Michaels board, and among the specialists themselves. A major conclusion drawn from the data was that, whereas nationally programmers were declining in status relative to analysts, within Michaels, the programmers' successful power-maintenance strategies prevented too extensive an encroachment on their task environment. A consequence of this was a feeling of status deprivation, of frustration, among the Michaels analysts.

This feeling, together with the analysts' awareness that previous computer decisions had released new resources into the computer groups' sphere of activities, and that the outcome of the administrative office decision would set the pattern of relationships between the computer technologists for several years to come, led them to take an assertive stand early in the decision process.

If the analysts were suspicious of the programmers' intentions, they were even more so of Kenny's. When Kenny made himself head of the new Management Services department he significantly increased the complexity of the Michaels computer environment. To the continuing conflict between the analyst and programmer groups was added the sociological enrichment of a third party—what is more, a third party given authority over the two warring factions.

If the analysts were to increase their standing through the 1966-8 decision they now had Kenny to think of as well. Kenny, however, had come to power partly through successfully supporting Newton in the 1964 tendering process. He had a great deal of investment in Newton, as Newton had in him. A number of unobtrusive measures showed the strength of his relationship with Newton prior to the later decision.

The analysts' expectation that Kenny would opt for Newton offered them a ready normative theme to play on in order to support their acquisitive demands for Wilson Electric. They argued both that Kenny was technically incompetent to make the decision and that his attachment to Newton was emotional. The norm in making such technical decisions is to be objective.

A look at the determinants and level of uncertainty in this innovative decision illustrates the difficulties of being objective. Where the solution to the problem is dynamic, where the goals that set the constraints for the problem are subject to change, where there is great technical complexity, and where the selection criteria are ill perceived and ultimately a matter of individual judgement, any self-interested demand can be clothed in respectability, be it a belief in a special relationship, or in the virtues of a particular type of input equipment, or in the maxim that those who spend most on research will always be at the forefront of the field.

Finally, the analysis has tried to show that, if a group is lacking in basic consensus, the selective application of outside pressures is likely to add to those divergencies. In this case, the marketing strategies of the computer manufacturers added to the divergent tendencies in the social structure of the Management Services department and further contributed to the disparities in the demand-generating process of this innovative decision.

CHAPTER 9

The Sources and Use of Power in an Innovative Decision Process

One of the major themes of this work has been an attempt to demonstrate the value of the concept of power for the study of organizations. In earlier chapters the theories of organizational decision-making presented by March and Simon (1958) and Cyert and March (1963) have been criticized for their neglect of power. While March and Simon completely ignore the role that powerful interests might play in a decision process, the Cyert and March theory does at least savour of political realism. However, our discussion of the latter work concluded that it left many pertinent questions unanswered (see pp. 9-11 above).

It was argued that to complement the political approach of Cyert and March would involve an attempt to explain processually the relationship between the strategies pursued by the various interested parties and the final decisional outcome. Such an analysis would have a dual focus. First, it would involve tracing out the generation of demands in the decision process. This has been the aim of the previous chapters. The second political component requires an analysis of the mobilization of support for the demands. The issue of power mobilization serves, then, as the theoretical and empirical focus of this, the final data chapter.

POWER MOBILIZATION

In Chapter 2 the point was made that power structures rest primarily not on a social consensus concerning expectations about privileges or rights between superiors and subordinates, but on the distribution of the resources by means of which compliance with demands can be enforced. The implication of this for our theory of decision-making as a political process is that a demand is politically feasible only if sufficient power can be mobilized and committed in its support. Such a process of mobilization is founded not only on the possession and control of system-relevant resources but also on skilful use of them. The successful use of power is a matter of tactical skill rather than merely of possession.

The present concern is to explain an actor's success in a competitive demand-generating process involving a differentiated innovating system acting in an advisory capacity to a leadership system. The issue here cannot be, in an absolute sense, why did Newton win out? To answer that question would have entailed a close look at the deliberations of the Michaels board. Unfortunately, research access was not forthcoming for that kind of study. The focus here is therefore the decision-making behaviour of the innovating groups in the context of the leadership system and the marketing strategies of the computer manufacturers. The following represent the general research questions to be asked of the data:

1. Since the formal organizational structure – Kenny – won out, what were the positional factors that enabled the winner to succeed? What resources did he possess? How did he use them?
2. What were the positional factors of the others such that they could not win? What resources did they possess? Did they have an inadequate perception of the way the Michaels social structure operated? Did they lose because they played the structure badly, or was it because they did not have the political access to play the structure at all?

Some theoretical elaboration will add precision to the above general questions. There is the issue of how resources may aid in generating support for a demand. Mechanic (1962: 352) has stated that, within organizations, power can be mobilized by controlling access to the resources of 'information, persons and instrumentalities'. Bucher (1970: 11) notes the importance of structural position as a component of power. Position has consequences mainly in terms of the other persons in a social system with whom a given incumbent is likely to interact. The amount of support a person achieves in a situation is likely to be conditional on the structure and nature of his direct and indirect interpersonal relationships. The assumption is that, in a competitive demand-generating process, the decisional outcome will not necessarily be a product of the greater worthiness or weight of the issues ranged to uphold one or other demand in the dispute, but may result from the nature of the linkages that opposing parties have with the individuals for whose support they are competing. Since, in a dispute, it is the legitimacy of a person's demand according to the centre of power that is crucial, our analysis will seek to show how the relative power of Kenny, Reilly, and Turner varied as a consequence of their differential access to the Michaels board.

Aside from the general factor of structural position and its corollary, extent of each actor's role set, the following analysis also considers the particular role of middleman between two different social systems. Kenny was, of course, the interface between the Michaels board and its technical advisers. In the context of a discussion of power relations, his role had both disadvantages and advantages.

The disadvantages related to the generalized problem of superiors, namely that their position gives them authority, but the use of authority requires interaction. Subordinate compliance is seldom automatic and unconsidered. To exercise his power the superior must be able to create a kind of legitimacy for himself. Such legitimacy is notoriously difficult to achieve in a boundary-spanning role.[1] As a group representative the superior often has to protect and project the values and standards of the group. And yet the contact he has with outside values and interests, coupled with his need for some acceptance by outsiders if he is to be an effective group representative, may place on him pressures to conform to norms contrary to his group's.

Laboratory studies by Julian and Hollander (1966; Hollander and Julian, 1969) and field-work by Kaplan (1959) and Glaser (1963) have established that a superior's competence in a major group activity, his 'interest in group members', and his 'interest in group activity' are all critical to his ability to legitimate his power. Such legitimation is an important factor in a superior's ability to generate support for and therefore compliance with his demands. We shall see that, if a superior is considered to make excessive demands, is held responsible for failures, and is thought of as being manipulative and seeking personal power, he is unlikely to receive group support.

Legitimation for the middleman is problematic. The essence of his role is to keep a foot in both the systems he spans. Suspicion of deviousness, if not deceitful activity, is inherent in the middleman's

---

[1] For examples from a variety of cultures, see Gluckman (1949), Kaplan (1959), Evan (1965), and Bailey (1969).

position. In terms of power mobilization, however, accusations of deviousness and inconsistent support from subordinates, while troublesome, may not be crucial. For the middleman it is the legitimation of his demands in the organization's centre of power that is critical. Here his *assessed stature* is likely to be important.

Earlier, it was argued that the blanket term 'advisory' had little analytical and empirical relevance in considering the computer specialist–manager relationship.[1] A person in Kenny's position does not merely advise; he persuades, negotiates, and exercises the power derived from his specialist expertise. Assuming for the moment that the computer specialist both is able to identify successfully with, and has access to, the centre of power in the organization, an important constraint on his ability to negotiate and persuade is likely to be his assessed stature in that centre of power. The components of assessed stature are likely to vary from position to position and task environment to task environment. The particular way in which respect is defined will depend on the value system of the group assessing the specialist. Achieving the requisite level of assessed stature is therefore likely to be especially difficult for the middleman faced as he is by conflicting pressures from different value systems.

Aside from the problem the innovating specialist has of achieving and maintaining his stature in a situation where he receives conflicting and ambiguous expectations,[2] there are also difficulties in using power derived from high stature. If it is important for the specialist to be able to identify correctly the attitudes and values he must emulate to achieve a high stature, it is equally essential for him to be able to perceive accurately when he has high and when low stature. The timing of a demand and the manner of its presentation may have a decisive impact on the support it receives.

The final theoretical issue to be raised to aid the analysis of power mobilization in the Michaels computer decision involves consideration of information control as a power resource derived from the structural position of the gatekeeper. Several authors have noted the importance of information as a power resource. Burns and Stalker (1961: 152), for example, point out that 'information may become an instrument for advancing, attacking or defending status'. French (1956), in his formalization of a theory of power, demonstrates that

---

[1] See also Pettigrew (1968) and Mumford and Ward (1968a).
[2] For an empirical example – operational researchers – see Pettigrew (1968).

the exercise of power is contingent upon communication connections. In four out of five cases, he finds congruence between the power and communication structures. Speaking of information control in decision-making situations, McCleery (1960: 51) states: 'Decisions reflect the interests that are communicated most effectively on the administrative level at which decisions are made.' Stinchcombe (1968: 151) is equally emphatic: 'The communication structure is the administrative apparatus of the system of power.'

Clearly, demands have to be communicated. They do not flow randomly through a system. They have a directional force through the system, usually to the centre of power. If the researcher is interested in the structural paths along which demands flow he needs to be aware of:

– who communicates with whom, about what, and when
– the determinants of those relationships.

An important phenomenon in communication structures is the gatekeeper. Easton (1965: 137) suggests that gatekeepers are likely to be those who 'have the greatest number and variety of interpersonal and organizational contacts'. Their role contains the possibility not only of opening and closing communication channels but also of collecting and reformulating information. We shall argue that Kenny was such a gatekeeper. His strategic placement as the communications link between the technical specialists and the Michaels board, together with his degree of political access, constituted his greatest advantages. With control over the information flow in the decision process, he was able to focus attention successfully on his demands and, at the same time, to hinder others from generating support for theirs.

The data on power mobilization are presented and discussed under four main headings:

1. The technical gatekeeper: information as a power resource
2. Political access: extent of role set as a power resource
3. Assessed stature
4. The marketing strategies of the computer manufacturers.

THE TECHNICAL GATEKEEPER: INFORMATION AS A POWER RESOURCE

In their discussions of information flow among technical groups Allen (1966) and Allen and Cohen (1969) refer to organizational boundary impedance, that is, the tendency for information from outside sources to fail to reach areas of the organization where it might be effectively used. Their recommendation for dealing with such impedance is to find the organization's technical gatekeeper. Such a suggestion ignores the possibility that the gatekeeper may himself be a structural source of impedance. He may use the information junction on which he sits as a power resource to further his own interests.

Wilensky (1967) is well aware that structural problems of hierarchy, specialization, and centralization are major sources of distortion and blockage of intelligence: 'Insofar as the problem of control – coordinating specialists, getting work done, securing compliance – is solved by rewards of status, power and promotion, the problem of obtaining accurate, critical intelligence is intensified. For information is a resource that symbolizes status, enhances authority and shapes careers. In reporting at every level, hierarchy is conducive to concealment and misrepresentation' (pp. 42-3). Earlier discussions on the March and Simon theory of organizational decision-making highlighted an ill-developed conception of the organization as an information-processing system. It was held that these authors show too much concern with the individual as an information-processing system and not enough with the organization in these terms. Cyert and March (1963: 71) recognize the existence of biasing in decision-making but argue that it will be controlled by counter-biasing. Lowe and Shaw (1968: 314), in a study of managerial biasing, found: 'Sales budgeting forecasts were accepted which were suspected of inaccuracy, and on this limited evidence we tentatively conclude that bias was not eliminated fully.' They support their conclusion by attacking the 'unrealistic' experiment that Cyert and March quote in arguing that counter-biasing will be successful.

It might be suggested that, in the specialist–manager interface where the information passed is likely to be complex and uncertain, it will be especially difficult for managers either to identify bias or to deal with it by counter-biasing. March and Simon imply this when they discuss uncertainty absorption: 'The more complex the data that are perceived and the less adequate the organizational language, the closer to the source of information will the uncertainty absorption take place' (1958: 166). Downs (1967) has also noted a relationship between distortion and uncertainty. He finds that under uncertain conditions the range of values a set of variables may assume cannot be reduced below a significant size. The greater the uncertainty, the wider this range is, and the more latitude officials have in emphasizing one part of it without being proved wrong.

The potential to bias information is maximal in the gatekeeper role where the information passed is complex and uncertain. Kenny occupied such a role. It was a major factor in his ability to control the decisional outcome. Kenny was a gatekeeper along two communication channels: first, the channel between his technical subordinates and the Michaels board, and, second, that between the computer manufacturers and the Michaels board (see diagram):

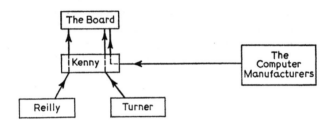

Since the computer manufacturers did not contact the Michaels board directly, but operated through Kenny, it would be useful to know the relative amount of correspondence Kenny had with each of them during the decision process. *Table 24* shows that, of the total correspondence Kenny received from and sent to computer manufacturers during 1966-8, 35·4 per cent was with Newton.

TABLE 24 *Amount of correspondence between Kenny and manufacturers:
during decision process*

Manufacturer	No. of items	% of items
Newton	29	35·4
NTL	22	26·8
BCD	15	18·3
Wilson Electric	9	11·0
American Electronics	6	7·3
Alpha	1	1·2

Although a relatively high percentage (26·8) of the correspondence was with NTL, much of this related to the NTL 200 that had been installed in Michaels in 1962 and does not concern the administrative office computer decision. NTL was eliminated fairly early on in the 1966-8 decision process and made only infrequent forays after that.

The finding that Kenny tended, in the period prior to the decision process, to correspond with the higher reaches of Newton and, in contrast, with the salesmen of the other manufacturers, is replicated for the 1966-8 period. *Table 25* shows that only a small proportion of the Newton correspondence was at salesman level, whereas most of his correspondence with all the other manufacturers was at this level. In the area manager column the positions are reversed: a high proportion of Newton communications are at this level, but there is relatively little contact with the managers of the other companies. The table shows further that Kenny's contacts with the Newton board were much fewer in the 1966-8 period compared with 1964-6. Presumably by this time Newton felt sufficiently sure of Kenny's support not to need regular contact with him at director level.

TABLE 25 *Correspondence between Kenny and manufacturers*
at three levels:
during decision process

Manufacturer	Salesmen	Manager	Director
	%	%	%
Newton	17·2	75·9	6·9
NTL	59·1	31·8	9·1
BCD	73·3	26·7	0
American Electronics	83·3	16·7	0
Alpha	100·0	0	0
Wilson Electric	100·0	0	0

While the different relationships Kenny had with the various computer manufacturers are an important factor in the decision process, more precise evidence of bias is likely to be found in how Kenny translated the inputs he received from the manufacturers and his subordinates into outputs for receipt by the Michaels board. An analysis was made of all available memos and technical reports sent by Kenny to the board during the 1966-8 period. A count was made of the number of times Kenny mentioned any of the manufacturers by name, and each manufacturer's proportion of the total number of mentions was calculated. The results are presented in *Table 26*. It will be seen that Kenny mentioned Newton's name to the board twice as many times as he did the name of any other manufacturer.

TABLE 26 *Manufacturers' names mentioned by Kenny in communications to the board: during decision process*

Manufacturer	No. of mentions	% of total
Newton	30	48·4
BCD	15	24·2
NTL	7	11·4
Wilson Electric	4	6·4
American Electronics	4	6·4
Alpha	2	3·2

Nearly half (48·4 per cent) of all Kenny's references to manufacturers' names were in fact to Newton. After Newton, BCD was mentioned most frequently, accounting for 24·2 per cent of all the occasions a name was given; Alpha was mentioned by name only twice. It is noteworthy that Wilson Electric, one of the two firms shortlisted in January 1967, and the manufacturer pushed hardest by the analysts between November 1966 and July 1967, was mentioned by name by Kenny only four times (representing 6·4 per cent of all the occasions a name was given).

More significant as evidence of self-interested informational biasing are the findings presented in *Table 27*. All the statements Kenny made about the manufacturers in his memos and technical reports to the Michaels board were content-analysed into positive, negative, and neutral categories, and percentages were calculated for each category by manufacturer. The inter-coder reliability score for the data was ·87. Again, the results clearly indicate the strength of Kenny's demand for Newton and his corresponding negative feelings towards the other computer suppliers. Of the statements Kenny made to the board about Newton, 71·4 per cent were positive, only 8·2 per cent were negative, and 20·4 per cent were neutral. With regard to three of the other manufacturers, the proportions of positive statements Kenny made were very low (under 15 per cent of the total); BCD was referred to slightly more favourably – 20 per cent of Kenny's comments about this company were positive. A substantially higher proportion (43 per cent) of Kenny's statements about Wilson Electric were positive. However, this last finding, together with the relatively low proportion (28·5 per cent) of negative statements this company received, must be qualified by two factors. In the first place, Kenny made only seven statements to the board about Wilson Electric; and, second, all of these were made in one memo early in January 1967. Kenny never mentioned Wilson Electric to the board in the period January – July 1967 when the analysts were putting in strong demands for that supplier. The reason for Kenny's rather low level of activity at that time will be considered when we look at the issue of assessed stature. The other main finding shown in *Table 27* is the consistently high level of negative comments Kenny fed to the board when discussing the other four manufacturers.

TABLE 27 *Analysis of Kenny's statements about the manufacturers in communications to the board: during decision process*

Manufacturer	Positive statements	Negative statements	Neutral statements
	%	%	%
Newton	71·4	8·2	20·4
Wilson Electric	43·0	28·5	28·5
BCD	20·0	52·0	28·0
American Electronics	14·3	71·4	14·3
NTL	9·9	63·6	26·5
Alpha	0	100·0	0

The final evidence concerning Kenny's effective use of his gate-keeping role is presented in *Table 28*. The content analysis of his statements was combined with a time-series analysis for two of the manufacturers. Of the six manufacturers, only Newton and BCD received consideration from the Management Services department throughout the whole period of the decision process. Kenny's negative and positive statements about these two manufacturers were therefore coded into three time periods with a view to obtaining evidence of any trend of feeling that Kenny might have communicated to the board about them. Time period 1 extended from December 1966 to August 1967; time period 2 was from September to December 1967; and time period 3 was from January to March 1968. The evidence is plain. *Table 28* shows that there was an increase, over the three time periods, in the proportion of positive comments Kenny made to the board about Newton – from 60 per cent, to 73·3 per cent, to 75 per cent, respectively. There was a corresponding decline, over the three periods, in the proportion of negative comments he made – from 20 per cent, to 6·7 per cent, to 4·2 per cent, respectively. The opposite trend was found in Kenny's reporting of his attitudes towards BCD. Over the three time periods, the proportion of positive statements he made about this company declined from 50 per cent, to 12·5 per cent, to zero, while the proportion of negative comments rose from 33·3 per cent, to 50 per cent, to 100 per cent. (The statements not included in these two sets of figures were in the neutral category.)

TABLE 28 *Analysis of Kenny's statements about Newton and BCD in communications to the board: at three time periods during decision process*

	Time period 1		Time period 2		Time period 3	
	Positive statements	Negative statements	Positive statements	Negative statements	Positive statements	Negative statements
	%	%	%	%	%	%
Newton	60·0	20·0	73·3	6·7	75·0	4·2
BCD	50·0	33·3	12·5	50·0	0	100·0

All these data illustrate how Kenny used the advantages of his gatekeeping role to feed data to the Michaels power centre that were advantageous to his own interests and disadvantageous to those of his opponents. McCleery (1960: 54) has noted that the gatekeeping position of the custodial force in a prison, between the warden and specialist service units, afforded the custodial people similar advantages. Its control over communication permitted the custodial force to adapt the efforts of other institutional units to the support of its own function and status. However, as Stinchcombe (1968) has suggested, an analysis of power relations cannot stop at highlighting the communications structure; placement in the communications structure needs to be linked to other forms of political access.

R

It has been shown that Kenny had almost complete control over the Management Services department's written contacts with the Michaels board and that he turned this to good account. In fact, the analysts sent only one report to the board between September 1966 and April 1968, and by then they were recommending Newton hardware. The programming manager, Turner, wrote a short memo in November 1967 pointing out the advantages and disadvantages of BCD hardware. This was tacked onto a more detailed report prepared by Kenny recommending Newton. Kenny certainly monopolized the written communication channels with the board.

McCleery also raised the issue of other forms of political access: 'Each superior reinforced his position in the hierarchy with a wider range of movement and wider access to personal contacts than that enjoyed by his subordinates. Status in both the official and the inmate communities was closely related to freedom of movement' (1960: 55). In the following section it is hoped to show how Kenny's communication advantages were compounded by advantages derived from the extent of his role set.

POLITICAL ACCESS: EXTENT OF ROLE SET AS A POWER RESOURCE

The general argument has been made that generating support for a demand is conditional on the structure and nature of an individual's direct and indirect interpersonal relationships. Not all relationships will be uniformly advantageous to an individual. For a variety of reasons certain people may want to help a particular individual seeking support more than others. It may be a matter of a marriage of convenience based on a commonality of interests. As well as being alert to common interests, the support-seeker must be sensitive to the relative power of the people he endeavours to attract. An accurate perception of the power distribution in the social arena in which he lives is therefore a necessary prerequisite for the man seeking powerful support for his demands. Along with a reasoned perception must come effective action. Bailey (1969: 108) makes this point well: 'Knowledge is power. The man who correctly understands how a particular structure works can prevent it from working or make it work differently with much less effort than a man who does not know these things. This may seem obvious yet actions are often taken without previous analysis and out of ignorance.'

Neither accurate perception nor careful action will do the power aspirant much good unless he has political access. The aim of this section is to indicate the relative power of the Michaels directors and then to discuss the relationships that Kenny, Reilly, and Turner had with individual board members prior to and during the decision process.

Perceptions of the Relative Power of the Board Members

I asked Kenny, Reilly, and Turner how they would rank the directors involved in the 1966-8 decision. There was consensus in their replies. Kenny said:

> 'Unless you could win over Brewster you were wasting your time. . . . Hall, I hardly regard him as a director. He doesn't carry a lot of weight. I talk with him very easily, "For Christ's sake what are you talking about, Chris", things like that. Both Taylor and Hall are directors, but Taylor is regarded as senior of the two.'

Reilly said:

> 'Brian Michael, and then the managing director [Brewster]. In terms of their commitment to computers, obviously Taylor and Hall. We're responsible to the managing director; we must influence him. Of Taylor and Hall, in general terms I'd put Taylor before Hall, but on specific jobs it may be one or the other.'

Turner's comment was:

> 'Brewster's obviously first, then Taylor, and finally Hall. Bill would put these two the other way round. All Hall ever does is agree with Brewster. Taylor is the so-called computer expert among the directors.'

It is significant that none of the three men mentioned the deputy chairman in his list. The deputy chairman played a part in the decision process after May 1967 when Kenny was made responsible to him instead of to Brewster. Although his name appears above Brewster's in the company letter-heading, in effective power terms he probably lies below Brewster but above Taylor and Hall. In lists of directors' names on memos sent from Kenny to the board, and in the minutes of a meeting prepared by Hall, the deputy chairman is given a place below Brewster but above Taylor and Hall. It is noticeable that Hall places himself below Taylor. Of the ten memos or reports sent by Kenny to the board during the decision process.

Taylor is placed above Hall in eight. In the company letter-heading Taylor's name appears above Hall's. From these various sources one might conclude that the board 'pecking order' is:

1. Brewster
2. The deputy chairman
3. Taylor
4. Hall.

Given that this list reflects the relative power of the board members, the next question is: 'What access do Kenny, Reilly, and Turner have to each of them?'

I asked Kenny about his relations with the directors as a group. He replied:

'Nobody has any relations with the directors in this company as a group. My relations with individuals differ enormously. With Brewster they are highly formalized. He can't have used my Christian name on more than two or three occasions. With Taylor they are also highly formal, but friendlier. We do at least have chats. With the deputy chairman they're much closer and have been for many years. We meet in each other's homes for dinner; there is quite a bit of contact socially.'

At the point I said to Kenny: 'What about Hall?' He replied:

'Oh, Chris! I hardly regard him as a director. He doesn't carry a lot of weight.'

I asked Reilly the more general question: 'What resources does Jim Kenny possess?' He answered:

'He's highly thought of by the deputy chairman. He's liked by a lot of people in the company ... He has his golfing relationship with Mills. He's liked by Brewster but not respected. The deputy chairman invites him out to dinner.'

Reilly said of his own relationships in the company:

'On every job you make new friends. I can go into the local pub anytime and meet somebody I know. I probably know more people in the company than Jim does, but I don't know the important people as well as he does.'

I asked Turner if he had any contact with the directors:

'I sometimes see Hall, but only rarely if he has to pop into Bill's office. I tend to see Taylor along with [the company statistician]. He's quite helpful. He tends to clamp down on the stock-control people because of what we say.'

In an attempt to back up the interview data with an 'objective' measure of the frequency of contacts Kenny, Reilly, and Turner had at various levels of the company, I asked them to keep diaries for a week. Each was given a precoded form with spaces for written and telephone communications both to and from themselves, and for face-to-face interactions. Unfortunately, I have misplaced Turner's forms, so a comparison can be made only between Kenny and Reilly. And at the last moment Kenny announced that he would be out of his office for one day of the chosen week, therefore he and Reilly are compared for four days only. The results are presented in *Table 29.*

TABLE 29 *Written, telephone, and face-to-face interactions of Kenny and Reilly with various others:*
over a four-day period during decision process

	Out-siders	Directors	Senior manage-ment	Manage-ment	M S dept managers	M S dept staff
	%	%	%	%	%	%
Kenny	20·0	10·7	21·3	36·0	8·0	4·0
Reilly	6·6	10·2	5·0	21·7	10·7	45·8

All interactions – written, telephone, and face-to-face – were totalled, and percentages were calculated for six categories representing contacts at different levels. The data show that, overall, Kenny has more contacts than Reilly with outsiders, Michaels directors, senior management, and management, and fewer contacts than Reilly with Management Services department managers and staff. At director level there is only 0·5 per cent difference in Kenny's favour. However, whereas Kenny had separate contacts with three of the more powerful directors, Brewster, Mills, and Taylor, all Reilly's interactions at this level were with, by general consensus, the weakest board member, Hall. In addition to noting that over half of Kenny's interactions were at senior management and management levels compared with under 30 per cent of Reilly's, it should be noted that a substantial proportion (45·8 per cent) of Reilly's interactions were with his own Systems department.

The general conclusion that may be drawn from our analysis of interview material, documents, and diaries is that Kenny's system of relationships is both more extensive and more power-laden than that either of his subordinates. Clearly, on this dimension Kenny was in a much better position to mobilize power for his demands. As we shall see, Kenny's power over his subordinates was not just a product of his wide contacts in the company.

Kenny's Excess of Power Resources

Kenny's position of dominance over Reilly was due to some extent to Reilly's inadequate relationships with his own staff. Ray Ashton said of Reilly:

> 'He has few social contacts in the department. We've been out to dinner with him and his wife once, and I think the only time he's been out with Jim was about ten years ago.'

Kenny indicated that some of Reilly's analysts preferred him to Reilly. Moreover, these analysts supplied him with information about Reilly's section:

> 'There are camps in the Systems department, mine and Bill's. Bill only has one kind of relationship with his staff. I've a wide range of contacts with them, a lot of cross relationships in a lot of different roles. Some of these contacts have come from being chairman of the company Welfare Club. All these contacts mean I've got a wide knowledge of the department. I get a lot of feedback from them.'

I asked Kenny to be more specific:

> 'Well, Colin Coles for example – my season ticket is next to his. Jimmy Archer – again it's football. And Roger Ivens – we have these common interests. Roger Ivens and Paul Mason have also had a lot to do with the pantomimes for the Welfare Club.'

The split in Reilly's section that Kenny mentioned was real enough. When I arrived to start the research I found it extremely difficult to get to know people in the 'footballer' side of the office.[1]

[1] Originally, the analysts had all been together in one office. However, the 'intellectuals' complained to Reilly that they could not do any serious work because of the endless chatter of the 'footballers' about sport. Reilly agreed to having the office split in two.

The two sections rarely met at the social level. It was clear that the 'intellectuals' had all the prestigious work in the department. Kenny's comment was:

> 'The split in Bill's department was no accident. He did it. Guys are given projects because of their attitudes.'

Kenny also felt rather more secure than Reilly because his career was not tied to Michaels; he had many outside contacts in a variety of business settings:

> 'I don't live here as an introverted isolate. I have an outside base. I don't have to rely on Michaels for my career.'

I asked Kenny if he thought that either of his two subordinates had any resources that they might use against him:

> 'Neil had two or three years ago [the interview was in 1969]. I was very dependent on his technical expertise. Losing him would have been a near disaster. Neil's always had considerable knowledge . . . On hardware certainly Neil is a much better adviser than Bill. Bill knows nothing about hardware in a deeply technical sense. He had nothing to do with the 200 or 350 decisions.
>
> I know Bill won't leave, therefore he's no resources at all. I doubt if he's ever had any. . . . I've told him to his face he won't leave. Consequently he's made these desperate attempts to improve his status . . . at certain times some of his staff thought that a palace revolution was possible. I doubt if anybody would think this now.'

Clearly, when the decision process started in 1966, Turner was the only member of Kenny's staff that Kenny felt dependent on. Turner still had the programmers' detailed technical expertise. Kenny had to go to him for this. As we shall see, during the decision process the coalitions Kenny and Turner formed helped to preserve both their positions from the aspiring analysts.

Political Access during the Decision Process

Kenny controlled the formal face-to-face interactions with the Michaels board as completely as he did the written communications. During the decision process he effectively gated out his two technical subordinates.

Table 30 shows who was present from the Management Services department at the board meetings that took place in connection with the administrative office computer decision in the period July 1966 to March 1968. It will be seen that Kenny attended all twelve of the meetings, while Reilly was present at only one and Turner at two. Moreover, Reilly and Turner did not attend meetings when Brewster, the managing director and by general consensus the key figure on the board, was present.

TABLE 30 *Attendance of Kenny, Reilly, and Turner*
at board meetings:
during decision process

Year	Month	Board members present	Mgt services staff present
1966	July	Brewster	Kenny
1967	5 Jan.	Brewster, Taylor, Hall	Kenny
	9 Jan.	Taylor, Hall	Kenny, Reilly, Turner
	June	Taylor, Hall, Nixon	Kenny
	20 Sept.	Brewster	Kenny
	4 Oct.	Brewster, Deputy chairman, Taylor, Hall	Kenny
	22 Nov.	Deputy chairman	Kenny, Turner
	7 Dec.	Brewster, Deputy chairman, Taylor, Hall	Kenny
1968	30 Jan.	Brewster, Taylor, Hall	Kenny
	2 Feb.	Brian Michael, Brewster	Kenny
	6 Feb.	Brewster, Deputy chairman	Kenny
	1 Mar.	Brewster, Deputy chairman, Thomas	Kenny

Being starved of political access in this way was a great source of annoyance and frustration to the analysts. Reilly commented after the meeting of 5 January:

'I was furious, and still am, about not being invited to the meeting. I've been involved with these proposals and the project for two years now. Kenny has only been concerned with them for the last three months. I knew that if the directors moved away from a rigid discussion of the proposal as it was set out on paper, Kenny would be lost.'

Not only were they helpless to put forward their own demands, but they were never sure what the directors said in the meetings. They certainly did not trust Kenny's interpretations of what had been said. I had asked Ashton what he thought was the most critical factor in the decision:

'Something which Jim told the management that we never found out about. We've got snippets of evidence to suggest that what Brewster told him is slightly different from what he tells us. This is particularly so over CRT. Jim always maintains that the CRT idea came from the board. The obvious thing for him to have said when CRTs were introduced was that they were uneconomic, but no, he was all for them. In the summer of 1967 he said to me: "I bet you £1 what we install has CRTs." '

Later, when Reilly was describing what happened in the decision process, he remarked:

'At this point Brewster said, or at least Jim said Brewster said, "Go CRTs". We'll never know whether Jim implanted this idea or not. It was claimed at the time that Brewster got the idea of CRT from watching a TV programme. In the privacy of his office Brewster might have made some faintly positive gesture in favour of CRT. This was enough for Jim.

As far as document readers were concerned, Brewster said that he didn't like all those noughts and crosses – but I'm doubtful if he ever did say this.'

The analysts had, of course, argued consistently against CRTs and in favour of document readers.

Reilly's response to Kenny's behaviour was to try to generate informal support at board level for his demands:

'While he [Jim] talks about freedom he never invites us to any meetings with the directors. Most of the contact I've had with Hall on the administrative office job I've generated myself.

Organizationally this is wrong. Jim resents the bypassing that goes on.'

Reilly tried unsuccessfully to use Hall to gain admittance to the board meeting in September 1967:

'After the January affair I was determined to get into the board meeting this time. Before I went on holiday I phoned up Hall and asked him if he thought there was going to be a meeting in the period I was on holiday. Hall said he didn't know but if I wanted to find out I had to phone him up sometime while I was on holiday.'

Kenny was aware of the clandestine meetings between Reilly and Hall. Reilly said that on one occasion, when Hall was in his office, Kenny was seen to walk past his room. Reilly had made to invite Kenny in, but Hall said, "We don't need him in here, do we?" I asked Kenny if Reilly had any contacts at board level:

'Bill went out of his way to see Chris [Hall] a lot. He really went out of his way. This was another example of his naïveté about political forces. As far as I was concerned he could sleep with Chris if he liked; it wouldn't count. Therefore I just let him get on with it. Chris doesn't like to come to me. He knocks diffidently at my door like a junior member of my staff. He feels he can go to Bill more easily. Bill sold him Wilson Electric.'

Ashton, Reilly's assistant, had this to say about the Hall–Reilly relationship:

'Bill's relationship with Hall is largely a result of Hall's inadequate contacts with Jim. Hall thinks Jim flannels him – talks down to him. Initially the contact started from Hall but now [1968] it's reciprocal. Hall is a fairly slippery customer to use – he is not a strong, sure person. He talks about the other directors as "them".'

Kenny saw no threat in Hall's meeting Reilly. He knew the former was not a powerful figure in Michaels. However, when in the midst of Reilly's demands for Wilson Electric, Reilly met the deputy chairman, Kenny acted very quickly:

'Bill has made an important political mistake recently. He has always seen me as an important barrier between himself and the directors. However, one day he met the deputy chairman in the lift, and the deputy chairman said to him, "Come and see me sometime". Bill told me this and I said, "Take no notice". The deputy chairman has sudden enthusiasms and then forgets all about them.

However, one day when I was away, Bill rang the deputy chairman and asked if he could see him. They had a long discussion, agreed things, and made plans. Later, when I returned and found out about this, I saw the deputy chairman and belted him, asking him what he was doing talking to my subordinates in my absence. He was appropriately apologetic. Bill now feels that I let him walk into this situation and then belted him about it, but I warned him in advance about letting the situation develop.'

Kenny then went on to say that Reilly was still pressuring him to make him his deputy.

Coalitions in the Management Services Department

The combination of Reilly's political mistakes and Kenny's extensive contacts and political skills meant that the systems manager had little success in mobilizing powerful support for his demands. Reilly also lost out within the Management Services department. As it became apparent that his demands for Wilson Electric would be unsuccessful, his erstwhile supporters in his own department turned against him.

On 15 May 1967, Ashton came to me and asked if we could meet in the pub after work:

'I've been having a terrible time with Bill these last few weeks. I'm fed up with his high-mindedness and rigid supervision. When a situation develops where there are two choices and it doesn't matter which one we take, Reilly always appears to go against us. We [Ashton and the other analysts] are getting really fed up with this.'

I asked Ashton why he thought Bill was so demanding:

'It's the corresponding pressure that's been put on him by Kenny. He's also looking for a way out with Wilson Electric. Bill's a Michaels man. He argues that almost anything is justified if it's for Michaels.... Bill's changed his whole attitude recently. A few months ago, faced with the situation we're in at the moment, where it looked as if Newton was about to get the contract on very dubious grounds, Bill would have gone all out for Wilson Electric and tried to force a decision on logical grounds. Now he's more concerned with not losing rather than winning. He thinks he's only got a great deal to lose in fighting for a lost cause.'

A more telling factor that weakened Reilly's position and strengthened Kenny's was the coalition the latter made with Turner during the decision process. Ignoring for the moment the fact that Kenny, Reilly, and Turner exist in a wider structure of relationships, they can be seen as a triad. If 1966 is taken as the base-line, the actual distribution of power between the three men can be represented, from the evidence set out in Chapter 7, in the following way:

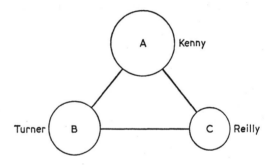

This situation, where A has greatest power but could be overthrown by a coalition of BC, has been re-created many times in the laboratory. Experiments by Mills (1953) and Caplow (1968) have repeatedly confirmed Simmel's (1950) generalization about the structural instability of triads. The pattern is to have a pair of combatants and an uncommitted witness to whom each appeals for support. Given the above power distributions in the laboratory, Caplow (1968: vi) has noted that 'coalitions of two weaker subjects against a stronger occur with predictable regularity'. However, he continues: 'In organized social activity, the tendency of the weak to combine against the strong is discouraged by various devices.'

In the organizational sphere, a major constraint on subordinates forming a revolutionary coalition is the superior's relations with, and therefore possible support from, another power base. It is difficult in an organization to imagine a completely isolated triad. A further limiting factor on a revolutionary coalition may be a conflict of interest between the two subordinates. Both these conditions existed in the Michaels case. Kenny appeared to have strong links with an outside power base – the directors – and there was a history of conflict between the analysts and programmers. In this sort of situation, argues Caplow (1968: 50), the instability within the triad will be dealt with through the formation of a conservative coalition AB. This is exactly what happened in the computer decision. It has been demonstrated that Turner, at various times, supported Kenny against Wilson Electric hardware and the Wilson Electric reader, in favour of teletypes, CRTs, and Newton.

Turner did come out in favour of BCD at the end of 1967, but, as Reilly said, Turner did it in an 'oblique way' and it was not a serious personal challenge to Kenny. I asked Turner why he and Bill did not combine on issues:

> 'That assumes that both people want to overcome the person at the apex. There's no drive to do this by me in particular. Bill has a go . . . Bill never had a chance with Wilson Electric. When he realized this he pestered me to make a challenge for BCD. My attitude was, if you're doing a job of the size the directors were considering, then you had to look at BCD. . . . I'm quite certain that if Jim thought I would go to the directors and say "You must go BCD" he would back down. He gambled that I would not go above his head.'

I asked Turner why he did not do this:

> 'It wasn't that important to me, or the company. Any advantages that there were for BCD were purely technical. They couldn't be measured on purely capital returns to the company. After all, this was a decision about the allocation of capital resources. It wasn't up to me.'

In sum, on the dimension of political access, Kenny's position was again far superior to that of either of his two subordinates. During the decision process he almost monopolized the formal contact his department had at board level, and at the same time he managed either to redirect or to prevent any power-related contacts that the aspiring Reilly attempted to make. Finally, while Reilly's energies were being wasted in cultivating a relationship with Hall, the weakest board member, Kenny and Turner were finding identities of interest on issues critical to the decisional outcome.

ASSESSED STATURE

It has been argued that the ability of a manager of a specialist group to persuade and negotiate successfully is very much a function of his assessed stature. High assessed stature is a form of power. In this section it is hoped to demonstrate how Kenny's assessed stature complicated the exercise of his power during the decision process.

That Kenny's assessed stature with the board was critical to both his own and his department's ability to make an impact seems clear enough. Reilly commented:

> 'The success of this department depends to a great extent on the reputation the department has among the directors. Since Kenny is the only person who really has any contacts with the directors, it's up to him. He's responsible for creating the right sort of reputation and image.'

The problem for the person in Kenny's position is to straddle the culture gap between his executive superiors and his technical subordinates. Several authors have noted the problems of the middle or marginal man. Dalton (1959: 248), for example, has observed: 'He must reconcile the complex outlooks and compromising techniques of his superiors with the relatively direct and uncompromising approaches of his juniors.' Kaplan (1959: 30) describes the situation thus: 'The scientific administrator is constantly caught in the crossfire between the demands of the organization as he sees them and the demands of scientists as they are transmitted in complaints, bickering and low morale.'

I asked Kenny what was the most important aspect of his work:

> 'I suppose it's being the interface between the technologists and management. There's an enormous communications gap between them. It's not a role which has to be interpreted, there are few precedents to help, you're creating patterns yourself. . . . The emotional conflicts are enormous. Considerable emotional stability is required. I am in a curiously privileged position yet I feel completely exposed. Endeavouring to change the outlook of the company has meant adopting a revolutionary role. This means you can't count on your subordinates going along with you. They endanger their jobs if they join in with my revolutionary behaviour.'

Like the scientists in the Kaplan (1959) and Glaser (1963) studies,

Reilly and Turner had a low opinion of their superior. They expressed their feelings in a number of normative themes.[1] Throughout the decision process, Reilly, in particular, referred to these themes in an attempt to discredit his superior's demands. According to the normative themes Kenny was:

- self-interested: he was more interested in his own future than in the department's future
- technically ill equipped to perform his role
- poor at dealing with the Michaels board.

I asked Reilly and Turner how they would describe the ideal head of Management Services. Reilly said:

'He has to be manager, but not in the heavy-handed sense; the accepted leader; a policy-maker. He has to have a good technical background and be able to communicate with others in the department. Above all he must be able to convince top management of the contribution the department can make. This is where Jim's greatest weakness lies. . . . He's not a very good manager, he's scared to take executive decisions. He makes ifs and buts all over the place. Witness my position and arguments with him about the research. He's limited technically; he's never gone through the grinding business of adding up the details to make a system.'

Turner's answer was:

'First, he should be respected by top management and able to convince them what he wants to do. Second, he should be able to get advice from the people who work for him and should have enough knowledge to be critical of it. Third, he should be a very good administrative manager.'

I asked Turner how Jim matched up to this ideal:

'There's one thing he does well, he can talk. He's a poor administrative manager and he doesn't know enough about the subject he's dealing with. He can come out with the buzz words though.'

The following are Reilly's and Turner's responses to the question: 'How has Jim's power varied over the years?' Reilly said:

'He had pretensions to being a director up until about two years

[1] See Bailey (1969: 104) for an extended discussion of normative themes.

ago [i.e. 1966]. He's now abandoned them.[1] His assessment of his prospects hasn't matched up to those he had when he came here. There are a whole host of reasons why this should have happened. The management have become severely disillusioned. The critical factors have been that in the management's view he doesn't accomplish things. All of the management came up the hard way. They've lived with the detail. Jim can't talk to them. They can thrash him every time.'

Turner remarked:

'His power has varied a great deal from time to time. It depends on how he's getting on with the top people what his status is in the company generally. The general impression is that they recognize he's a good talker and respect his opinion but think of him as an egghead. They're continually worried about this – Jim sailing off on a new toy. Brewster has told him, "The trouble with you is you're not a businessman." '

Reilly and Turner thus both acknowledged that Kenny's assessed stature with the board was critical to the amount and exercise of his power. Turner was also able to identify the incidents during the 1966-8 decision process which, for a time at least, lowered Kenny's stature and complicated his attempts to generate support for his demands.

The incidents related to the period January–July 1967 and involved Kenny's responsibility for bringing in consultants whose performance turned out to be less than adequate. In that period the analysts made their most assertive demands for Wilson Electric hardware and reading machines. As we have seen, Kenny's position at the time was not helped by Newton's inability to deal with the input problem. The analysts were well aware of Kenny's low position with the board. This may have been the reason why they were pushing so hard. In an interview on 3 January 1967, Ashton pointed out Kenny's weak position and gave reasons for it:

'Jim's position in the company is pretty weak at the moment. A bill's just arrived from the SWIFT people for £4500. This is for producing a typed report of seventy pages indicating very little that we didn't know already. Michaels are questioning this bill and, as Jim Kenny was responsible for bringing them in, he may have some rather awkward questions to answer.

[1] Kenny has acknowledged this to me.

Kenny's also brought some consultants in to do some programming. They're far behind schedule; there's even the possibility they may not get the job done. The company appears to be breaking up because of some internal squabbles between the directors. There's a feeling that Jim may get into trouble about this as well.'

He did! On 10 March Kenny indicated his concern for his position:

'Brewster could say I'm costing the company a lot of money. This could inihibit computer developments.'

At the beginning of April, Kenny was called to see Brewster:

'He said we're too academic. We devise model schemes but don't put any into operation. I tried to convince him that we implemented everything we were allowed to.'

Two weeks later Brewster used a memo to express his concern about the programming job:

'I must continue to contend that we are held up because we cannot get programming completed and would suggest that we have got into a frame of mind because the present work which we are programming has turned out to be of marathon duration.'

Bailey (1969: 60) has noted the importance of the relationship between timing and what he calls political credit. The person seeking to mobilize power must be careful to make his assertions at a time when he has the resources to enforce his will. Kenny was aware of this. I asked him to describe the strategy he used to deal with the directors:

'It depends on the situation. The crucial factor is "Where does the power lie?" For a long time it was Mr Brewster.[1] Unless you could win over Brewster you were wasting your time. The deputy chairman is an easy friend to cultivate; you can convince him of anything. With Brewster your case had to be thought out, completely buttoned up, otherwise it meant disaster. . . . It's a matter of understanding their approach, their attitudes, and working out the necessary action. You've got to ask yourself, "What am I trying to get out of this situation?" You then say, "What's the best thing I can hope for?", and go for that. . . . The most difficult aspect is determining at what stage one pursues an issue. This

[1] This interview was in 1969. Brewster retired as managing director the year after the administrative office computer decision was taken.

S

isn't just a matter of retreating into your expertise but of the kinds of tactic you play.'

The tactic that Kenny played between January and September 1967, when his stature was low, was to keep out of the directors' way. The reader will recall that there was only one board meeting in that period. This was arranged after the directors had complained that Kenny was not keeping them informed of developments on the administrative office job. Just before the important September meeting Reilly and Turner had this to say about Kenny's behaviour:

> 'The impending meeting with the directors has been built into a summit conference. What should have been happening over the last few months is frequent consultations with the directors to keep them up to date with the latest situation. Jim Kenny's just about to dive off the top board without any idea if there's any water below. If he'd had frequent contacts with the board he could have known the temperature of the water, he would have known whether to put his hand in bare or gloved – now he's likely to get scalded.'

In fact, he did not. Kenny was a better all-weather sailor than his subordinates thought. He was wise enough to sit in port while the storm was raging against him. The man with low stature does not make demands on the system that threatens him.

The data reported in this section indicate that while information control, political access, and extent of role set are all important factors enabling a person to mobilize support for his demands, they need to be considered in the context of the person's assessed stature in the social arena in which he lives. This finding appears to corroborate Bucher's (1970: 33) recent suggestion 'that the extensiveness of a role set is a necessary but not sufficient condition for power, and that assessed stature is the more critical variable'. I feel that I have done little more than hint at the use of assessed stature as an explanatory variable. It would seem to be a concept highly relevant to any further studies of power relations involving executives and specialists. In particular, it offers a way of conceptualizing changes in a specialist's power over time.[1]

---

[1] See Pettigrew (1972c) for further theoretical discussion of the concept of assessed stature.

THE MARKETING STRATEGIES OF THE COMPUTER MANUFACTURERS

The preceding analysis of power mobilization in the Michaels computer decision has relied almost entirely on intra-firm behaviour. It would be unrealistic, however, to suggest that the marketing strategies of the computer manufacturers had no impact on the decisional outcome. Relative political access and relative knowledge of the Michaels social structure were just as critical to the manufacturers' attempts to generate support for their demands as they were to Kenny, Reilly, and Turner.

It is clear that the manufacturers had differential access to the Michaels power structure. It is also evident that they had differential knowledge of its operation. These were key factors. In terms of their knowledge of the Michaels power structure, the gap between Newton and BCD, on the one hand, and Wilson Electric, on the other, was enormous. The Wilson Electric people appeared to be completely insensitive to the power-related forces that were obviously structuring the decisional outcome. After the decision had been made, I interviewed the BCD and Wilson Electric salesmen. The extent of the difference between their sales approaches can be gauged from the answer each gave to the question: 'What strategy did you use on the Michaels job?'

The Wilson Electric approach was phrased entirely in technical language:

'We considered the system and what it needed in terms of hardware and what our opposition were likely to be quoting. Really it was a systems-oriented job. We knew BCD were weak at the low end in cost performance and this influenced the sort of machine we quoted, and the price. Our basic approach was to design the system as cheaply as possible. We used our document reader because we had it and the others didn't.'

The BCD answer was phrased entirely in terms of intra-firm strategy:

'We never thought we'd win over Kenny so we worked hard on the technical people and at the same time fed Kenny information and attempted not to put a foot wrong. We had Kenny round here a few times but you could tell he was just going through the motions. He wasn't really listening to us. Maddams made all the contacts; he had good relations with Neil. They would meet frequently in the "Cat and Fiddle" for a half-pint. On the basis that Reilly was somebody you could convince over a short period, we worked on him in a short burst near the end.'

The Wilson Electric salesman later acknowledged the naïveté of his company's strategy:

'A lot of our approach was just straightforward, because in price performance terms we were clearly out on our own to such an extent that all we had to do was tell them. We thought this would be enough. Technical excellence and an advanced product we thought was enough. It says a lot about our naïveté about selling.'

I asked him if he had sized up the power structure in Michaels:

'No, not at all, although we would now. We did that job with blinkers on. We went for technical problems, the ones we could understand. If I'd gone into the situation now, I would have come to the conclusion that it wasn't worth bothering about. We neglected politics. The trouble is these things are so difficult to disentangle.'

Assuming that the man who correctly understands how a particular structure works can most effectively use it to his advantage, I asked the two salesmen a further question about the social structure in Michaels: 'Whose advice would you say Kenny valued most?' The Wilson Electric salesman replied:

'I got the impression that Bill was slightly senior mainly because of the way he used to talk to Neil. If Neil didn't turn up for a meeting Bill would get him on the phone and say, "Where the hell are you? There's a meeting on" – or words to that effect. Back at the end of 1965 when we called on Kenny he only asked one man in – Turner. If I had to give a yes–no answer, I'd say he paid more attention to Bill.'

The BCD salesman commented:

'I think Kenny trusted Neil more because Bill and Kenny didn't like one another.'

The BCD man was correct. When I asked Kenny about his two subordinates he replied:

'On hardware certainly Neil is a much better adviser than Bill. Bill knows nothing about hardware in a deeply technical sense.

He had nothing to do with the 200 or 350 decisions.'

BCD and Wilson Electric shared one major problem – how to gain access to powerful figures in Michaels. BCD was the more successful of the two, but it could not compete with the insuperable advantages held, in this respect, by Newton.

The Wilson Electric people spent most of their time with Ashton and Reilly. Their salesman commented:

'I never dealt with Michaels above the Bill Reilly level, with the exception of a few contacts with Kenny. It was very much an arms-length contact. We never got close to Kenny. Looking back now our whole relations were thoroughly unhealthy because they were so much at arms length. I was pretty raw at handling an account of that size.'

I asked: 'Were your visits with any special individuals?'

'Most certainly. With Bill. Neil couldn't have been present on more than one in five of our visits. We were friendly with Neil as well as Bill, but Kenny had them under his thumb. They protested, but it didn't really affect the issue.'

BCD had a long-term policy of working on Turner. This was partly a result of the outcome of the 1964 decision, when Kenny used Newton to topple Ramsbottom and BCD. The BCD salesman recalled:

'There was a big power struggle between Kenny and Ramsbottom. Kenny won it by doing a switch on Ramsbottom. The fact that BCD came out of it badly was just unfortunate.'

This experience drove BCD towards Neil:

'Neil always appeared to be the technical wizard. Based on this we kept up a long-term policy of always supplying Neil with the data on what we had to offer on the basis that, next time round, we would technically be in a good position. We certainly got the technical backing of Neil on this last thing.'

The technical backing of Neil Turner was not enough. BCD needed contacts at board level. With Kenny in between, this was very difficult:

'We didn't contact any of the directors. Kenny made it apparent he didn't like it. There was no good contacting them anyway unless you had something very specific they were likely to be interested in.'

When they found out that they had not been shortlisted, the general strategy adopted by the BCD people was:

'... to ignore the machine and concentrate on the software and the peripherals, plus the "people who'd done it before" seminar for the Michaels board.'

This seminar, arranged in November 1967, was the specific device BCD used to gain access to the Michaels directors. It will be recalled that Hall was the only director to turn up, and I asked the BCD salesman why, in his opinion, this had happened:

'Because we played it through Kenny. He agreed that we could approach only the deputy chairman and Hall. The idea was that the BCD men from Europe and America would talk about computer objectives and not just machines and how they were used. Kenny liked this because he wanted these objectives pursued in Michaels. We contacted Brewster after the Newton decision had been made in April 1968. He wrote back to say that Mr Kenny had considered all the facts and that he could see no point in a meeting. We pointed out that a decision of this magnitude couldn't be made on emotional grounds.'

If BCD had difficulty in reaching the Michaels board, Wilson Electric could not even arrange meetings between its senior management and Kenny. The Wilson Electric salesman has already described his relationship with Kenny 'as taking place at arms length'. In fact, in June 1967, Kenny agreed to such a meeting, but only under pressure from Reilly, and in order to tell Wilson Electric that they were wasting their time:

'I have agreed to meet Wilson Electric because of Bill's persuasion. I shall say to them: "You must understand the realities of the situation. There is every reason why we should buy Newton. Therefore, you must show us overwhelming advantages." The reality is, however, that no one will say, "Newton is a heap of junk. We never want to have a machine like that again." '

Wilson Electric was still writing to Kenny in January 1968. By that time, however, Kenny was passing the company's letters over to Reilly with pencilled comments such as: 'Is there much point in following this up?' 'The problem arises as to whether we should go through with this visit.'

Both Wilson Electric and BCD pursued Kenny relentlessly. An indication of the strength of their pursuit can be seen in the change in their passion ratios from 1964-6 to 1966-8. The passion ratio, as explained in the previous chapter, was a measure of the reciprocity of the relationships between Kenny and the various manufacturers, calculated on the basis of the correspondence Kenny received from, and sent to, each computer supplier. The higher the ratio of correspondence in to out, the greater the strength of the suitor's desire as compared with the maiden's response. *Table 31* shows the passion ratios for BCD, Wilson Electric, and Newton for the 1964-6 and 1966-8 periods. It is clear that, both before and during the decision process, Kenny received more letters from Newton than from either of the other companies, but he also sent more letters to Newton. BCD and Wilson Electric, on the other hand, were strong, but frustrated, suitors during the decision process: they made many advances but received very few responses in kind. In both time periods, then, the Kenny–Newton relationship was more balanced and stable.

TABLE 31 *Passion ratios: Kenny and three manufacturers: 1964–6 and 1966–8 compared*

	Correspondence 1964–6		Passion ratio in : out	Correspondence 1966–8		Passion ratio in : out
BCD	In	14	2·3 : 1	In	13	6·5 : 1
	Out	6		Out	2	
Wilson Electric	In	11	1·1 : 1	In	7	3·5 : 1
	Out	10		Out	2	
Newton	In	35	1·7 : 1	In	19	1·9 : 1
	Out	20		Out	10	

Letter-writing was not the only means by which BCD pursued Kenny. Kenny described, at the end of March 1968, the tremendous efforts the company was still making to try to persuade Michaels to buy BCD instead of Newton:

'I received a phone call from Mike Curran, area manager, who was in Majorca at the time. When I went to London two weeks ago I was met at the Euston barrier by a BCD representative. BCD have also phoned me up at home. They have tried to get me to see Barlow, their assistant general manager.'

Wilson Electric and BCD were helped in their efforts by the out-of-work chats they had with Reilly and Turner. The Wilson Electric salesman said:

'Bill Reilly let more out of the bag than he should have done. Bill used to tell me how well Kenny got on with Newton. I got on very well with Bill and he used to tell me that Jim was up to some of his usual tricks again. You don't often get on those terms with a manager.'

The BCD man commented:

'We had a lot of feedback from the technical people. We had known Bill and Neil for well over seven years. Neil was the main feedback, but Bill was as well to some extent. There was no sneaky chat. Relations had been built up over a number of years. It was just a matter of having an open chat over a beer.'

No amount of information feedback could retrieve the situation for BCD and Wilson Electric. Without the support of Kenny and access to key members of the Michaels board, there was little hope that their demands would be met. Fetter, the Newton area director, was asked what he thought of the sales strategies of his two competitors in the tendering process:

'Wilson Electric were mistaken in their sales approach. They should have realized that they couldn't get the Michaels contract and withdrawn from the situation. I would have done this if I'd been in their position. This is what BCD did. They didn't fight for the main hardware contract but instead offered to supply any peripheral equipment that was required. . . . Wilson Electric had to focus on Reilly because Kenny had clearly indicated he wasn't interested. . . . It wasn't possible for Wilson Electric to go above Kenny to the directors because they would merely refer the salesman back to Kenny.'[1]

The Newton salesman, Sam Allison, had three main advantages:

[1] Brewster did this when BCD contacted him in March and April 1968.

1. Kenny was committed to buying Newton before the decision process started.

2. Newton had access to an important member of the Michaels board.

3. From September 1967 until the decision was made, Allison was virtually a full-time member of the Management Services department staff. He used his close contact with Neil to good effect.

Allison described his strategy like this:

> 'We'd won the first battle before Michaels even asked us to work out a set of proposals for the job. Jim Kenny was closely identified with Newton.
>
> We felt sure of Kenny, so this left us with Neil and Bill to win over to make sure we got the order. Everybody in Newton knew that Neil was technically a very good man; in fact, when I first met him I was rather frightened of him for this reason. Knowing that Wilson Electric at that time had nothing very spectacular to offer in software and support, the proper approach to make towards Neil was an "honest Joe" one. We knew Neil would quickly see through anything that Wilson Electric had to offer, and so all I had to do was to be as honest as I could with Neil. I knew that just by telling him the truth we could still be much better than Wilson Electric.'

Allison's account is so close to the feelings expressed earlier by Neil that it sounds very much like an after-the-fact rationalization. Neil did not trust the Wilson Electric pronouncements on software. He said himself that that was why he rejected them. The Wilson Electric salesman later admitted that he could not get across to Neil:

> 'We only saw Neil when we discussed software, and that wasn't very often. He used to ask odd questions. We never felt we struck up any rapport with him – well, anyway, not the sort of rapport that Sam Allison did. In programming, as you know, the languages can be very specialized. The jargon he used was Newton jargon. We never really got over this problem. Neil seemed to be less interested than Bill. He didn't turn up for meetings and things like that.'

Of his contacts with Reilly, Allison said:

> 'We knew that all Wilson Electric had to offer was data prepara-
> tion equipment – their reading machines – therefore, they had to
> concentrate their approach on the man interested in this area in
> Michaels, Reilly. We used a soft-sell approach with him. . . .
> Reilly did in fact become fantastically enthusiastic for Wilson
> Electric, but when he had waited long enough to test the Larco
> reader, he immediately became just as enthusiastic for this. This
> was quite in line with Bill's personality; he tends to be highly
> erratic and extreme.'

As soon as Neil expressed an interest in BCD, Allison hardly left
his side:

> 'I suppose you've noticed the close attention I've been giving
> Neil in the last few months. This lot around here don't appear to
> have noticed this. Amazing, isn't it? I've had to keep close tabs
> on Neil because of his friendship with the BCD salesmen. I know
> for a fact that Neil sees quite a lot of them and they may be
> talking about what we've been quoting. I've been trying to coun-
> teract this the best way I can.'

In fact, Allison's behaviour caused some embarrassment among the
programmers. A senior programmer remarked:

> 'It's been really embarrassing having Allison around so often.
> One afternoon when Neil was out I answered the phone seven
> times from the local BCD salespeople. Sam was there. He knew
> all this was going on. There was also an occasion a fortnight ago
> when the BCD salesman walked into the office to see Neil, and
> Sam Allison was there as well. Allison walked out of the room.'

The final advantage held by Newton was access to the Michaels
board. Allison refused to tell me who their contact was:

> 'The contact was made when Michaels bought the Newton 350.
> We've kept it going since then. This has meant that we've not
> been entirely dependent on Kenny. It's also meant that Kenny
> has felt more secure than he would have done, knowing we have
> contacts at the director level. Neil and Bill don't know anything
> about this.'

SUMMARY AND CONCLUSION

In earlier chapters it has been argued that the theoretically most developed analyses of organizational decision-making yet proposed, those of March and Simon (1958) and Cyert and March (1963), are lacking in certain respects. The main criticism of March and Simon's model concerned their attempt to impose a theory of individual decision-making on the firm and call it a theory of organizational decision-making. In terms of the present interest in innovative decision-making, the approach of Cyert and March seemed a more valuable one. Their conception of organizational decision-making as a political process raised many interesting questions. It also left many unanswered. The Cyert and March theory lacked depth of presentation, particularly with regard to the determinants of conflict in the decision process. Little attention was given to the role of power, and there was little discussion of the generation of support and of how the structure of the organization might limit such a process.

This analysis has tried to complement the Cyert and March theory by dealing with the issue of power mobilization in the context of an innovative decision process. The view held is that an adequate theory of organizational decision-making should assume that decisions are made not by individuals or by role occupants, but via processes that are affected by properties of the unit or units in which the decision is to be made. Decision-making in organizations is not merely a thought process that balances goals and means, or a choice process in which the environment is discriminated as a limit to choice only through the mind of the decision-maker. Rather, it may be understood as a political process that balances various power vectors.

I have argued that the processes of demand generation and power mobilization are essential to any theory of the politics of organizational decision-making. Decisional outcomes evolve out of the processes of power mobilization attempted by each party in support of its demand. This analysis has tried to show that generating support for a demand is very much a matter of strategy and structure. Perception constitutes the crucial link between strategy and structure. Strategies are formulated on the basis of perceptions. Accuracy here is critical. Those who correctly understand how a structure operates are in a much better position to make it work to their advantage. Political sensitivity, however, is not enough. There is the issue of access. Individuals are differentially located in the organization's structure. This means that not all potential supporters are approachable. Perception and structural location may give strategies their impetus; equally they may act as constraints on political behaviour.

Demands are generated and processed in the context of social structures in which individuals are differentially located and have, by implication, access to varying amounts of the resources that are the bases of power. A demand is politically feasible only if sufficient power can be mobilized and committed in its support. This involves, on the one hand, negotiating with the organization's power centre and undermining an opponent's support, and, on the other hand, modifying the demand until its power requirement can be assembled.

I have tried to show that where a demand is voiced, who articulates it, who hears it, and how widely it is diffused are all crucial determinants of the way in which it is received and processed. In particular, attention has been focused on the structural position of the technical gatekeeper, in order to demonstrate the advantages this position gives him when he is seeking support for his demands. Control over information was a critical resource used by Kenny for mobilizing power. Because he sat at the junction of the communication channels between his subordinates, the manufacturers, and the board, Kenny was able to exert biases in favour of his own demands and at the same time feed the board negative information about the demands of his opponents.

This strategy could not have brought success on its own. Kenny was also able to control the face-to-face interactions of his subordinates and the computer salesmen, and he virtually dominated face-to-face interactions with the board. A further critical variable for Kenny was his assessed stature. His control over the information flow in the decision process, his more extensive role set, and his easier access to the locus of power in Michaels have to be considered in relation to how he was thought of by key members of the board. His ability to negotiate and persuade in face-to-face interactions rested on his assessed stature with the Michaels board.

CHAPTER 10

Conclusion

The Social Sciences have tended to neglect the way the limits
and flows of time intersect the persistent and changeful qualities
of human enterprises for reasons that are only partly clear. It is
approximately accurate to say that the dominance of static
models in social analysis has resulted in scant attention to the
temporal order of social life.

Wilbert E. Moore (1963: v)

The focus of this study has been social process. The concern has
been to show the elaboration of social structure over time. This
change process has been explored in terms of the varying degrees
and intensities of association and dissociation between certain
groups and individuals over time. As Blau (1964: 336) has suggested, interdependencies involve both reciprocity and imbalance.
Incompatible requirements in social structures lead to recurrent
reorganizations.

The theoretical questions raised have been expressed in the
language of social conflict, power, and decision-making. Specific
questions have involved tracing out the sources of the emergence
and decline of contending groups. Changes in the level of hostility
between the disparate groups have been a point of focus, as have the
reasons for those hostilities. Attention was given to the forms of
social action, intended and unintended, that contributed to the
attainment, maintenance, and dissolution of power. The preceding
analysis also dealt with the implications of those power changes for
the distribution of status between the conflicting parties. Finally,
the analysis has explored the nature of the 'political' in the context
of an innovative decision process. This was attempted by raising
theoretical issues associated with the generation of demands and
the mobilization of power. The overall aim has been to link the

political processes in the innovative decision to the preceding
analysis of social change. The emphasis has been on the organization
as an ongoing system with a past, a present, and a future. This view
has implied that sound theory must take into account the history and
the future of a system and relate them to the present.

Such theoretical concerns have required a particular methodological approach. It is the nature of the phenomena under investigation,
together with the objectives of the study, that must determine what
approaches are taken, and what materials are gathered by what
methods. As Scott (1965: 284) has suggested, there should be some
measure of association between problem definition, study design,
kinds of data gathered, and investigator role. There are two principal ways of studying social processes: sustained participation in the
field over time, and some form of historical investigation. Both
methods were used here.

Again, the various theoretical issues raised by the conception
presented of decision-making as a political process have required a
detailed immersion in a particular social context. While power is an
ever-present phenomenon in organizations, people are often loath to
discuss its use. The researcher has to build up stable, trustful
relationships with the people in his field-setting before they will
discuss their perceptions and/or their participation in political
processes. In an important sense, the theory dictates sustained
researcher participation. If the goal is to map out over time the
power resources possessed and controlled by the various participants
in a decision process, together with the ways in which they use those
resources in either furthering their own interests or weakening the
interests of others, some sort of observational research would seem
necessary.

Scott (1965), in his chapter on field methods in the *Handbook of
Organizations*, has endorsed this line of argument: 'Another
difference which may mark the manner in which research problems
are defined is the extent to which the investigator is concerned with
changes over time in the phenomena explained. In general, if the
system under examination is relatively small and change is considered an important element of the study design, sustained participation by the researcher will be the more satisfactory approach.'
On the question of models of social process he observes: 'To the
extent that the models developed focus on social processes, the most

important contribution of field research in the future may be the collection of detailed descriptive information' (1965: 269).

It has not been the aim of this research to provide the reader with detailed descriptive information about particular events in Brian Michaels. Rather, the purpose of the study has been to use Michaels as a setting in which to examine ideas about the processual aspects of specialization, conflict, power, and innovative decision-making. Nevertheless, when research is carried out in a single organization, there is the issue of the potential generality of the findings.

Fortunately, generality is something over which the researcher has a certain amount of control. As Erikson (1966: vii) has so crisply stated: 'Human events themselves are neither general nor particular until some student arranges them to fit the logic of his own approach.' The present research has used a variety of mechanisms in an attempt to create the conditions for, and stress, the general quality of the findings. First, the study has a strong theoretical content. Second, there has been a careful interaction of theory and data during the data-gathering and data-analysis phases of the research. Third, the findings have been reported in such a way that they can be discussed and evaluated along with research in similar fields. Fourth, not only has pre-existing theory been used to explain the rudiments of the Michaels setting, but an attempt has been made to develop a general theoretical approach that can be applied in other studies of social process. My sustained participation in the research setting added greatly, I consider, to my chances of developing, as distinct from solely verifying, theoretical insights. A continual process of interaction of theory and data was possible, and multiple methods could be employed with the aim of improving the validity of the findings and the reliability of the conclusions. Finally, the preceding analysis has utilized a form of the comparative method.

Webb *et al.* (1966: 5), in their discussion of research methodology, remark that 'the goal of the social scientist is always to achieve interpretable comparisons'. Lipset *et al.* (1956: 426) and Mouzelis (1967: 68) suggest that this can be done by examining relations between variables through time. Lipset has used historical data to test the relationship between high occupational stratification and intense political cleavage. In the present study, time-based data were used to explore the relationship between extent of interdependence and level of perceived hostility between two occupational groups. The anthropologist Harris (1968: 530) holds that, through the historical perspective, 'there emerges a conception of how the parts of sociocultural systems relate to each other in general and specific terms, for we observe the phenomena of parallel and convergent development and note how the changes in one part are regularly succeeded by changes in another'. Here it was possible to explore the impact of a changing technology on the emergence of the specialties of programming and systems analysis, and eventually to examine how changes in their relative power had consequences for their relative status.

Scott (1965: 269) has questioned the convenient dichotomy between hypothesis-testing and exploratory studies. When one is faced with characterizing a given piece of research, the distinction seems to lose a great deal of its theoretical crispness: 'Most field researchers "explore" and "test" concurrently, and one is often hard put to determine where one activity leaves off and another begins.' He goes on: 'More importantly, as organization theory develops, the researcher should be less and less inclined to think in terms of one or more hypotheses guiding his inquiry and begin to work with theoretical models which generate numerous implications, each of which becomes a proposition guiding field observations.'

The present research began with a conception of *homo sociologicus* which had important implications both for the model of organizations put forward and for the theoretical questions asked of innovative decisions. Unlike the conception of man presented by Parsons (1964) and Merton (1957a), this view of the individual does not assume that he is constrained either by a coherent and consistent normative system or by immovable social structural forces. As Kapferer (1969b: 228) rightly suggests, Merton's (1957a) treatment of structure and function 'runs the risk of viewing structure as something which exists above the individual, determining his behaviour and lying beyond his control'. The focus here is on man faced with only an imperfectly conceived and partially communicated range of acceptable or expected behaviours: 'In place of being a mere medium for the operation of determining factors that play upon him, the human being is seen as an active organism in his own right, facing, dealing with, and acting toward the objects he indicates' (Blumer, 1969: 236).

Such a view of man implies neither a preoccupation with personal idiosyncrasies nor an end to structural analysis. Rather, the emphasis is on man operating the variability and ambiguity in the social arena of his action; on man constrained but purposeful; on man shaped by situational constraints, prior expectations, and historical experiences of past interaction, but also differentially interpreting those forces often in self-interested terms.

This recognition of variability in social structure opens the door to a strategic conception of behaviour. As Van Velsen (1967: 142) observes: 'The norms of society do not constitute a consistent and coherent whole; they are vague and discrepant. It is this fact which allows for their manipulation by members of a society in furthering their own aims, without necessarily impairing its apparently enduring structure of social relationships.' This use of the word strategy does not imply rational choice-making. Strategies are bounded by structural, informational, and perceptual factors. Strategic behaviour is limited by the constraints of access imposed by man's location in a social structure. Structure acts as a source of both opportunity and constraint.

A great deal of the argument in this work has relied upon the proposition that poorly institutionalized social systems are likely to facilitate power-related conflicts. The two examples of poorly institutionalized social systems discussed were the social conditions surrounding the emergence of the specialties of programming and systems analysis, and the innovative decision process. According to Eisenstadt (1965: 40) 'The institutionalization of any social system means that certain norms, sanctions, and organizations which regulate the access to different positions and establish certain norms of exchange are set up and that policies through which these norms can be upheld and applied to a relatively large and complex variety of social situations are implemented.' Eistentadt's theoretical approach has a processual form: "Any institutionalization necessarily entails efforts to maintain the boundaries of the system, through continuous attempts to mobilize resources from different groups and individuals and to maintain the legitimacy of its values, symbols and norms. But continuous implementation of these policies may affect the positions of different groups in the society and give rise to continuous shifts in the balance of power among them . . .' (1965: 42). The contradictions and conflicts that arise during this process of institutionalization are also partly founded on each system's relations with its environments: 'Each institutional system is especially sensitive, in terms of dependence on resources and

T

maintenance of its own boundaries, to certain aspects of its relations
to its environment' (1965: 43).

My conceptualization of specialization as an emergent process
complements the work of Wilensky and Lebeaux (1965) and Strauss
et al. (1964) on, respectively, the social work and psychiatric professions. Moreover, both the present work and the above two studies
provide a useful emphasis on intra-specialist relationships when the
dominant focus of the literature is currently the specialist–manager
interface.[1]

The social arena in which the Michaels programmers and analysts
interacted was regarded as poorly institutionalized in the sense that
there was no clear-cut set of mutually acceptable expectations about
how the duties should be allocated between the two groups. Each
group had vague and often discrepant beliefs about how the task
environment should be shared. Conflicts developed over their
different perceptions of the reality of their interdependence. Much
of this conflict was expressed in attitudinal and value differences.
There was also the issue of power. As the technological environment
in which they operated changed, so the distribution of power
resources between the two groups altered. Ultimately their relative
status changed with the shifts in the balance of power. Neither
party remained completely content with the initial task interdependence or chose to remain inert as its technological resource
base altered. It was shown that the programmers attempted to use
various power-maintenance strategies to protect themselves against
the acquisitive strategies of the analysts.

While both Wilensky and Lebeaux (1965) and Strauss *et al.* (1964)
discuss the emergent qualities of specialist groups, neither study is
able to demonstrate clearly either how the level of hostility between
such groups increases over time with the degree of their interdependence, or how the strategic behaviour of the groups affects the nature
of their task environment over time. The literature on power is also
striking for the absence of an attempt to show the instability and
imbalance in power relations. In a recent book, Perrow (1970: 67)
describes the gap in the organizational power literature as a failure
to take into account 'the ability of those who once gain power to
manipulate the source of uncertainty, at least over a span of, say,

[1] For example, Burns and Stalker (1961), Box and Cotgrove (1966), Dutton
and Walton (1966), Pelz and Andrews (1966), and Lynton (1969).

ten to fifteen years'. The present analysis has attempted to deal in part with that deficiency in the literature.

This research has tried to put forward a conception of decision-making as a political process. Many of the theoretical insights are contextually bound in the sense that they are most applicable to large-scale innovative decisions and, in particular, to those involving a decision unit composed of an executive leadership system and a differentiated innovating system. This is not a severe limitation. The interface between executives and specialists would seem to be a general problem.

Innovative decisions were seen to be a special source of political behaviour in the sense that the dynamics of their process and their outcomes had an impact on the organization's distribution of resources. Following Burns (1961), political behaviour was defined as behaviour by individuals, or, in collective terms, by sub-units, within an organization that makes a claim against the resource-sharing system of the organization. The kinds of resources up for redistribution may vary from situation to situation. They may be salaries, promotion opportunities, capital expenditure, new equipment, or control over people, information, or new areas of a business.

This view of resource allocation does not assume a zero-sum conception of power. Nor is it assumed that when an innovative decision brings about an increase in the size of the resource cake held by a differentiated group of specialists, one group must necessarily gain all the new resources and the other groups none. The power of all can be increased. Allocation, however, remains a critical problem, for the existing distribution of power is always an important factor in determining who will gain a disproportionate share of new resources as these become available. Consideration was therefore given in this study both to the pattern of distribution of power prior to the 1966-8 computer decision and to the dynamics of its use during the decision.

While the view of innovative decision-making presented here has emphasized the political behaviour that such decisions are likely to release, I have suggested that the general form of my theoretical argument may add to existing conceptualizations of organizational decision-making. On several occasions I have indicated the partial nature of the March and Simon (1958) and Cyert and March (1963) theories. Complementing their approach has involved an attempt to link the strategies of the various interested parties to a particular decisional outcome. I have sought to do this by tracing out, first, the generation of demands and, second, the mobilization of power in the decision process.

It was hypothesized that the more complex and differentiated a political structure is, the more likely are disparate demands to be made. Such disparities were a product of organizational position, professional training, and adherence to subgroup values and reference groups. Further critical factors discussed included the history of social relationships, likes, dislikes, and organizational attachments of those involved in the demand-generating process, and the level of uncertainty surrounding the decision. This uncertainty was a product of a complex political structure, a technically complex set of problems, the dynamic nature of the technical environment in which the decision was being made, and the selective intervention of external forces.

Both the March and Simon (1958) and Cyert and March (1963) conceptions of organizational decision-making are weak on conflict and power; though the former is more so than the latter. The earlier appraisal of the Cyert and March theory concluded that, while the authors' approach savoured of political realism, it lacked depth of presentation on several important dimensions. In particular, the authors ignore role and communication structures, give little attention to the impact of external affiliations on organizational behaviour, and do not discuss the organizational structure of the firm or, therefore, the membership of the bargaining subgroups in the coalition. Finally, although Cyert and March use the language of political science when they talk of demand and support, they do not attempt to develop the use of these concepts in their theory. In particular, they offer a sparse presentation of the processual aspects of demand generation, and give no consideration to the forms of strategic behaviour used in mobilizing support for a demand, or to how the organizational structure might limit such a process.

The analysis of power mobilization in Chapter 9 was an attempt to deal with some of those deficiencies. It tried to show that generating support for a demand is very much a matter of strategy and structure. Perception seemed to be the crucial link between strategy and structure. Those who accurately understand how a structure operates are in a much better position to make it work to their advantage than those who do not. However, it is of little consequence to use a variety of normative themes to threaten the basis in terms of which powerful men present themselves to others, if the position one occupies in the organization's structure limits one's contact with those relevant others. Political access is clearly a fundamental factor in any theory of power mobilization.

One of the most important features of structural location highlighted in this study was the role of the technical gatekeeper. Control over information was a critical resource used by Kenny for mobilizing power for his demands. Because he sat at the junction of the communication channels between his subordinates, the manufacturers, and the board, he was able to exert biases in favour of his own demands and at the same time feed the board negative information about the demands of his opponents.

A further critical variable influencing the decision process was Kenny's assessed stature. The analysis in Chapter 9 tried to show that while information control, political access, and extent of role set are all important factors enabling a person to mobilize support for his demands, they need to be considered in the context of the person's assessed stature in the social arena in which he lives. This finding would seem to be particularly applicable to the specialist, placed as he is in a rather ambiguous authority position within the organization. Assessed stature is a concept that has general applicability in discussions of power relations involving executives and specialists. In particular, it offers a way of conceptualizing variability in a specialist's credibility over time.

It is hoped that this research has been able to demonstrate the value to social scientists of analysing man's behaviour over time. This has been a neglected strategy. A major consequence is that many theories lack processual development. However, it is impossible to construct and test theories of social process unless the researcher has a longitudinal research design. In many fields this entails the use of multiple methods for studying ongoing processes and historical methods for delving into the past. Only then will it be a realistic goal to analyse, as Moore (1963: v) has suggested, how 'the limits and flows of time intersect the persistent and changeful qualities of human enterprises'.

References

ALLEN, T. J. (1965). Problem Solving Strategies in Parallel Research and Development Projects. *Working Paper No. 126-65.* Cambridge, Mass.: Sloan School, MIT. June.

ALLEN, T. J. (1966). The Differential Performance of Information Channels in the Transfer of Technology. *Working Paper No. 196-66.* Cambridge, Mass.: Sloan School, MIT. June.

ALLEN, T. J. (1969). Meeting the Technical Information Needs of Research and Development Projects. *Working Paper No. 431-69.* Cambridge, Mass.: Sloan School, MIT. November.

ALLEN, T. J., and COHEN, S. I. (1969). Information Flow in Research and Development Laboratories. *Administrative Science Quarterly* **14**(1): 12-21.

ARGYRIS, C. (1962). *Interpersonal Competence and Organizational Effectiveness.* Homewood, Ill.: Irwin Dorsey.

ARGYRIS, C. (1965). *Organization and Innovation.* Homewood, Ill.: Irwin Dorsey.

ARGYRIS, C. (1968). Some Unintended Consequences of Rigorous Research. *Psychological Bulletin* **70**(3): 185-97.

BAILEY, F. G. (1969). *Stratagems and Spoils: A Social Anthropology of Politics.* Oxford: Blackwell.

BANKS, J. A., and BANKS, O. (1964). Feminism and Social Change: A Case Study of a Social Movement. In G. K. Zollschman and W. Hirsch (eds.), *Exploration in Social Change.* Boston: Houghton Mifflin.

BANNESTER, D. M. (1969). Socio-dynamics: An Integrating Theorem of Power, Authority, Interinfluence and Love. *American Sociological Review* **24**: 374-93.

BARNARD, C. I. (1938). *The Functions of the Executive.* Cambridge, Mass.: Harvard University Press.

BARNES, L. B. (1963). *Organizational Systems and Engineering Groups*. Cambridge, Mass.: Harvard University Press.

BASS, B. A. (1960). *Leadership, Psychology, and Organizational Behavior*. New York: Harper.

BECKER, H. S. (1958). Culture Case Study and Greek History. *American Sociological Review* **23**: 489-504.

BECKER, H. S. (1963). *Outsiders: Studies in the Sociology of Deviance*. New York: Free Press.

BECKER, H. S., and CARPER, J. W. (1956) The Development of Identification with an Occupation. *American Journal of Sociology* **61** (4): 289-98.

BERKHOFER, R. F. (1969). *A Behavioral Approach to Historical Analysis*. New York: Free Press.

BLAKE, R. R., SHEPARD, H. A., and MOUTON, J. S. (1964). *Managing Intergroup Conflict in Industry*. Houston, Texas: Gulf Publishing.

BLAU, P. M. (1955). *The Dynamics of Bureaucracy*. Chicago: University of Chicago Press.

BLAU, P. M. (1964). *Exchange and Power in Social Life*. New York: Wiley.

BLAU, P. M. (1967). The Research Process in the Study of 'The Dynamics of Bureaucracy'. In P. E. Hammond (ed.), *Sociologists at Work*. New York: Doubleday.

BLUMER, H. (1953). Psychological Importance of the Human Group. In M. Sherif and M. O. Wilson (eds.), *Group Relations at the Crossroads*. New York: Harper & Row, pp. 199-207

BLUMER, H. (1969). Sociological Implications of the Thought of George Herbert Mead. In W. L. Wallace (ed.), *Sociological Theory*. Chicago: Aldine.

BORING, E. G. (1963). *History, Psychology and Science*. New York: Wiley.

BOWDEN, B. (1970). The Language of Computers. *American Scientist* **58**: 43-53.

BOX, S., and COTGROVE, S. (1966). Scientific Identity, Occupational Selection and Role Strain. *British Journal of Sociology* **17**(2): 20-28.

BRAYBROOKE, D., and LINDBLOM, C. E. (1963). *A Strategy of Decision*. New York: Free Press.

BROWN, R. (1963). *Explanation in Social Science*. Chicago: Aldine.

BRUNER, J. S. (1957). On Perceptual Readiness. *Psychological Review* **22**: 123-52.

BRUNER, J. S., and POSTMAN, L. (1949). On the Perception of Incongruity: A Paradigm. *Journal of Personality* **18**: 206-23.

BUCHER, R. (1970). Social Process and Power in a Medical School. In M. N. Zald (ed.), *Power in Organizations.* Nashville, Tennessee: University of Vanderbilt Press.

BUCKLEY, W. (1967). *Sociology and Modern Systems Theory.* Englewood Cliffs, N.J.: Prentice-Hall.

BUDD, R. W., THORP, R. K., and DONOHEW, L. (1967). *Content Analysis of Communications.* London: Collier–Macmillan.

BUMSTEAD, D. C. (1969). Organisational Aspects of the Management of Industrial Research and Development. Unpublished M.A. thesis, University of Manchester.

BURNS, T. (1955). The Reference of Conduct in Small Groups: Cliques and Cabals in Occupational Milieux. *Human Relations* **8**: 467-86.

BURNS, T. (1961). Micropolitics: Mechanisms of Institutional Change. *Administrative Science Quarterly* **6**(3): 257-81.

BURNS, T. (1962). Ends and Means in Management: Internal Politics and Organizational Pathology. Mimeo, University of Edinburgh Social Sciences Research Centre.

BURNS, T. (1965). On the Plurality of Social Systems. In J. R. Lawrence (ed.), *Operational Research and the Social Sciences.* London: Tavistock.

BURNS, T., and STALKER, G. (1961). *The Management of Innovation.* London: Tavistock. Second edition, 1966.

CAHILL, R. S., and GOLDSTEIN, M. N. (1964). Notes on a Theory of Political Actualization: A Paradigm of the Political Process. In W. J. Gore and J. W. Dyson (eds.), *The Making of Decisions.* New York: Free Press.

CAMPBELL, D. T. (1969). Reforms as Experiments. *American Psychologist* **24**(4): 409-29.

CAMPBELL, D. T., and FISKE, D. W. (1959) Convergent and Discriminant Validation by the Multitrait – Multimethod Matrix. *Psychological Bulletin* **56**: 81-105.

CAMPBELL, D. T., and STANLEY, J. C. (1963). *Experimental and Quasi-experimental Designs for Research.* Chicago: Rand McNally.

CAPLOW, T. (1968). *Two against One: Coalitions in Triads.* Englewood Cliffs, N.J.: Prentice-Hall.

CHANDLER, A. D. (1962). *Strategy and Structure.* Cambridge, Mass.: MIT Press.

CHAPMAN, R. A. (1968). *Decision Making*. London: Routledge and Kegan Paul.

COCHRAN, T. C. *et al.* (1954). *The Social Sciences in Historical Study*. New York: Social Science Research Council, Bulletin 64.

COHEN, A. K. (1965). The Sociology of the Deviant Act: Anomie and Beyond. *American Sociological Review* **30**: 5-14.

COLEMAN, J. S. (1957). *Community Conflict*. Glencoe: Free Press.

COLLINS, B. E., and GUETZKOW, M. (1964). *A Social Psychology of Group Processes for Decision Making*. New York: Wiley.

Computer Bulletin (1967). The Education and Training of Systems Analysts. **11**(1): 11-19.

CONSTANTINE, L. L. (1968). The Programming Profession, Programming Theory, and Programming Education. *Computers and Automation*, pp. 14-19.

COOPER, W. W., HITCH, C., BAUMOL, W. J., SHUBIK, M., SCHELLING, T. C., VALAVANIS, S., and ELLSBERG, D. (1958). Economics and Operations Research: A Symposium. *Review of Economics and Statistics* **40**: 195-229.

COSER, L. A. (1956). *The Functions of Social Conflict*. London: Routledge and Kegan Paul.

COSER, L. A. (1964). The Termination of Conflict. In W. J. Gore and J. W. Dyson (eds.), *The Making of Decisions*. New York: Free Press.

COTTRELL, F. (1962). Social Groupings of Railroad Employees. In S. Nosow and W. H. Form (eds.), *Man, Work, and Society*. New York: Basic Books.

CROSS, J. E. (1969). *The Economics of Bargaining*. New York: Basic Books.

CROZIER, M. (1964). *The Bureaucratic Phenomenon*. Chicago: University of Chicago Press; London: Tavistock.

CYERT, R. M., and MARCH, J. G. (1963). *A Behavioral Theory of the Firm*. Engelwood Cliffs, N.J.: Prentice-Hall.

DAHL, R. A. (1957). The Concept of Power. *Behavioral Science* **2**: 201-18.

DAHL, R. A. (1961). *Who Governs?* New Haven, Conn.: Yale University Press.

DAHL, R. A. (1967). The Politics of Planning. In *Decisions and Decision Makers in the Modern State*. Paris: UNESCO.

DAHL, R. A. (1968). Power. In *International Encyclopedia of the Social Sciences*, Vol. 12, New York: Macmillan, pp. 405-15.

DALTON, M. (1950). Conflict between Staff and Line Managerial Officers. *American Sociological Review* 15: 342-51.

DALTON, M. (1959). *Men who Manage*. New York: Wiley.

DALTON, M. (1967). Preconceptions and Methods in Men who Manage. In P. E. Hammond (ed.), *Sociologists at Work*. New York: Doubleday.

DANTO, A. C. (1965). *Analytical Philosophy of History*. Cambridge: Cambridge University Press.

DEARBORN, D. C., and SIMON, H. A. (1958). Selective Perceptions: A Note on the Departmental Identification of Executives. *Sociometry* 21: 140-4.

DENZIN, NORMAN K. (1970). *The Research Act*. Chicago: Aldine.

DEPARTMENT OF EDUCATION AND SCIENCE (1967). *Computer Science*. London: HMSO.

DEPARTMENT OF EMPLOYMENT AND PRODUCTIVITY (1969). *The Training of Systems Analysts*. London: HMSO.

DEVONS, E. (1950). *Planning in Practice*. Cambridge: Cambridge University Press.

DILL, W. R. (1958). Environment as an Influence on Managerial Autonomy. *Administrative Science Quarterly* 2(4): 409-43.

DILL, W. R. (1962). Impact of Environment on Organizational Development. In S. Mailick and E. M. Van Ness (eds.), *Concepts and Issues in Administrative Behavior*. Englewood Cliffs, N.J.: Prentice-Hall.

DIMOCK, M. (1952). Expanding Jurisdiction: A Case Study in Bureaucratic Conflict. In R. K. Merton *et al.* (eds.), *Reader in Bureaucracy*. Glencoe, Ill.: Free Press, pp. 282-90.

DOWNS, A. (1967). *Inside Bureaucracy*. Boston: Little, Brown.

DUBNO, P. (1965). Leadership, Group Effectiveness and Speed of Decision. *Journal of Social Psychology* 65: 351-60.

DUNCAN, R. (1970). A Cybernetic-operant Model of Organizational Learning: An Exploration of how Organizations Learn to Adapt to the Uncertainty in their Environment. Unpublished paper, Yale University.

DUTTON, J. M., and WALTON, R. E. (1966). Interdepartmental Conflict and Cooperation: Two contrasting Studies. *Human Organization* 25(3): 207-20.

EASTON, D. A. (1965). *A Systems Analysis of Political Life*. New York: Wiley.

EDWARDS, W., and TVERSKY, A. (eds.) (1967). *Decision Making*. Harmondsworth: Penguin Books.

EISENTSTADT, S. N. (1965). *Essays in Comparative Institutions*. New York: Wiley.

EMERSON, R. M. (1962). Power–Dependence Relations. *American Sociological Review* 27: 31-41.

EPHRON, L. R. (1961). Group Conflict in Organizations: A Critical Appraisal of Recent Theories. *Berkeley Journal of Sociology* 6: 53-72.

ERIKSON, K. T. (1966). *Wayward Puritans: A Study in the Sociology of Deviance*. New York: Wiley.

EVAN, W. M. (1962). Role Strain and the Norm of Reciprocity in Research Organizations. *American Journal of Sociology* 68: 346-54.

EVAN, W. M. (1965). Superior–Subordinate Conflict in Research Organizations. *Administrative Science Quarterly* 10: 53-64.

FRENCH, DAVID H. (1962). Ambiguity and Irrelevancy in Factional Conflict. In M. Sherif (ed.), *Intergroup Relations and Leadership*. New York: Wiley.

FRENCH, J. R. P. (1956). A Formal Theory of Power. *Psychological Review* 63: 181-94.

FRISCHMUTH, D. S., and ALLEN, T. J. (1968). A Model for the Description and Evaluation of Technical Problem Solving. Working Paper. Cambridge, Mass.: Sloan School, MIT.

GAMSON, W. A. (1968). *Power and Discontent*. Homewood, Ill.: Dorsey.

GARFINKEL, H. (1967). *Studies in Ethnomethodology*. Englewood Cliffs, N.J.: Prentice-Hall.

GIBSON, Q. (1960). *The Logic of Social Enquiry*. London: Routledge and Kegan Paul.

GIDDENS, A. (1968). 'Power' in the Recent Writings of Talcott Parsons. *Sociology* 2(3): 257-72.

GLASER, B. G. (1963). Attraction, Autonomy, and Reciprocity in the Scientist–Supervisor Relationship. *Administrative Science Quarterly* 8: 379-98.

GLASER, B. G. (1964), *Organizational Scientists: Their Professional Careers*. Indianapolis: Bobbs Merrill.

GLASER, B. G. (1968). *Organizational Careers: A Sourcebook for Theory*. Chicago: Aldine.

GLASER, B. G., and STRAUSS, A. L. (1965). *Awareness of Dying.* Chicago: Aldine.

GLASER, B. G., and STRAUSS, A. L. (1967). *The Discovery of Grounded Theory: Strategies for Qualitative Research.* Chicago: Aldine.

GLUCKMAN, M. (1949). The Village Headman in British Central Africa. *Africa* **19**(2): 89-106.

GLUCKMAN, M. (1956). *Custom and Conflict in Africa.* Oxford: Blackwell.

GLUCKMAN, M. (1965). *Politics, Law and Ritual in Tribal Society.* Chicago: Aldine.

GOLD, R. L. (1958). Roles in Sociological Field Observations. *Social Forces* **36**: 217-23.

GOLDNER, F. H. (1961). Industrial Relations and the Organization of Management. Unpublished Ph.D. dissertation, University of California, Berkeley.

GOLDSTEIN, B., and FARLEE, C. (1970). The Hospital as a Negotiated Order. Paper presented at Eastern Sociological Association meeting, New York.

GOODE, W. J. (1960a). A Theory of Role Strain. *American Sociological Review* **25**: 483-96.

GOODE, W. J. (1960b). Encroachment, Charlatanism, and Emerging Professions: Psychology, Sociology, and Medicine. *American Sociological Review* **25**: 902-14.

GORDON, G., and BECKER, S. (1964). Changes in Medical Practice bring Shifts in the Patterns of Power. *The Modern Hospital* **102** (2).

GORE, W. J. (1956). Administrative Decision Making in Federal Field Offices. *Public Administration Review* **16**: 281-91.

GORE, W. J., and DYSON J. W. (1964). *The Making of Decisions.* New York: Free Press.

GORE, W. J., and SILANDER, F. S. (1959). A Bibliographic Essay on Decision Making. *Administrative Science Quarterly* **4**(1): 97-121.

GOULDNER, A. W. (1964). *Patterns of Industrial Bureaucracy.* New York: Free Press.

GOULDNER, A. W. (1965a). *Wildcat Strike.* New York: Harper.

GOULDNER, A. W. (1965b). Organizational Analysis. In R. K. Merton *et al.* (eds.), *Sociology Today: Problems and Prospects.* New York: Harper.

GROSS, N., MASON, W. S., and MCEACHERN, A. W. (1958). *Explorations in Role Analysis.* New York: Wiley.

HARRIS, M. (1968). *The Rise of Anthropological Theory: A History of Theories of Culture.* New York: Crowell.

HAWLEY, W. D., and WIRT, F. M. (eds.) (1968). *The Search for Community Power.* Englewood Cliffs, N.J.: Prentice-Hall.

HAYS, W. L. (1963). *Statistics for Psychologists.* New York: Holt, Rinehart, and Winston.

HERZBERG, F., MAUSNER, B., and SNYDERMAN, B. (1959). *The Motivation to Work.* New York: Wiley

HICKSON, D. J. (1966). A Convergence in Organization Theory. *Administrative Science Quarterly* 11: 224-37.

HILL, S. R. (1966). *The Distributive System.* Oxford: Pergamon Press.

HOLLANDER, E. P., and JULIAN, J. W. (1969). Contemporary Trends in the Analysis of Leadership Processes. *Psychological Bulletin* 71 (5): 387-97.

HOLTZMAN, W. H. (1963). Statistical Models for the Study of Change in the Single Case. In C. W. Harris (ed.), *Problems in Measuring Change.* Madison: University of Wisconsin Press.

HOMANS, G. C. (1949). The Strategy of Industrial Sociology. *American Journal of Sociology* 54: 330-39.

HOMANS, G. C. (1967). *The Nature of Social Science.* New York: Harbinger.

HORWITZ, M. (1964). Managing Hostility in the Laboratory and the Refinery. In R. L. Kahn and E. Boulding (eds.), *Power and Conflict in Organizations.* New York: Basic Books; London: Tavistock.

HOWER, R. M., and ORTH, C. D. (1963). *Managers and Scientists.* Cambridge, Mass.: Harvard University Press.

JOBLING, R. G. (1969). Some Sociological Aspects of University Development in England. *Sociological Review* 17(1): 11-26.

JULIAN, J. W., and HOLLANDER, E. P. (1966). A Study of Some Role Dimensions of Leader–Follower Relations. *Technical Report No. 3.* State University of New York at Buffalo.

KAHN, R. L. (1964). Field Studies of Power in Organizations. In R. L. Kahn and E. Boulding (eds.), *Power and Conflict in Organizations.* New York: Basic Books; London: Tavistock.

KAHN, R. L., and CANNELL, C. F. (1962). *The Dynamics of Interviewing: Theory, Technique and Case.* New York: Wiley.

KAHN, R. L., WOLFE, D. M., SNOEK, R. P., DIEDRICK, J., and ROSENTHAL, R. A. (1964). *Organizational Stress.* New York: Wiley.

KAPFERER, B. (1969a). Norms and the Manipulation of Relationships in Work Context. In J. C. Mitchell (Ed.), *Social Networks in Urban Situations*. Manchester: Manchester University Press.

KAPFERER, B. (1969b). Urban Africans at Work. Unpublished Ph.D. thesis, University of Manchester, Department of Social Anthropology.

KAPLAN, N. (1959). The Role of Research Administrator. *Administrative Science Quarterly* 4: 20-42.

KAPLAN, N. (1965). Professional Scientists in Industry. *Social Problems* 13(1).

KELMAN, H. C. (1968). *A Time to Speak: On Human Values and Social Research.* San Francisco: Jossey Bass.

KNIGHT, K. E. (1967). A Descriptive Model of the Intra-firm Innovation Process. *Journal of Business* 40(4): 478-96.

KORNHAUSER, W. (1962). *Scientists in Industry*. Berkeley: University of California Press.

KRUPP, S. (1961). *Patterns in Organizational Analysis*. Philadelphia: Clifton.

LANDSBERGER, H. A. (1961). The Horizontal Dimension in a Bureaucracy. *Administrative Science Quarterly* 6: 298-332.

LAWRENCE, P. R., and LORSCH, J. W. (1967). *Organization and Environment: Managing Differentiation and Integration.* Cambridge, Mass.: Harvard University Press.

LEHMAN, E. W. (1969). Toward a Macro Sociology of Power. *American Sociological Review* 34(4): 453-65.

LEWIN, K. (1951). *Field Theory in Social Science.* Edited by D. Cartwright. New York: Harper.

LINDBLOM, C. E. (1959). The Science of Muddling Through. *Public Administration Review* 19: 79-88.

LIPSET, S. M. (1968). History and Sociology: Some Methodological Considerations. In S. M. Lipset and R. Hofstadter (eds.), *Sociology and History: Methods.* New York: Basic Books.

LIPSET, S. M., TROW, M., and COLEMAN, J. (1956). *Union Democracy.* Glencoe, Ill.: Free Press.

LOASBY, B. J. (1968). The Decision-maker in the Organization. *Journal of Management Studies* 5(3): 352-64.

LOMBARD, G. F. (1955). *Behavior in a Selling Group.* Cambridge, Mass.: Harvard University Press.

LONG, N. E. (1958). The Local Community as an Ecology of Games. *American Journal of Sociology* 64(3): 251-61.

LONG, N. E. (1962). The Administrative Organization as a Political System. In S. Mailick and E. H. Van Ness (eds.), *Concepts and Issues in Administrative Behavior*. Englewood Cliffs, N.J.: Prentice-Hall.

LOWE, E. A., and SHAW, R. W. (1968). An Analysis of Managerial Biasing: Evidence from a Company's Budgeting Process. *Journal of Management Studies* 5(3): 304-15.

LOWIE, R. (1917). Oral Tradition and History. *Journal of American Folklore* 30: 161-7.

LUCE, R. D., and RAIFFA, H. (1957). *Games and Decisions*. New York: Wiley.

LUPTON, T. (1963). *On the Shop Floor*. Oxford: Pergamon.

LUPTON, T. (1966). *Management and the Social Sciences*. London: Lyon Grand and Green.

LYNTON, R. P. (1969). Linking an Innovative Subsystem into the System. *Administrative Science Quarterly* 14(3): 398-416.

MCCLEERY, R. (1960). Communication Patterns as Basis of Systems of Authority and Power. In *Theoretical Studies in Social Organization of the Prison*. New York: Social Science Research Council, Pamphlet 15.

MCIVER, R. M. (1964). *Social Causation*. New York: Harper & Row.

MCNEMAR, Q. (1963). *Psychological Statistics*. New York: Wiley.

MACK, R. W. (1954). Ecological Patterns in an Industrial Shop. *Social Forces* 32: 351-6.

MAILICK, S., and VAN NESS, E. H. (1962). *Concepts and Issues in Administrative Behavior*. Englewood Cliffs, N.J.: Prentice-Hall.

MALINOWSKI, B. (1944). *A Scientific Theory of Culture and Other Essays*. Chapel Hill: University of North Carolina Press.

MANN, F. C. (1968). The Computer Personnel. Unpublished paper given at a conference at Oberhausen, Germany.

MARCH, J. G. (1957). Measurement Concepts in the Theory of Influence. *Journal of Politics* 19: 202-6.

MARCH, J. G. (1962). The Business Firm as a Political Coalition. *Journal of Politics* 24: 662-78.

MARCH, J. G., and SIMON, H. A. (1958). *Organizations*. New York: Wiley.

MARSHALL, T. H. (1969). Reflections on Power. *Sociology* 3 (2): 141-55.

MARTIN, N. H., and STRAUSS, A. (1956). Patterns of Mobility within Industrial Organizations. *Journal of Business* 29(2): 101-10.

286 *The Politics of Organizational Decision-making*

MECHANIC. D. (1962). Sources of Power of Lower Participants in Complex Organizations. *Administrative Science Quarterly* **7**: 349-64.

MERTON, R. K. (1957a). *Social Theory and Social Structure*. Glencoe, Ill.: Free Press.

MERTON, R. K. (1957b). The Role-Set. *British Journal of Sociology* **8**: 106-20.

MICHELS, R. (1949). *Political Parties*. Glencoe, Ill.: Free Press.

MILLER, E. J. (1959). Technology, Territory, and Time: The Internal Differentiation of Complex Production Systems. *Human Relations* **12**: 243-72.

MILLER, E. J., and RICE, A. K. (1967). *Systems of Organization*. London: Tavistock.

MILLER, G. A. (1967). Professionals in Bureaucracy: Alienation among Industrial Scientists. *American Sociological Review* **32** (6): 755-68.

MILLER, S. M. (1969). The Participant Observer and 'Over-rapport'. In G. J. McCall and J. L. Simmons (eds.), *Issues in Participant Observation: A Text and Reader*. Reading, Mass.: Addison-Wesley.

MILLS, C. W. (1951). *White Collar*. New York: Oxford University Press.

MILLS, T. M. (1953). Power Relations in Three-person Groups. *American Sociological Review* **18**: 351-7.

MITCHELL, J. C. (1956). *The Yao Village*. Manchester: Manchester University Press.

MOORE, W. E. (1963). *Man, Time and Society*. New York: Wiley.

MOUZELIS, N. P. (1967). *Organization and Bureaucracy*. London: Routledge and Kegan Paul; Chicago: Aldine, 1968.

MUMFORD, E., and BANKS, O. (1967). *The Computer and the Clerk*. London: Routledge and Kegan Paul.

MUMFORD, E., and WARD, T. (1966). Computer Technologists: Dilemmas of a New Role. *Journal of Management Studies* **3**: 244-55.

MUMFORD, E., and WARD, T. (1968a). Computer People and their Impact. *New Society* **12**(313): 443-5.

MUMFORD, E., and WARD, T. (1968b). *Computers: Planning for People*. London: Batsford.

MYERS, C. (1967). *The Impact of Computers on Management*. Cambridge, Mass.: MIT Press.

MYERS, R. C. (1946). Interpersonal Relations in the Building Industry. *Applied Anthropology,* Spring.

MYERS, R. C. (1952). Myth and Status Systems in Industry. In R. K. Merton *et al.* (eds), *Reader in Bureaucracy.* Glencoe, Ill.: Free Press.

NADEL, S. F. (1957). *The Theory of Social Structure.* Glencoe, Ill.: Free Press; London: Cohen and West.

NICHOLAS, R. W. (1966). Segmentary Factional Political Systems. In M. J. Swartz, V. W. Turner, and A. Tuden (eds.), *Political Anthropology.* Chicago: Aldine.

NORTH, R. C., HOLSTI, O. R., ZANINOVICH, M. G., and ZINNES, D. A. (1963). *Content Analysis: A Handbook with Applications for the Study of International Crisis.* Chicago: Northwestern University Press.

OLESEN, V. L., and WHITTAKER, E. W. (1967). Role-making in Participant Observation: Processes in the Research–Actor Relationship. *Human Organization* 26(4): 273-81.

OLESEN, V. L., and WHITTAKER, E. W. (1968). *The Silent Dialogue: A Study in the Social Psychology of Professional Socialization.* San Francisco: Jossey Bass.

PARSONS, T. (1964). *The Social System.* New York: Free Press.

PARSONS, T. (1967). *Sociological Theory and Modern Society.* New York: Free Press.

PEABODY, R. L. (1964). *Organizational Authority.* New York: Atherton Press.

PELZ, DONALD C., and ANDREWS, FRANK M. (1966). *Scientists in Organizations: Productive Climates for R & D.* New York: Wiley.

PERROW, C. (1970). Departmental Power and Perspective in Industrial Firms. In M. N. Zald (ed.), *Power in Organizations.* Nashville, Tennessee: University of Vanderbilt Press.

PETTIGREW, A. M. (1967). The Outsiders. *Personnel and Training Management,* pp. 30-33, November.

PETTIGREW, A. M. (1968). Inter-group Conflict and Role Strain. *Journal of Management Studies* 5(2): 205-18.

PETTIGREW, A. M. (1972a). Managing under Stress. *Management Today,* April.

PETTIGREW, A. M. (1972b). Information Control as a Power Resource. *Sociology* 6(2): 187-204.

PETTIGREW, A. M. (1972c). Stress and Power in the Internal

U

288   *The Politics of Organizational Decision-making*

Consultant–Client Relationship. Paper presented to the European Federation Productivity Services Research Conference, Stresa, Italy. (Under editorial review.)

PETTIGREW, A. M., and GATES, S. (1968). A Survey of Computer Installations in Five British Insurance Companies. Unpublished paper, Manchester Business School.

POLSBY, N. W. (1963). *Community Power and Political Theory.* New Haven, Conn.: Yale University Press.

PONDY, L. R. (1967). Organizational Conflict: Concepts and Models. *Administrative Science Quarterly* 12(2): 296-320.

PREISS, J. J., and EHRLICH, H. J. (1966). *An Examination of Role Theory: The Case of the State Police.* Lincoln: University of Nebraska Press.

RADCLIFFE-BROWN, A. R. (1952). *Structure and Function in Primitive Society.* London: Cohen and West.

RAMSOY, O. (1963). *Social Groups as System and Subsystem.* New York: Free Press.

REX, J. (1961). *Key Problems in Sociological Theory.* London: Routledge and Kegan Paul.

ROBINSON, F. (1968). The Role of the Systems Analyst. *Data Processing,* pp. 228-33, September/October.

SAYLES, L. R. (1958). *The Behavior of Industrial Work Groups.* New York: Wiley.

SCHEFF, T. J. (1961). Control over Policy by Attendants in a Mental Hospital. *Journal of Health and Human Behavior,* pp. 93-105.

SCHELLING, T. C. (1960). *The Srategy of Conflict.* Cambridge, Mass.: Harvard University Press.

SCHLESINGER, A. M., JR. (1959). *The Age of Roosevelt.* Vol. II, *The Coming of the New Deal.* Boston: Houghton Mifflin.

SCOTT, W. R. (1965). Field Methods in the Study of Organizations. In J. G. March (ed.), *Handbook of Organizations.* Chicago: Rand McNally.

SELZNICK, P. (1966). *TVA and the Grass Roots.* New York: Harper.

SHERIF, M. (1966). *In Common Predicament: Social Psychology of Intergroup Conflict and Cooperation.* Boston: Houghton Mifflin.

SHERIF, M., HARVEY, O. J., WHITE, B. J., HOOD, W. R., and SHERIF, C. V. (1961). *Intergroup Conflict and Cooperation: The Robbers Cave Experiment.* Norman: University of Oklahoma Book Exchange.

SHUBIK, M. (1959). *Strategy and Market Structure.* New York: Wiley.

SHUBIK, M. (1961). Approaches to the Study of Decision-making Relevant to the Firm. *Journal of Business* **34**, April.

SIEGEL, B. J., and BEALS, A. R. (1960). Conflict and Factionalist Dispute. *Journal of the Royal Anthropological Institute* **90**: 107-17.

SIEGEL, S. (1956). *Non-parametric Statistics for the Behavioral Scientist*. New York: McGraw-Hill.

SIEGEL, S., and FOURAKER, L. (1960). *Bargaining and Group Decision Making*. New York: Macmillan.

SILVERMAN, D. (1968). Formal Organizations or Industrial Sociology: Towards a Social Action Analysis of Organizations. *Sociology* **2**(2): 221-38.

SIMMEL, G. (1950). *The Sociology of Georg Simmel*. Translated and edited by K. H. Wolff. Glencoe, Ill.: Free Press.

SIMON, H. A. (1955a). A Behavioral Model of Rational Choice. *Quarterly Journal of Economics* **69**(1).

SIMON, H. A. (1955b). Recent Advances in Organization Theory. In S. K. Bailey (ed.), *Research Frontiers in Politics and Government*. Washington: Brookings Institute, pp. 23-44.

SIMON, H. A. (1957). *Administrative Behavior*. New York: Macmillan.

SIMON, H. A. (1960). *The New Science of Management Decision*. New York: Harper.

SMITH, H. L. (1962). Contingencies of Professional Differentiation. In S. Nosow and W. H. Form (eds.), *Man, Work, and Society*. New York: Basic Books.

SMITH, M. G. (1962). History and Social Anthropology. *Journal of the Royal Anthropological Institute* **92**: 73-85.

SNOEK, J. D. (1966). Role Strain in Diversified Role Sets. *American Journal of Sociology* **71**(4): 363-72.

SNYDER, R. C., and PAIGE, G. D. (1958). The US Decision to Meet Aggression in Korea. *Administrative Science Quarterly* **3**: 341-78.

SOELBERG, P. (1963). The Structure of Individual Goals: Implications for Organizational Theory. In G. Fisk (ed.), *The Psychology of Management Decision*. New York: Wiley.

SOUTHALL, A. W. (1954). Alur Tradition and its Historical Significance. *Uganda Journal* **18**: 137-65.

STEWART, R. (1968). Diary-keeping as a Training Tool for Managers. *Journal of Management Studies* **5**(3): 295-304.

290   *The Politics of Organizational Decision-making*

STINCHOMBE, A. L. (1968). *Constructing Social Theories.* New York: Harcourt, Brace, and World.

STRAUSS, A. et al. (1963). The Hospital and its Negotiated Order. In E. Freidson (ed.), *The Hospital in Modern Society.* New York: Free Press.

STRAUSS, A., SCHATZMAN, L., BUCHER, R., EHRLICH, D., and SABSHIN, M. (1964). *Psychiatric Ideologies and Institutions.* New York: Free Press.

STRAUSS, G. (1962). Tactics of Lateral Relationships: The Purchasing Agent. *Administrative Science Quarterly* 7: 161-86.

STRAUSS, G. (1964). Work Flow Frictions, Interfunctional Rivalry, and Professionalism: A Case Study of Purchasing Agents. *Human Organization* 23(2): 137-49.

SWARTZ, M. J., TURNER, V. W., and TUDEN, A. (eds.) (1966). *Political Anthropology.* Chicago: Aldine.

SYKES, G. M. (1961). The Corruption of Authority and Rehabilitation. In A. Etzioni (ed.), *Complex Organizations.* New York: Holt, Rinehart, and Winston.

THOMAS, W. I., and ZNANIECKI, F. (1927). *The Polish Peasant.* New York: Alfred Knopf.

THOMPSON, E. P. (1963). *The Making of the English Working Class.* London: Gollancz; New York: Pantheon, 1964; Harmondsworth: Penguin Books, 1970.

THOMPSON, J. D. (1967). *Organizations in Action.* New York: McGraw-Hill.

THOMPSON, V. A. (1961). Hierarchy, Specialization, and Organizational Conflict. *Administrative Science Quarterly* 5(4): 485-521.

THRUPP, S. (1957). History and Sociology: New Opportunities for Cooperation. *American Journal of Sociology* 63: 11-16.

TURNER, R. (1952). Role-taking: Process versus Conformity. In A. Rose (ed.), *Human Behavior and Social Processes.* Boston: Houghton Mifflin.

TURNER, V. W. (1957). *Schism and Continuity in an African Society.* Manchester: Manchester University Press.

TURNER, V. W. (1969). *The Ritual Process.* Chicago: Aldine.

UDY, S. H. (1959). Review of 'Organizations'. *American Journal of Sociology* 65: 222.

VANSINA, J. (1965): *Oral Tradition: A Study in Historical Methodology.* Chicago: Audine.

VAN VELSEN, J. (1967). The Extended-case Method and Situational

Analysis. In A. L. Epstein (ed.), *The Craft of Social Anthropology*. London: Tavistock, pp. 129-49.

VIDICH, A. J. (1969). Participant Observation and the Collection and Interpretation of Data. In G. J. McCall and J. L. Simmons (eds.), *Issues in Participant Observation: A Text and Reader*. Reading, Mass.: Addison-Wesley.

VOGT, E. Z. (1960). On the Concept of Structure and Process in Cultural Anthropology. *American Anthropologist* 62: 18-33.

VON NEUMANN, J., and MORGENSTERN, O. (1944). *Theory of Games and Economic Behavior*. Princeton: Princeton University Press.

WAGNER, H. (1969). *Principles of Operations Research*. Englewood Cliffs, N.J.: Prentice-Hall.

WALTER, B. (1966). Internal Control Relations in Administrative Hierarchies. *Administrative Science Quarterly* 11(2): 179-206.

WALTON, R. E. (1965). Theory of Conflict in Lateral Organizational Relationships. In J. R. Lawrence (ed.), *Operational Research and the Social Sciences*. London: Tavistock.

WARD, T. B. (1968). The Role of Management Services in Instituting Change. Unpublished paper, December.

WARREN, D. I. (1968). Power, Visibility and Conformity in Formal Organizations. *American Sociological Review* 33(6): 951-70.

WASSERMAN, P., and SILANDER, F. S. (1964). *Decision-making: An Annotated Bibliography*. Ithaca, New York: Graduate School of Industrial and Public Administration, Cornell University.

WEBB, E. J. (1966). Unconventionality, Triangulation and Inference. In *The Proceedings of the 1966 Invitational Conference on Testing Problems*. Princeton, N.J.

WEBB, E. J., CAMPBELL, D. T., SCHWARTZ, R. D., and SECHREST, L. (1966). *Unobtrusive Measures: Non-reactive Research in the Social Sciences*. Chicago: Rand McNally.

WEBER, C. E. (1965). Intraorganizational Decision Processes Influencing the EDP Staff Budget. *Management Science* 12(4): 869-93.

WEISS, D. J., and DAWIS, R. V. (1960). On Objective Validation of Factual Interview Data. *Journal of Applied Psychology* 44: 381-5.

WHITE, H. (1961). Management Conflict and Sociometric Structure. *American Journal of Sociology* 67(2): 185-99.

WHYTE, W. F. (1948). *Human Relations in the Restaurant Industry*. New York: McGraw-Hill.

WHYTE, W. F. (1955). *Street Corner Society*. Chicago: University of Chicago Press.

WILDAVSKY, A. (1964). *The Politics of the Budgetary Process.*
Boston: Little, Brown.

WILENSKY, H. L. (1967). *Organizational Intelligence.* New York:
Basic Books.

WILENSKY, H. L., and LEBEAUX, C. N. (1965). *Industrial Society and
Social Welfare.* New York: Free Press.

WILLIAMS, R. M. (1947). The Reduction of Intergroup Tension.
New York: Social Science Research Council, Bulletin 57.

WILLIAMS, T. H. (1969). *Huey Long.* New York: Alfred Knopf.

Working Party 10, British Computer Society (1967). The Education
and Training of Systems Analysts. *Computer Bulletin* **11**(1):
11-19.

WRONG, D. H. (1968). Some Problems in Defining Social Power.
American Journal of Sociology **73**(6): 673-81.

ZALD, M. N. (1962). Power Balance and Staff Conflict in Correctional
Institutions. *Administrative Science Quarterly* **7**: 22-49.

ZALD, M. N. (1969). The Power and Functions of Boards of Directors: A Theoretical Synthesis. *American Journal of Sociology* **75**
(1).

ZANDER, A., COHEN, A., and STATLAND, E. (1966). Accommodative
Relationships. In H. Vollmer and D. L. Mills (eds.), *Professional-
ization.* Englewood Cliffs, N.J.: Prentice-Hall.

ZELDITCH, M. (1969). Some Methodological Problems of Field
Studies. In G. J. McCall and J. L. Simmons (eds.), *Issues in
Participant Observation: A Text and Reader.* Reading, Mass.:
Addison-Wesley.

Author Index

Subject Index

aspiration-level goals, 10
assessed stature, 64, 232, 252–6
authority
  definitions of, 24–5
  locus of, 170
autonomy, *v.* integration, 13

bargaining subgroups, 10, 15, 18
Behavioral Theory of the firm, A, 9
biasing, 234–5
boundary relevance, 219 *and n.*
boundary-spanning role, 231 *and n.*
Brian Michaels
  allocation of resources in computer
    activities, 196–9
  Computer department
    formation, 36–7, 83–5
    investigation of by consultants,
      158
    management of, 86, 146–7
  and computer manufacturers
    correspondence with, 201–5, 235–7
    marketing strategies of, 77, 224–6,
      257–64
  computer purchase decisions
    NTL 200
      effects on O & M officer-pro-
        grammer relations, 104–8
      installation, 39, 67*n.*
      making the decision, 101–4
    Newton 350
      making the decision, 113–16,
        158
      and management of O & M
        department, 198–9
    SE 100
      effects, 36–9
      making the decision, 32–5
      operational problems, 97–8
    1966–8

author's summary and conclusions, 227–8
commitments to manufacturers,
  199–207
conflicting preferences, 170–92
consultants brought in, 209, 254
evaluating criteria, 222–3
existing antagonisms, 207–11
input equipment, 46, 49–51,
  171, 184, 186–7, 192, 208–
  11, 214–15
making the decision, 42–51
programmer-analyst issue, the,
  211–15
conflict at work, *see particularly* 41,
  45, 77, 78, 207
departmental executives
  contacts with other staff, 242–4
  contacts with own staff, 244–5
  perceptions of directors, 240–4
  relative political access, 245–9
directors
  dependence on programmers, 141–
    143
  as perceived by executives, 241–4
  power strategies, 84–5
  relationship with O & M manage-
    ment, 255–6
  strategy towards O & M depart-
    ment, 153–7
  support policies, 113, 115–16
  use of uncertainty, 145–6
geographical location of departments, 40
history of, 32
interdependence in
  programmer-analyst, 82
  programmer-O & M officer, 104–8,
    117–18, 197
labour turnover, 74, 148–9

297

chase decisions, 1966–8
computer installation in general, 21, 121, 197
computer languages, 137
computer manufacturers and Michaels, *see under* Brian Michaels
computer programmers, in general, 21
computer programmer in Michaels, *see under* Brian Michaels
computer purchase decisions in Michaels, *see under* Brian Michaels
computer salesmen, as participant observers, 60
computer–technologist–manager relationship, 14–15, 232
computer technologists, 14–15, 77
computer technology, changes in
  backing and fast stores, 220
  effect on programmer–analyst relationship, 73–4, 100–1, 136
  effect on programmers, 21, 77
  and power-maintenance strategies, 149–53
  at time of SE 100 purchase in Michaels, 97–8
conflict
  and ambiguity, 224
  behaviour, statements about, 74
  and existing antagonisms, 78, 207
  and incomparability, 8
  intergroup, 12, 13, 80, 107–8
  in Michaels, *see under* Brian Michaels
  and research environment, 56
  resolution of, 9
  and unacceptability, 8
  an uncertainty, 224–6
  and value predispositions, 8
  control of information, *see* information control

demand-generating process, the, 17, 22, 168–228 *passim*, 230–1, 240, 256, 265–6, 274–5
demands
  defined, 169
  disparity in, 168–9, 192–4, 215–17
  distinguished from interest, 168
  support for, 169
  timing and presentation, 232, 255
dependency, 26–9, 139–40

ecological mechanisms, 146 *and n.*
economics and game theory, 3–4

emergent occupational groups, 106–7
environment, definition of, 217, 218. *See also* task environment
exchange imbalance, 141
exchange theory, 3
executives and change agents, 169
extended case method, the, 2
extent of role set, 64, 231, 240–56

factionalism, 224–5
functional autonomy, 144–8

gatekeeper, the
  and information as a power resource, 233–40, 266
  in Michaels, 64–5, 235–9, 275
  and potential bias, 235
  and power, 232, 233

Handbook of Organizations, 268
hierarchy, and information control, 234
historian–social scientist relationship, 80–1
historical explanation, 79–81, 194–9, 215–17
historical research, 66–7

inclusive systems, 12, 21, 31
'incrementalism', 194, 199
Index of Average Earnings, 71–2, 120
information control, 64–5, 169, 215, 232–40, 266, 275
innovating subsystems, 12, 21, 31
innovation, defined, 11
innovative decisions
  complexity and uncertainty in, 217–224
  non-programmed, 11–15
  political behaviour in, 21–2
  and resource-sharing, 196
  sources and uses of power in, 229–66
institutionalization, 116, 117, 271
institutional process, the, 3
interdependence
  between sub-units, 17
  in innovative decision-making, 219
  in Michaels, *see under* Brian Michaels, programmers *and* (systems) analysts
  'reality' of, 21
  in theories of organization, 8, 12–13
intergroup conflict, *see under* conflict
interpersonal relationships, 240

inter-specialist relationships, 117, 272

longitudinal research, *see under* research methods

Management Services department in Michaels, *see under* Brian Michaels
managers, in general, 14–15
'managing dependency', 104
mating search process, the, 226
middleman, role of, 231–2, 252
motivation, 6
myths, generation of, 150–2

National Computer Centre, 121
negotiation process, the, 3
negotiation, over task environment, 116–17
newspaper advertisments, as indicators of status in computer industry, 70–1, 120–5, 128–35
non-programmed innovative decisions, *see under* innovative decisions
normative functionalism, 2
normative themes, 228, 253 *and n.*

occupational identity, 100, 117
occupational specialization, as an emergent process, 76–83
occupational status differences, *see under* status
operationalizing power, *see under* power
organizational boundary impedance, 233–4
organizational decision-making
  complexity of structure and, 217–23
  complexity of task and, 12
  and conflict, 7–9
  non-programmed innovative decisions, 11–15
  power as a major variable in, 8–9
  satisficing in, 7, 8
  search behaviour in, 7
  structural differentiation, effects of on, 12–15, 168–9, 193–4, 234, 266, 274–5
  structural sources of instability in, 8
  theories of, 5–11, 21–2
    author's, 196 *and passim*
    Cyert and March, 9–11, 21–2, 234
    March and Simon, 6–9, 21–2, 234
    psychological, 5, 6

uncertainties during, 9, 11, 217–23
organizational goals
  Cyert and March's theory of, 10
  as constraints in decision-making, 222
Organizations, 6, 9, 196
organizations, the study of
  author's approach to, 2, 4, 17 *and passim*
  behaviour in, 3–4
  historical data in, 2–3
  as political systems, 16–22
  as resource-sharing systems, 20
Organization and Methods department in Michaels, *see under* Brian Michaels

participant–observer role, the, 56–61
passion ratios, 202, 261
Patterns of Industrial Bureaucracy, 109
perceived hostility–interdependence relationship, 118
perceptions in Michaels, *see under* Brian Michaels
perceptual identification, 195
political access, *see under* power
political behaviour in organizations
  controls on, 19–20
  definition of, 17–18, 169
  legitimation of, 56
  studies of, 16–17
political commitments, 18, 19
political processes in decision-making, 16–31
power
  and assessed stature, 232, 252–6
  author's views, 30–1
  conflicts, 20
  and communication structures, 233
  definitions of, 23–5
  distribution, 170
  expert, 28, 29–30, 138
  and extent of role set, 27, 231, 240–56
  holders, identification of, 56
  and information control, 28, 232–3
  legitimation, 144, 231–2
  -maintenance strategies, 69, 149–53
  mobilization, 229–33
  operationalizing, 63–5, 74
  in organizational decision-making, 23–30
    Cyert and March's theory, 10
    as a major variable, 8–9

Milton Keynes UK
Ingram Content Group UK Ltd.
UKHW020000071024
449327UK00031B/2597

9 780415 488358